SECOND EDITION

TRAINING for YOUNG DISTANCE RUNNERS

Happy Birthday Ceci ! Love, Neil 2012

Larry Greene

Russ Pate

HUMAN KINETICS

Library of Congress Cataloging-in-Publication Data

Greene, Laurence S., 1960-
 Training for young distance runners / Larry Greene and Russ Pate.-- 2nd ed.
   p. cm.
 Includes bibliographical references and index.
 ISBN 0-7360-5091-4 (soft cover)
 1. Running for children. 2. Marathon running--Training. I. Pate, Russell R. II. Title.
 GV1061.18.C45G74 2004
 796.42'4'083--dc22

                                    2004003137
 ISBN-10: 0-7360-5091-4
 ISBN-13: 978-0-7360-5091-3

Acquisitions Editor: Martin Barnard; **Developmental Editor:** Leigh LaHood; **Copyeditor:** Alisha Jeddeloh; **Proofreader:** Coree Clark; **Indexer:** Betty Frizzéll; **Permission Manager:** Toni Harte; **Graphic Designer:** Robert Reuther; **Graphic Artist:** Francine Hamerski; **Photo Manager:** Dan Wendt; **Cover Designer:** Keith Blomberg; **Photographer (cover):** © SportsChrome; **Photographer (interior):** Kelly Huff, unless otherwise noted; photos on pages 5, 16, 27, 36, 43, 72, 78, 91, 144, 149, 166, 186, 196, 203, and 211 © Human Kinetics; photos on pages 12, 38, 56, 74, 92, 134, 150, 172, 188, and 205 courtesy of the featured coaches; **Art Manager:** Kareema McLendon; **Illustrator:** Kareema McLendon; **Printer:** Sheridan Books

Human Kinetics books are available at special discounts for bulk purchase. Special editions or book excerpts can also be created to specification. For details, contact the Special Sales Manager at Human Kinetics.

Printed in the United States of America   10   9

The paper in this book is certified under a sustainable forestry program.

Human Kinetics
Web site: www.HumanKinetics.com

United States: Human Kinetics
P.O. Box 5076
Champaign, IL 61825-5076
800-747-4457
e-mail: humank@hkusa.com

Canada: Human Kinetics
475 Devonshire Road, Unit 100
Windsor, ON N8Y 2L5
800-465-7301 (in Canada only)
e-mail: info@hkcanada.com

Europe: Human Kinetics
107 Bradford Road
Stanningley
Leeds LS28 6AT, United Kingdom
+44 (0)113 255 5665
e-mail: hk@hkeurope.com

Australia: Human Kinetics
57A Price Avenue
Lower Mitcham, South Australia 5062
08 8372 0999
e-mail: info@hkaustralia.com

New Zealand: Human Kinetics
P.O. Box 80
Torrens Park, South Australia 5062
0800 222 062
e-mail: info@hknewzealand.com

I dedicate this book to the memory of Libby—my running partner and my best friend, forever.

Larry Greene

To my children, Colin and Amy, the young runners who inspire their dad and stimulate his interest in the topic of this book.

Russ Pate

CONTENTS

ACKNOWLEDGMENTS

We can't say enough to thank the outstanding staff at Human Kinetics who reviewed, edited, designed, and produced the first and second editions of *Training for Young Distance Runners*. Special thanks to Ted Miller, Martin Barnard, Ann Brodsky, and Leigh LaHood.

We're grateful to all of the coaches who shared valuable insights and information about their programs. Thanks also to Cyndi Long for input on nutrition for young runners and to Jinger Gottschall for helpful ideas about running technique.

For their endless encouragement, support, and love, I thank my family: Christy, Mom, Dad, and David.

—Larry Greene

I would like to extend sincerest thanks to my colleagues in the Department of Exercise Science at the University of South Carolina and to the graduate students with whom we are honored to work. It is the personal support and intellectual stimulation provided by these people that have enabled me to pursue professional projects such as this book.

In addition, I wish to acknowledge the coaches who are responsible for developing in me a lifelong love of running. They are my father, Robert Pate, who guided me into track and field and who helped me survive the inevitable losses that come to young athletes; John Chew, who showed me how to enjoy distance running and who introduced me to the sport's wonderful culture; and the late Vern Cox of Springfield College, who brought to his coaching a remarkable ability to make each athlete feel like the most important one on the planet.

—Russ Pate

INTRODUCTION

- At what age should kids start training for competitive distance running?
- What distances should young runners cover in training and competition?
- Should young runners do high-intensity interval training? If so, what are good interval workouts?
- Is weight training beneficial or harmful for young runners?
- How important is technique?
- What sorts of foods should growing endurance athletes eat for performance and health?
- Do girls and boys have different training and nutritional needs?
- What are the best approaches to developing mental fitness for distance running?

These are just a few of the questions that motivated us to write the first edition of *Training for Young Distance Runners*, which was published in 1996. Back in 1993, when we started to plan the book, there was no comprehensive resource with the answers to these questions. We sought to provide coaches, parents, and young runners with the best information and training guidelines, because we knew that a well-informed resource on training for young runners would lead to many positive results. For example, as young runners we experienced the unparalleled feelings of satisfaction and confidence that come from working hard to accomplish performance goals in cross country, track, and road racing. That hard work and dedication in our youth have served us well in our personal, family, and professional adult lives. We also knew that the spirited teamwork and camaraderie that made running so much fun in our youth are the foundation of true friendships, some of which last forever. And from our work as exercise scientists we knew that sound training and nutrition in the teenage years set the stage for a lifetime of physical fitness and good health. We were motivated to write the first edition, as well as this new edition, by the desire to share these great gifts of running.

What's New to This Edition?

When we set out to write this edition we began by wondering whether the motivating questions for the first edition were still relevant for coaches, parents, and young runners. We discovered that the key questions haven't changed over the years, and in most cases our answers haven't changed either. Based on continued nutrition research and the advice of expert dietitians, for example, we still recommend that young endurance athletes eat a diet that is high in complex carbohydrates and low in fat. In some cases, however, we've revised and further developed our answers to the old questions because new research has filled in knowledge gaps. Consider the question about whether young runners should do high-intensity interval training. When we wrote the first edition, the existing research indicated that compared to adult runners, young runners are extremely limited in producing energy to fuel high-intensity work. The research showed that children and adolescents lack important enzymes and hormones necessary to produce energy anaerobically.

In recent years, however, research has revealed physiological mechanisms in children and adolescents that compensate for their lower capacity to perform anaerobic work. Recent research has even shown that young runners' bodies can adapt favorably to high-intensity training. We discuss these new developments in more detail in the second chapter. Then in later chapters where we guide you through the steps of designing training programs and individual workouts, we use this research to slightly increase the recommended amount of high-intensity interval training. (As in the first edition, we still don't recommend a lot of high-intensity training for beginners because it can cause musculoskeletal injuries.)

Between the publication of the first and second editions, the biggest difference in information on training young distance runners is its now widespread availability. The Internet has extensive forums for sharing information and talking about running. We see many interesting ideas and approaches to training on Web sites and in chat rooms for runners. But we also see misleading and unsupported recommendations for how young runners should train. More than ever, we're convinced that the best approaches are based on sound scientific research and the experiences of established coaches and runners. Like the first edition, this book will help you understand the scientific basis of distance running and how to creatively apply scientific knowledge to designing effective training programs.

The Art and Science of Training Young Distance Runners

Two major themes that convey our philosophy of training young runners run through this book. First, the best outcomes depend on taking a developmental approach, which means that all training and competitive experiences should promote gradual progression toward the young runner's ultimate goals and potential, whether that means making the junior varsity team or the Olympic team. In the developmental approach, the most important goal of all is self-improvement. Attaining this goal not only depends on training that builds physiological and psychological fitness, it equally depends on training that promotes health and positive attitudes about physical activity, teamwork, and competition.

The second theme is that successful training for young runners involves the art of applying science. The great gifts of running don't come from half-baked, seat-of-the-pants training programs. Instead, they come from the inspired and creative application of scientific information as well as from the knowledge and experience of great coaches, parents, and runners. In this book we provide the scientific principles and guidelines as well as the insights of experts to help you determine the best types and amounts of training for individual athletes. We don't offer a paint-by-numbers approach with a lot of lists of daily training sessions. Instead, we present principles and procedures to help you apply the science of running to the art of designing and carrying out training programs. With the scientific background as your canvas, you can become the artist by using your creativity to develop masterpieces: young endurance athletes who have developed the fitness and skill to perform at their greatest potential.

PART I

RUNNING RESEARCH

We know that you have questions about training for young distance runners, and we're eager to answer them. But we'd like to begin by asking you a few questions:

▌ If you're a coach, how did you go about planning yesterday's training session? What factors influenced your choice of training methods and loads? How will you design training sessions for tomorrow, next week, next month, and next year?

▌ If you're a parent, how do you know whether you're providing nutrition for your child that promotes optimal health and running performance? If your child asks you for advice about training, how can you be certain that you're guiding her down the right track?

▌ If you're a runner, what do you need to know about your

body and about training to plan the most appropriate workouts? How do you know for sure that you're training in ways that capitalize on your strengths and correct your weaknesses?

Over many years we've heard different answers to these questions—answers that reflect various approaches to developing training programs for runners, from using intuition to copying elite runners to applying science. Each of these methods has benefits. For example, we know excellent coaches who, simply by their natural insight, feel that training should be fun and interesting, so their programs include games, contests, and variety in training methods and settings. Often, however, the intuitive approach can lead to unsuccessful, if not downright harmful, outcomes. Intuition is the basis for the flawed "more is better" philosophy of training: If 40 miles per week helps you improve, 80 miles will help you improve twice as much. In addition, intuition leads to the misconception that children and adolescents are just small versions of adults, so they should train by the same methods that adult runners use, just scaled down a bit.

A more common approach is to model training on the methods of elite runners. To an extent, this approach can be effective. For example, if you learn that a world-class runner does weight training, you might add weight training to your schedule. But modeling large chunks of your training program on someone else's is usually a recipe for poor performance and injuries. Closely following an elite runner's training program works only if you're already an elite runner, with similar physiological characteristics and technical skills as well as similar levels of fitness and motivation.

In contrast to using intuition and adopting the methods of elite runners, our approach to training young runners is based on *knowing running,* or applying scientific knowledge about the physical and psychological capacities of young endurance athletes. In addition, having been runners ourselves for more than 60 combined years and having competed at the national and international levels, we base our approach on experience, knowledge that comes from trial and error as well as trial and success.

In the long run, a knowledge-based approach leads to the best outcomes by far. If you're a coach or parent trying to answer young runners' questions about why they're doing particular types of training or eating certain foods, pure intuition and modeling give you only one, extremely limited, answer for each approach: "Because it feels right," and "Because what's-his-name, a world-class runner, does it." In contrast, our approach offers a wellspring of established knowledge and experience from which you can confidently draw your answers to a runner's questions. When you understand the scientific foundations of distance running, you'll become more creative in designing your program, and your experience coaching or parenting young runners will be much more satisfying. If you're a runner, knowing how your body and mind respond to training gives you an advantage over your competitors and makes your experience more interesting and fun.

We've devoted part I of this book to the scientific foundations of distance running, focusing on developmental principles for training and racing (chapter 1); running physiology (chapter 2); proper nutrition for growing and endurance athletes (chapter 3); mental fitness (chapter 4); and biomechanics, or technique (chapter 5). These chapters provide the knowledge necessary for understanding the training methods and procedures for designing programs in part II.

Peak Development

The greatest single challenge in training young distance runners is accounting for the physical and psychological changes that occur during adolescence. These developmental changes greatly influence nutritional needs as well as physiological, psychological, and biomechanical capacities, so you need to know a little about growth and maturation to determine the best training for adolescents. In this chapter we discuss 10 developmental principles that guide training and racing for young distance runners.

Developmental Principle 1: Limit Training Before Puberty

We're often asked what the best age is for kids to begin training for cross country, road racing, and the distance events in track and field. That's a tough question because there is limited scientific research on the subject and anecdotes simply aren't reliable. Even so, the question is too important to overlook, because researchers and doctors have raised many concerns about the effects of competitive running on young runners. We developed our answer to the question of when training should begin by considering these questions: At what age are young people physically capable of running long distances? Do they adapt physiologically to training? What are the long-term psychological effects of training and racing at a young age? Are any health risks associated with early participation in distance running?

You might be surprised to know that children as young as six years are physiologically well suited for aerobic activities such as distance running.

We know this from research on children's $\dot{V}O_2$max, which is a measure of how much oxygen the muscles are able to use to fuel their contractions during maximal exercise. Individuals with high $\dot{V}O_2$max values have superior aerobic fitness, which means that their heart and vasculature can supply their muscles with a sufficient amount of oxygen-rich blood and their muscles can quickly process the oxygen to generate energy. $\dot{V}O_2$max is vital to success in distance running because muscles fatigue quickly if their demand for oxygen is not fully met. (We examine the relationship between $\dot{V}O_2$max and fatigue more closely in chapter 2.)

Research shows that, pound for pound, normally active 6- to 8-year-olds have $\dot{V}O_2$max values as high as, or sometimes even higher than, recreational adult runners who train 30 to 40 miles a week. Based on these findings, some exercise physiologists contend that children are natural endurance athletes. This view is backed by age-group records for distance races, such as U.S. marathon records for young runners. The records for 8-year-olds are 3:37:26 for boys and 3:13:24 for girls; for 11-year-olds the record is 2:47:17 for boys and 3:03:55 for girls. Many adult marathoners have trained extensively for years without reaching these marks.

Research also shows that young children adapt physiologically to endurance training in several ways that, at least theoretically, will improve their running performance. Before puberty, for example, children who perform moderate levels of endurance training will experience about a 10 percent increase in $\dot{V}O_2$max, slightly less than the 15 percent increase observed, on average, in adults. You might conclude from this information that young children are capable of training for and competing in long distance races, but before you start planning programs for 8-year-olds, consider a few important points:

▌ Neither scientific nor anecdotal evidence suggests that distance runners must start training at a young age to reach their greatest potential. Most world-class runners did not begin training until they were in their mid- to late-teens. And, with very few exceptions, the children who have held age-group records for the 5K through the marathon have not developed into elite adult runners.

▌ Research consistently shows that, before puberty, physiological adaptations to training aren't always correlated with performance in long-distance events. For prepubescent children, the factors that best predict distance-running performance are simply related to physical maturity: Taller, stronger, and faster children lead the pack in distance races, just as they excel in other sports like basketball, baseball, and soccer.

▌ While many children have naturally high levels of aerobic fitness, making them physiologically capable of performing low-intensity endurance activities, they are very limited in generating energy for high-intensity

Although children as young as six are capable of attaining high levels of aerobic fitness through training, it's better to limit the amount and scope of training until age 12 to 14.

activities such as an 800-meter race. The body has two primary systems for producing energy during exercise: the aerobic system, which operates when a sufficient amount of oxygen is available to the muscles, and the anaerobic system, which operates when the oxygen supply cannot keep up with the muscles' demand during high-intensity activity. One of the most consistent findings in pediatric exercise science is that the anaerobic system is not fully developed in children because it relies on enzymes and hormones that are released and accumulate during puberty.

▎ Physically immature youth who undertake systematic training are at high risk for injuries, abnormal growth and maturation, and psychological burnout.

These points convince us that youths who haven't yet reached puberty should not train systematically for distance running. One reason for limiting training before puberty is that normal pubertal development can improve running performance on its own (see table 1.1). For example, the growth spurt of the lungs and heart, which occurs at an average age of 11.5 years in girls and 13.5 years in boys, boosts the delivery of oxygen-rich blood to the muscles, which naturally increases $\dot{V}O_2$max. Another example is the elevated levels of growth hormone, which enable stronger muscle contractions, increasing running speed and efficiency.

TABLE 1.1—Hallmarks of Puberty

Hallmark	Characteristics	AVERAGE AGE	
		Girls	Boys
Beginning of pubertal growth spurt	Accelerated skeletal growth of the arms, legs, feet, and trunk	10.5	12.5
Peak height velocity	Sharpest increase in the rate of height gain	11.5	13.5
Growth spurt of the cardiopulmonary system	Accelerated growth of the heart and lungs in diameter and volume	11.5	13.5
Beginning development of secondary sex characteristics	Growth of reproductive organs; breast development and widening of the hips in females; appearance of facial hair, widening of the shoulders, and lowering of voice in males	10.5	11.5
Menarche	Onset of menstruation	12.5-13.0	—
End of pubertal growth	Skeletal growth diminishes or ceases	15.5	17.5

Not all developmental changes automatically improve running performance, a point that also supports curbing early training. Take rapid growth in height—at the average age of 10.5 for girls and 12.5 for boys, the growth rate increases dramatically from approximately 5.5 centimeters (2.1 inches) per year to approximately 10.5 to 12 centimeters (4.1 to 4.7 inches) per year. The highest rate of growth, which is called peak height velocity, occurs at around age 11.5 for girls and 13.5 for boys. Now consider the 13-year-old boy who grows 4 inches over a single summer—suddenly he's all legs. The growth spurt should improve his running by increasing leg length and thus stride length. However, he now has trouble coordinating his longer legs because the nervous system, which controls movement, doesn't immediately adapt to changes in limb length. Also, during the growth spurt different body parts grow at different rates. The feet and legs, for example, usually lengthen faster than the trunk, making many teenagers seem gangly or awkward. These developmental changes cause the rapidly growing runner to temporarily perform *worse* because his uncoordinated stride wastes energy, causing early fatigue.

Rapid limb growth also means that children who train intensely for distance running are at high risk for muscular and skeletal injury. Bones lengthen at each end in soft tissue called epiphyseal growth plates, which are very weak before and during the pubertal growth spurt. If the growth plates are stressed by heavy loads of running, fractures can occur. The growing athlete's joints and muscles are also susceptible to injury because muscle mass and strength develop more slowly than bone. Eventually the epiphyseal growth plates will ossify, or harden, and muscle mass will increase, but until these two critical growth processes are complete, youth risk serious injury from excessive training.

Training before puberty can also affect sex-specific hormones, disrupting physiological development. Estrogen, for example, is a hormone that ensures normal growth and development in girls. Under certain conditions, including insufficient energy replacement through diet, some female runners do not experience the cyclic increases in estrogen that should begin during puberty. Girls who train excessively and do not consume a sufficient number of calories can not only experience delayed menarche, they can also experience amenorrhea, or cessation of menstruation. Although researchers have not discovered all of the long-term health effects of these conditions, they have linked them with extremely low bone density, because estrogen promotes bone development, much of which occurs during puberty. In the short term, low bone density can lead to stress fractures. In the long term, it can lead to osteoporosis, a severely disabling bone disease.

Fortunately, most young runners will avoid harmful levels of training. They'll stop pushing themselves long before reaching their limits. However, we've known at least a few young runners who were self-motivated to push to extremes, and we've known coaches and parents who pushed young runners too far. For these children, running injuries are common. Psychological burnout is an even more likely outcome. Take the 10-year-old who's running 40 miles a week and racing 10Ks on a regular basis. Eventually he'll grow tired of running, especially because improvement depends on increasing training loads over time. If a child is running 40 miles a week at age 10, at age 16 he'll need to run 70, or maybe even 90 or 100 miles, in order to keep improving. That much running leaves little time for activities other than school, sleep, and eating. When training becomes that consuming, it isn't fun any more, and most youths will drop out of running.

By the age of 12 for girls and 14 for boys, most youth will have experienced key developmental changes that enable them to safely begin a low-mileage, low-intensity training program, leaving lots of room for gradual improvement over time. This doesn't mean that younger children shouldn't participate in distance running; they just shouldn't train systematically. Beginning at age 8 or 9, children who enjoy running may participate in fun runs and organized track and field programs that last a few months each year. Future distance runners will benefit from participating not only in middle-distance races (up to a mile), but also in sprinting, jumping, and throwing events. When track season is over, they should participate in soccer, basketball, and other youth sports, because it's important to develop all-around physical fitness before beginning specialized training for track and cross country (see developmental principle 3).

Developmental Principle 2: Consider Individual Differences

Table 1.1 on page 6 shows the average ages at which key developmental changes occur. Striking individual differences characterize these hall-marks of puberty. For example, two 12-year-old boys on the same cross country team might begin puberty 5 or 6 years apart. The early-matur-ing boy might show the first signs of puberty at age 10, while his late-maturing teammate might not get there until 15 or 16. The boys are the same chronological age, but they are very different in terms of biological age, or physical maturity. To develop effective programs, coaches must have a good sense of each individual's biological age and physical readi-ness for training. A herd approach, where everyone on the team does the same workout, can be harmful, especially when late-maturing youth try to keep up with early-maturing teammates who have gained advantages in size, muscle development, and physiological fitness. An awareness of individual differences in development is also critical for those who coach both girls and boys, because some pubertal changes influence running performance differently in girls and boys.

Determining precise biological age requires specialized medical equipment and expertise. However, coaches can still gain a good sense of their athletes' biological ages by being aware of the hallmarks of puberty. The obvious changes in secondary sex characteristics, such as breast development in girls and the appearance of facial hair in boys, indicate that puberty is underway. Also, as we discussed earlier, the pubertal growth spurt is a particularly important stage of development. Coaches should regularly measure their athletes' height to avoid overtraining during periods of rapid growth.

Besides accounting for individual differences in biological age, coaches must consider training age, which refers to the number of years that an athlete has been training regularly. A 16-year-old who has been training since 13 has a training age of 3 years, whereas a 16-year-old who just came out for the team 6 months ago has a training age of .5 years. Even though these two runners are the same biological age, they should train differently. The newcomer's program should include fewer miles and a greater emphasis on general training.

Developmental Principle 3: Emphasize General Fitness for Beginners

People tend to think of running as a natural movement that requires little athletic skill, unlike hitting a home run or sinking a three-pointer. From this perspective, runners just need a lot of endurance and willpower to

Effects of Puberty on Performance in Boys and Girls

Boys and girls experience several common developmental changes that lead to improved running performance, including increases in limb length and height, muscle mass, and dimensions of the heart and lungs. However, due to the effects of sex-specific hormones that are released during puberty—estrogen in girls and testosterone in boys—some changes tend to favor boys. For example, testosterone stimulates greater production of hemoglobin, an iron-containing protein in red blood cells. Hemoglobin is the vehicle for transporting oxygen in the blood, so blood with a higher concentration of hemoglobin can carry more oxygen to the working muscles. As a result of increased testosterone levels during puberty, then, boys experience an automatic improvement in $\dot{V}O_2$max, while in girls hemoglobin levels remain the same or decline.

Testosterone also stimulates muscle growth and the ability to produce anaerobic energy. At puberty, girls do get a little boost because their bodies produce a small amount of testosterone, but boys are at a much greater advantage because they produce far more testosterone than girls.

As a result of increased estrogen levels during puberty, girls tend to experience greater deposits of body fat. The average body-fat composition of 6-year-old girls is 14 percent, which increases to 25 percent in 17-year-olds. In contrast, body-fat composition averages only 11 percent in 6-year-old boys and 15 percent in 17-year-old boys. Runners who have relatively high percentages of body fat are at a disadvantage because fat is dead weight—it increases the energy required for distance running.

Estrogen also stimulates widening of the pelvic bones in young women. A wider pelvis can lead to misalignment of the legs, which worsens running technique and increases the risk of hip, knee, and ankle injuries.

These differences in the effects of puberty on boys and girls certainly don't mean that girl runners are doomed to poor performance and injuries. In most high school events, if the best girl runners competed in boy's races, they would place fairly high. Also, research clearly shows that girls who train for endurance sports have a significantly lower body-fat percentage than their nonathletic peers. Girls who train effectively experience marked increases in $\dot{V}O_2$max, which compensate for the slight decreases in hemoglobin that they experience. The same goes for the increased risk of injury girls face as a result of wider hips: Smart training prevents injuries.

Even so, the differences between the sexes are important because they call for individualized training. Because puberty has a small influence on muscle mass and strength in girls, they will benefit from a relatively high load of strength endurance training, including weight training, circuit training, and hill running. Training for flexibility and technique should be emphasized for girls who develop misalignment of the legs. And while sound nutrition is the key to success for all runners, it can play a more important role in performance for girls than for boys (see more about nutrition in chapter 3).

succeed, so their primary training method should be piling on the miles. The more you learn about the science of distance running, however, the more you appreciate that performance is determined by various physical and psychological capacities that reflect athletic skills, including neuromuscular control, specialized forms of speed and strength, proper technique, and of course, endurance.

Consider the ability to control the elastic, spring-like properties of muscles and tendons, one athletic skill that underlies peak performance in distance running. The calf, thigh, and buttock muscles and their tendons stretch when the foot contacts the ground during the running stride. The stretched leg muscles generate force by contracting, or shortening, to propel the body upward and forward in the takeoff phase of the running stride. This active muscle contraction requires energy that is created through metabolic processes, or the breakdown of stored dietary nutrients, primarily carbohydrates and fats. In training and competition, distance runners can easily deplete a critical source of nutrient energy called glycogen, resulting in fatigue. Skilled runners, however, can generate propulsive force without completely relying on metabolic energy, sparing glycogen and thus delaying fatigue. Like stretching a rubber band, lengthening the calf, thigh, and gluteal muscles and their connected tendons creates elastic energy that can be used for powerful recoil, which helps propel the runner's body upward and forward. Runners who can take advantage of the elastic energy in their muscles and tendons get something like a free ride—their legs behave like a bouncing ball or a pogo stick, generating force without using up precious metabolic energy sources.

The ability to use elastic energy isn't automatic. It requires great muscle strength and neuromuscular control, or the ability to precisely time muscle contractions. Just before the foot contacts the ground, a skilled runner generates neural commands to contract the muscles that will be stretched on impact. These contractions stiffen the springs, so to speak, of the muscles and tendons for more powerful recoil. Runners can't develop this skill by piling on the training miles. In fact, research shows that long, slow distance running dampens the springiness of muscles and tendons, impairing their ability to generate elastic energy. Runners can develop this skill instead through methods such as circuit training and technique drills. Also, games such as basketball and ultimate Frisbee train the neuromuscular system to take advantage of elastic energy. (You'll learn how to incorporate these methods into training programs in part II.)

Figure 1.1 illustrates the fitness capacities that are essential for success in distance running. In the lower part of the figure are general fitness capacities, which can be developed through training that doesn't directly simulate the physical and mental demands of a distance race. Consider cardiovascular fitness, the capacity of the heart and the vascular system (arteries, capillaries, and veins) to supply the muscles with sufficient oxygen-rich blood and rapidly remove metabolic waste products like lactic acid. To develop this general capacity, runners don't always need to run; instead, they can try swimming, bike riding, or even in-line skating. Or, to develop strength endurance, the capacity to generate forceful muscle contractions over a long time under conditions that demand a high power output, such as running uphill or in sand, runners can lift weights or do circuit training.

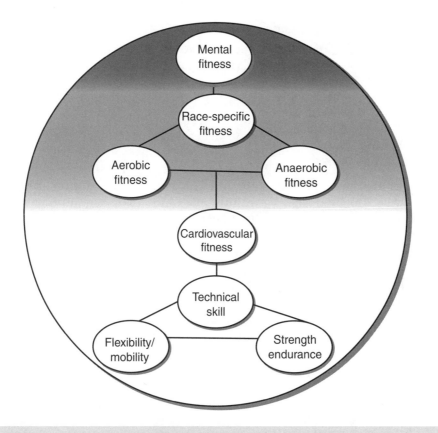

FIGURE 1.1 General fitness capacities are in the white background, and race-specific fitness capacities are in the shaded backgrounds.

In the middle part of figure 1.1 are race-specific fitness capacities, which can be developed through training that simulates the demands of competition. To develop race-specific fitness, runners must train by covering competitive distances at racing speeds, using high-intensity interval training, or participating in time trials or actual competitions.

The top part of figure 1.1 represents mental fitness, which is essential for success in distance running. Mental fitness is so important that an entire developmental principle, 6, is devoted to it.

Programs for young runners should emphasize general capacities because they form a fitness base that helps the athlete undertake specialized, high-intensity training. Consider an 800-meter runner's interval training session for developing race-specific fitness: 4 × 200 meters at 800-meter race pace, with a 20-second recovery period between each 200. To perform this high-intensity session successfully and safely, the runner must have strong general fitness, including ample flexibility and sound technique to move her limbs through the extensive range of motion required for such fast running. If her hamstring muscles are tight and her

Heathwood Hall Episcopal School

Location: Columbia, South Carolina

Coach: Ed Prytherch

In South Carolina junior high students can participate in high school track and cross country, so in
his 15 years as a high school coach, Ed Prytherch
has enjoyed the opportunity of working with runners spanning a wide range of ages, fitness levels,
and experience. A Heathwood Hall team, such as
the girls' teams that won the state cross country
championship in 2000 and finished second in 1999, might include runners as young
as 12 and as old as 18. By designing training programs that meet a wide variety
of individual needs, Prytherch has gained keen insights into the development of
young runners. Although training is tailored to the individual, three themes define
the program at Heathwood Hall: all-around physical fitness, technical skill, and a
psychological fortitude that revives the golden age of endurance athletics.

Prytherch encourages his runners to develop all-around fitness by participating
in other sports, such as soccer, lacrosse, and basketball. "The runners who also play
other sports tend to be more robust—they don't get injured. For the younger kids
especially, the problem with focusing only on running is that the movement is one-
dimensional. It doesn't encourage agility, mobility, and balanced muscle strength,"
he says. In addition to participating in other sports, the Heathwood Hall runners
develop general fitness through unique methods that Prytherch works into their training program. In the early phases of preparation for cross country, one day a week is
set aside for games, such as ultimate Frisbee and different kinds of tag. In the early
phases of preparation for track, most Fridays are Try-Another-Event Day. Prytherch
says, "I tell my runners, 'come try the high jump,' and 'come try the hurdles,' which
improves their overall fitness and prevents them from becoming mentally stale."

Although he includes all forms of training in his program, Prytherch stresses
technique drills and hill running. "It's free improvement," he says. "Everyone can
get better by using power more efficiently." The Heathwood Hall runners perform
technique drills, which each focus on a specific aspect of form, before every workout.
"I ask them to think about one thing at a time, and I give them feedback on that one
thing," Prytherch says. A technique session typically begins with 20-meter drills in
which the athletes run tall, with "tummies tight and butts tucked in. Then, when
they're doing that nicely, we work the arms," he says. "In the next set of drills I tell
them to imagine running in shallow water and having to pick their feet up high. The
last drill involves focusing on pulling the foot back before it contacts the ground. If
they're doing this drill right, I can see the heel accelerate."

Prytherch's philosophy on mental fitness is influenced by legendary coaches such
as Percy Cerutty, who guided fellow Australian Herb Elliot to a 1,500-meter gold
medal in the 1960 Olympic Games. Cerutty viewed sport as a vehicle for building
strong personal qualities. According to Prytherch, "Modern society offers fewer
opportunities for young people to develop courage and mental toughness. Endurance athletics helps young people develop valuable personal qualities that will stay
with them for the rest of their lives. I feel that facilitating this process is the most
important thing that I do as a coach."

range of motion at the hip joint is limited, she risks straining or tearing those muscles. If her technique is wanting—let's say she's overstriding, which creates a braking action with every foot strike—she'll waste energy and fatigue quickly. Clearly, without basic strength endurance and neuromuscular control, her running technique suffers. In addition, if she hasn't developed cardiovascular endurance, she won't recover adequately during the 20-second interval between the 200s.

When we focus on how to design training in part II, you'll see that methods for developing general fitness capacities are especially important for beginners and for all runners in the initial stages of preparing for upcoming competitive seasons. However, this emphasis doesn't mean that a beginner's program should not include race-specific methods like high-intensity interval training. We recommend mixing all the types of training throughout a season, starting out with a relatively low percentage of specialized training and increasing it gradually.

Developmental Principle 4: Increase Training Loads Gradually

Designing successful training programs is a matter of determining appropriate workloads, which are defined by volume, intensity, and frequency. Volume means the amount of training, which includes the number of miles or kilometers covered. Intensity refers to the effort exerted, which is reflected in the speed of a run. Frequency is defined by how often the athlete trains. There are two reasons for starting with manageable training loads and increasing them gradually. First, athletes who do too much too soon limit their potential for building up to advanced training loads, and second, the three components must systematically increase in order for the athlete to improve.

Marsha is a 15-year-old whose training age is 1.5 years. Marsha currently averages 18 miles over four days of training per week, including the moderate-intensity running she does to develop cardiovascular endurance as well as the high-intensity running that she does to develop anaerobic fitness and race-specific fitness. To ensure progressive improvement, Marsha's coach will increase her weekly volume over time: 26 miles (age 16), 34 miles (age 17), and 42 miles (age 18). As the total volume increases, so should the intensity and frequency. At age 15, Marsha might do one fast interval session per week to develop anaerobic power and race-specific fitness. By 17 or 18, she might do two or three interval sessions per week. In addition, Marsha's overall frequency of training might increase from four to six or seven days per week between ages 15 and 18.

Because no simple formula exists for determining optimal increases in training loads, the best coaches weigh many factors, including the runner's developmental status, motivation, history of responding to certain types of training, and potential for handling training loads over a career. This sort of planning is guided by well-defined goals. The process of setting individualized goals and designing the optimal training loads for achieving them is called periodization. Part II will guide you through periodization step-by-step.

Developmental Principle 5: Increase Competition Distances Gradually

For developing racing fitness and skill, we advise starting with shorter races and increasing the distances from season to season and year to year. In track competition, for example, beginners should focus on the shortest distance race—800 meters. With training and experience, runners can move up in distance if they show promise at and enjoy the longer races. Why start out with short races? The young runner must learn that successful racing means running as fast as you can over a given distance without slowing down and losing form. It's very difficult for beginners to accomplish this objective in a long race like 5,000 meters because they simply lack the concentration and pacing skills to maintain a fast pace for that long.

Table 1.2 provides guidelines for increasing distance with chronological and training age. These guidelines are flexible. For example, a 12-year-old who has just begun competing doesn't always have to run 800 meters. He will benefit from participating on occasion in other races, from 400 to 3,000 meters. Whatever the distance, a key focus in competition should be to run the race at the fastest pace possible—a pace that is neither too easy nor too hard to maintain. By starting out with shorter races, beginners will learn this focus more quickly than if they try to trudge through longer events.

TABLE 1.2—Recommended Racing Distances for Track

Chronological age (years)	Training age (years)	Racing distance (meters)
12 to 14	Up to 2	800 to 1,500-1,600
14 to 16	2 to 4	800 to 3,000-3,200
16 to 18	4 to 6	800 to 5,000

Developmental Principle 6:
Emphasize Training for Mental Fitness

While the physiological demands of distance running are obvious, physiological fitness alone is insufficient. Physiological fitness must be matched by mental fitness, which is characterized by supreme willpower and motivation, self-confidence, the ability to regulate how "psyched up" one gets, skill in controlling effort and pace, and intelligence in formulating and executing racing tactics. While training for physiological fitness has its limits, training for mental fitness isn't as restricted by developmental factors. Remember that physiological adaptations to training, such as increases in $\dot{V}O_2$max, don't necessarily predict improved running performance, at least until young runners are physically mature. Also, recall that runners who do a lot of physical training during periods of rapid physical growth and maturation risk musculoskeletal injuries. Young runners have much to gain by developing mental fitness, as you'll soon see.

Young runners have a lot of room for improvement in mental fitness because of their age—they simply have not had the deep and varied experiences in training and competition that build mental fitness. For example, one of the most important mental fitness skills in running is pacing. From studies on optimal patterns of energy expenditure during endurance activities, and from observing the pacing tactics of elite adult distance runners, we know that evenly paced running is optimal, but pacing is a skill that many young runners lack. They often run too fast in the early stages of training sessions and races. Particularly in track races, elite adult runners are able to judge and adjust their effort and speed in order to precisely hit target splits, such as 400-meter splits, along the way to achieving their final time goals. How many 14-year-old runners do you know who can do that?

The ability to precisely control effort and pace over a long distance requires extraordinary mental fitness. Just think about what's involved in pacing. The runner must continuously concentrate on how fast her limbs are moving, how hard she's breathing, and how fatigued she feels. Then she must compare this sensory information with a mental representation, based on memory, of how the effort should feel for the pace to be on target. Split times really help in determining and adjusting pace, but doing math on splits when you're fatigued is no simple mental task. Young runners can develop these skills through race-specific training methods. We provide examples of these methods in chapter 4 and part II.

Developmental Principle 7: Emphasize Proper Technique

We've talked about how young people are well suited for distance running because they have naturally high levels of aerobic fitness, indicated by their high $\dot{V}O_2$max measures. However, this advantage can be easily offset by another physiological determinant of performance, running economy, which reflects movement efficiency. Children and adolescents are inefficient runners; numerous studies demonstrate that young runners use significantly more oxygen than adult runners, which wastes energy and causes early fatigue. Having a high $\dot{V}O_2$max is like having a huge bag of money that you're hauling off to spend at your favorite store. Poor running economy, or a high oxygen cost for running at submaximal speeds, is like having a hole in the bottom of that bag. If you waste your fortune, it obviously doesn't count for much in the long run.

Two key focuses of training for young runners are mental conditioning and proper technique.

A major cause of poor running economy in youths is flawed technique, including overstriding, turning motions of the upper body, and flailing arms. These biomechanical flaws waste energy either by slowing the runner's forward progression or by diverting muscle force to counterproductive movements. Many flaws in running form are related to developmental factors. Earlier in this chapter, for example, we discussed how the adolescent growth spurt can temporarily impair coordination, thereby worsening running technique. Rapid growth can also weaken postural muscles in the abdomen and back, which are essential for stabilizing the upper body and avoiding counterproductive movements. Sufficient technique training, especially for beginners, is necessary in order to break bad habits and to prevent runners from acquiring wasteful movement patterns that will be difficult to correct later on.

In addition to improving performance by conserving energy, technique training can prevent injuries. Flaws such as overstriding place excessive stress on bones, joints, and muscles. Sound technique smoothes out the distribution of forces loaded on the musculoskeletal system, reducing injury risk. In chapter 5, we discuss the details of how technique influences performance and injury risks, and we present tips for optimal running form. Chapter 6 covers specific technique drills and other methods, such as weight, circuit, and flexibility and mobility training, that are critical to developing efficient running form.

Developmental Principle 8: Set Your Sights on Self-Improvement

Perhaps, like us, you're in the habit of going for long runs on weekend mornings—along endless country roads, deserted city streets, or winding mountain trails—feeling like you're the sole person on earth. If so, you know that runners dream fantastic dreams. If you're a young runner, maybe you dream of qualifying for your state championship, earning a college scholarship, or even winning a medal in the Olympic Games. Dreams are powerful fuel for pushing through the long runs, the exhausting interval sessions, and the last stages of grueling races. The reality, of course, is that only a small percentage of today's young runners will develop into tomorrow's Olympic athletes, and those who do reach the world's elite ranks get considerable help from their genes. Even so, all young runners can be on par with elite runners on at least one account: focusing on self-improvement as the most important measure of success.

Next time you read an article about a world-class runner or see one being interviewed on television, pay attention to what she talks about. It won't be about the competitors, the championships, the medals, or the money. Instead she'll focus on ways to improve. "I need to work on my kick, because I know that I can run faster over the last 400," she'll say. "I'm losing form going uphill, so I need to include more hill training in my program," or, "I'm letting my nerves get to me too much before races, so I'm planning to experiment with relaxation techniques."

The bottom line is that self-improvement from day to day, season to season, and year to year paves the road to your highest goals and results in unparalleled satisfaction, making the hard work worthwhile and, yes, even enjoyable.

Developmental Principle 9: Never Compromise Health

Without question, training for young distance runners should be designed for peak performance, but given the physical demands of running, a fine line often separates peak performance from injury and illness. To keep their athletes on the right side of the line, coaches must adhere to the philosophy that training should never compromise health. In the long run, there is no more important objective of youth sport than influencing values and behaviors in ways that ensure a healthy lifestyle in adulthood. Participating in cross country and track is especially valuable considering the high incidence of diseases that are linked to physical inactivity, including obesity, high blood pressure, coronary heart disease, diabetes, and even some forms of cancer. If you're a parent or a coach, you can pave the young runner's path to a physically active life by emphasizing healthy training practices such as increasing training loads gradually, including methods such as technique and strength training that are geared toward injury prevention, stressing optimal nutrition, watching for signs of overtraining, and forcing athletes to rest if they are injured or ill.

Developmental Principle 10: Make It Fun

The adage "last but not least" applies doubly here. That's because none of the previous principles has much practical value if young runners don't view their experiences as fun. All of the knowledge in the world about the science of distance running doesn't amount to much unless the coach knows how to make training interesting and enjoyable. For young runners to have fun, the coach must possess personal skills such as a caring attitude, a creative imagination, and a knockout sense of humor. Part II includes suggestions for making training fun with games, contests, and special events.

Striding Ahead

Developing training programs for young distance runners is best informed by knowledge about human development, specifically adolescent growth and maturation. We've stressed this point in the 10 developmental principles, which form the foundation of our philosophy on training young runners. You'll see these principles in action in part II, guiding our specific recommendations for training. First, however, we'll help you learn more about the science of distance running and its physiological basis, which is necessary for understanding the reasons behind our recommendations.

CHAPTER 2

Teen Physiology

On May 27, 2001, Alan Webb, a high school boy from Reston, Virginia, shocked the running world. Racing in an international field at the prestigious Prefontaine Classic in Oregon, Webb ran the mile in 3:53.43, beating the U.S. high school record of 3:55.3 set 36 years earlier by the legendary Jim Ryun. When you consider that a 5:00 mile is impressive for high school boys, Webb's 3:53.43 is truly astounding. One way to comprehend this achievement is to break it into 100-meter segments. A 3:53 mile strings together 16 consecutive 100s, averaging 14.5 seconds for each, plus another 9 meters to reach 1,609 meters, which equals 1 mile. At that pace you'd cover the mile at 3:53.35, breaking Alan Webb's record by almost 1/10th of a second.

Maybe that seems at least a little less daunting. After all, many high school boys can run 100 meters in 14.5 seconds. But why can't they keep up the pace for another 1,509 meters? What processes in the heart, lungs, blood, and muscles generate the energy to sustain such fast-paced running over long distances? What factors cause the fatigue that 99.99 percent of all runners will experience trying to break Alan Webb's record? Knowing the answers to these questions automatically taps you into a wellspring of insights and ideas for training the runner's body to generate sufficient energy and defy fatigue. That's our focus in this chapter on running physiology. Before you read on, make sure that you're well rested, because our physiology lesson guides you through an attempt at breaking the U.S. high school record for the mile run.

A Fantasy Run for the Record

"Last call for the mile run," announces the starter as the first-rate field, including you, toes the starting line. The stadium is packed, the air is filled with expectation, the track is fast, and the weather couldn't be better. It's a perfect day to set the high school record in the mile run. Again, for boys the challenge is to string together 16 nonstop 100-meter runs (plus another 9 meters) averaging 14.5 seconds for each, or 58 seconds for each 400 meters, to break the tape in 3:53.35. For girls the equivalent challenge is to average 17.1 seconds per 100 meters, or 68.4 seconds per 400. That's the pace for a 4:35.14 mile, which is 1/10th of a second under the U.S. high school record set by Polly Plumer in 1982.

The starting pistol fires and before you know it you're 20 meters down the track. Settling into target pace, a wave of confidence sweeps over you because, so far at least, this is easy. Your leg muscles generate powerful forces against the track that propel you upward and forward. If you can only sustain the same amount of force in each muscle contraction for every stride to the finish line, the record will be yours. You'll rely on the competition to bring out your best effort, you'll need the crowd to spur you on, and you'll have to draw on supreme determination and willpower to defy fatigue. If we reduce the task to the bare essentials, though, your body will need to produce a certain chemical compound at a fast enough rate for you to cross the finish line in record time. This compound is called adenosine triphosphate, or ATP.

Got ATP?

ATP molecules in muscle cells are split in a complex process to release energy that enables muscles to contract. Muscles are composed of parallel bundles of fibers, which consist of muscle cells (see figure 2.1). Each fiber is surrounded by nerve endings and capillaries so that muscle cells receive neural input as well as nutrients and oxygen in the blood. Muscle fibers consist of protein filaments called myosin and actin. The interaction of these myofilaments is the basic mechanism of muscle contraction.

A voluntary muscle contraction begins with neural signals that travel from the motor cortex in the brain to the nerve endings in muscle fibers. The neural signals trigger an intricate series of biochemical events that enable myosin and actin to overlap and bind with each other. As shown in figure 2.2, a cross-bridge is formed between myosin and actin. Although many chemical substances and reactions are involved, a muscle contraction essentially depends on energy from ATP. Catalyzed by an enzyme called myosin ATPase, the splitting of ATP releases energy that causes the end, or "head," of the myosin cross-bridge to bend and generate tension against the actin myofilament. This action, called the power stroke, causes actin and myosin to slide past each other, shortening the muscle fiber. This process occurs in millions of muscle fibers within a single muscle, causing the entire muscle to contract. Contracting muscles generate force that pulls on attached tendons, which then pull on the bones to which they are attached, resulting in limb movement and, ultimately, the running stride.

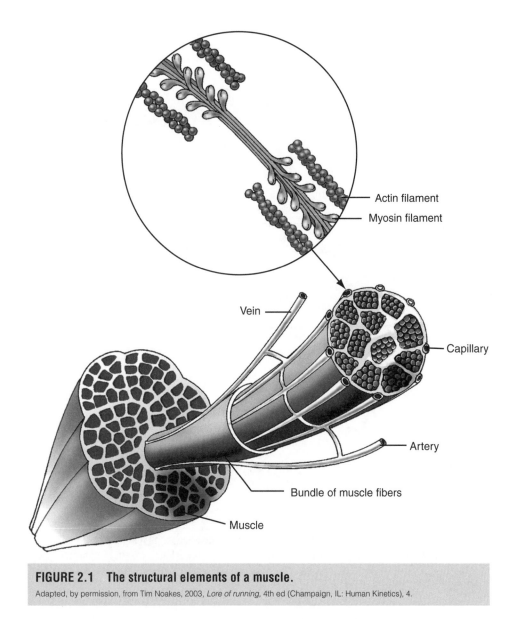

FIGURE 2.1 The structural elements of a muscle.

Adapted, by permission, from Tim Noakes, 2003, *Lore of running*, 4th ed (Champaign, IL: Human Kinetics), 4.

Your record run depends on ATP to sustain muscle contractions that are forceful enough to move your body at a speed of 14.5 seconds (boys) or 17.1 seconds (girls) per 100 meters over a mile. But there's a catch: Very little of this precious substance is stored for immediate use in the muscles. In a mile race, if you had to rely on immediate ATP stores as your only source of energy, you'd reach about 20 meters before experiencing complete fatigue—you literally would be unable to take another step. At least you'd reach the 20-meter mark side-by-side with Alan Webb or Polly Plumer, because the muscles of elite runners don't contain appreciably more ATP than anyone else's muscles.

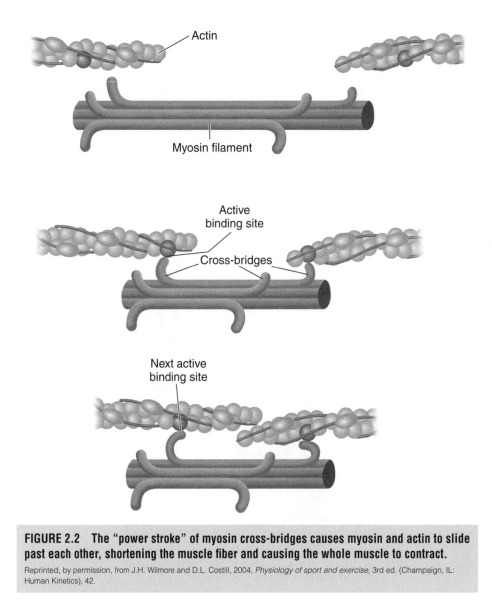

FIGURE 2.2 The "power stroke" of myosin cross-bridges causes myosin and actin to slide past each other, shortening the muscle fiber and causing the whole muscle to contract.

Reprinted, by permission, from J.H. Wilmore and D.L. Costill, 2004, *Physiology of sport and exercise*, 3rd ed. (Champaign, IL: Human Kinetics), 42.

Replenishing ATP With Creatine Phosphate

Fortunately, you don't have to worry about running out of fuel at the 20-meter mark of a distance race, because the body can replenish its ATP stores. The rate at which ATP is replenished determines whether runners have sufficient energy to sustain fast-paced efforts. When stored ATP is hydrolyzed, or split in the presence of water, the products are energy for muscle contraction and two molecules, adenosine diphosphate (ADP) and phosphate (see figure 2.3). To replenish ATP rapidly the body must have a source of energy to bind the phosphate molecule back to ADP. One immediately available energy source is creatine phospate (CP).

Phosphate

$$\text{ATP} + H_2O \rightarrow \text{ADP} + H_3PO_4$$

FIGURE 2.3 The ATP molecule is hydrolyzed, or split by water, yielding ADP and phosphate. To re-form ATP, energy is required to bind the phosphate to ADP.

The phosphate molecule in CP binds with ADP to re-form ATP (see figure 2.4). This ATP-CP energy system will get you past the 20-meter mark in a distance race, but it won't get you much farther. Like ATP, CP is stored in very small amounts in the muscles. Creatine, which is necessary to form CP, is naturally synthesized in the body, so if your diet includes at least a little meat, which contains creatine, your muscles likely have enough CP to reach about 50 meters on pace for the mile record. You've probably heard about power athletes, such as football players and sprinters, taking creatine supplements to boost CP levels, which can increase strength and speed. Distance runners, however, won't benefit from creatine supplementation, because CP contributes relatively little energy to events over 100 meters. In addition, creatine supplements increase body weight through water accumulation and muscle gain, and carrying the extra weight can drain distance runners' energy. At the 50-meter mark, then, our prospects for a new mile record are looking bleak. But don't despair—food and oxygen are coming to the rescue.

$$\text{CP} + \text{ADP} \rightarrow \text{ATP} + \text{creatine}$$

FIGURE 2.4 Creatine phosphate is an immediate source of energy for binding phosphate to ADP. When creatine phosphate stores are exhausted, the energy for producing ATP must come from the body's stored carbohydrates and fats.

Energy From Food and Oxygen

A 100-meter sprinter meets her energy demands with stored ATP and CP. In contrast, middle-distance (800 to 1,500 meters) and long-distance (3,000 to 5,000 meters) runners rely on nutrient metabolism, or the breakdown of stored food, to replenish ATP. The primary nutrient energy sources for young distance runners are carbohydrates and fat. The body has three systems, or metabolic pathways, for making ATP through carbohydrate and fat metabolism: anaerobic glycolysis, aerobic glycolysis, and aerobic lipolysis. The three pathways, which are actually a series of biochemical reactions occurring in muscle cells, are categorized by two factors: whether they use oxygen (aerobic metabolism) or do not use oxygen (anaerobic metabolism), and whether carbohydrates or fat supply the energy.

▌ *Anaerobic glycolysis* is the breakdown of carbohydrates to form ATP when oxygen is not present in the muscle cell. Dietary carbohydrates, found in breads, pasta, rice, potatoes, fruits, and vegetables, are stored in the muscles and liver as glycogen, which is composed of smaller molecules called glucose.

▌ *Aerobic glycolysis* is the breakdown of carbohydrates to form ATP when oxygen is present in the muscle cell. Exercise intensity, or effort, determines whether glycolysis will be aerobic or anaerobic. Higher-intensity running taxes the cardiovascular system to where it can't supply the muscles with oxygen-rich blood fast enough, so anaerobic glycolysis kicks in. For example, as a runner expends more effort, such as by speeding up or starting an uphill climb, the anaerobic pathway works to produce more ATP.

▌ *Aerobic lipolysis* is the breakdown of fat to form ATP when oxygen is present in the muscle cell. As we discuss shortly, running intensity determines whether aerobic metabolism will use carbohydrates or fat.

Oxygen is the star player in the game of energy metabolism. It's like the seven-foot, six-inch basketball center whose team scores big when he's in the offensive court, but who sometimes can't get down the court fast enough. When that happens the team doesn't score as much. Although the analogy isn't perfect, it's one way to think about ATP production for

Breathe Naturally

Because more oxygen in the working muscles results in more ATP, you might wonder whether runners should adjust their breathing to maximize oxygen intake. The best advice is to let breathing occur naturally, preferably through both the mouth and the nose. Research shows that under normal circumstances, the runner's natural breathing pattern brings more than enough air into the lungs to fully load oxygen onto hemoglobin, which carries oxygen in red blood cells. Changing breathing patterns won't load any more oxygen onto hemoglobin and therefore won't result in more oxygen being delivered to the muscles.

Research also shows that under normal circumstances distance runners don't gain any advantage from wearing nasal strips that open up the nasal passages to bring more air into the lungs. It's possible, however, that nasal strips will ease breathing in runners who have congestion from colds or allergies. The main condition that raises major concerns about breathing is exercise-induced asthma, which should be treated by a physician.

distance running. If oxygen is not present in muscle cells, only a small amount of ATP will be produced. In fact, anaerobic glycolysis yields only two ATP molecules per molecule of glucose. Now consider the score when oxygen is present:

- ▮ aerobic glycolysis → 36 ATP molecules per glucose molecule
- ▮ aerobic lipolysis → 130 ATP molecules per fat molecule

At first glance, these numbers point to aerobic lipolysis as the optimal energy pathway for the journey from 50 meters to the finish line of our fantasy mile. However, to use that pathway to supply enough energy for a mile race (or any race up to 10,000 meters), you'd have to slow your pace so drastically that the record would simply be unattainable. Although aerobic lipolysis yields 65 times more ATP than anaerobic glycolysis and 18 times more ATP than aerobic glycolysis, it is slow and inefficient compared to anaerobic and aerobic glycolysis.

Measuring $\dot{V}O_2$max

In chapter 1 we introduced $\dot{V}O_2$max as an indicator of aerobic fitness, pointing out that many children and adolescents have naturally high $\dot{V}O_2$max values. Throughout the book we discuss $\dot{V}O_2$max as a standard for gauging intensity in training and competition, so you might find it helpful to know how exercise scientists measure $\dot{V}O_2$max. In a typical test, the subject runs on a treadmill as the experimenter progressively increases the treadmill speed and raises its grade. The subject wears a mouthpiece connected to a computer that measures the volume of inspired and expired oxygen. As the running intensity increases so does the volume of oxygen consumed, or used by the muscles to make ATP aerobically. At a critical point in the test, an increase in intensity is not

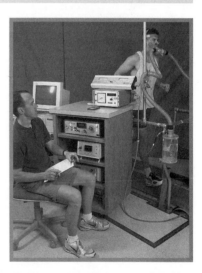

accompanied by an increase in oxygen consumption; the extra energy required to run faster or up a steeper grade must then come solely from the anaerobic pathway.

When the oxygen consumption plateaus, the experimenter notes this landmark as the $\dot{V}O_2$max. The measure is then expressed as the maximal volume of oxygen used by the muscles over a one-minute period. For an elite young runner this volume might be around 4,000 milliliters of oxygen per minute. To compare $\dot{V}O_2$max across individuals who weigh different amounts, exercise scientists express the absolute volume relative to each individual's body weight. So, for a boy who weighs 62 kilograms and has an absolute $\dot{V}O_2$max of 4,000 milliliters per minute, weight-relative $\dot{V}O_2$max is 64.5 milliliters per kilogram per minute (4,000/62 = 64.5).

One reason is that the primary energy source for aerobic lipolysis, fatty acids stored in adipose tissue, is typically situated far from the working muscles, such as in the abdominal region. It takes a significant amount of time to break down and transport these fatty acids to the muscles through the bloodstream. In a mile race, the muscles need tremendous amounts of ATP at extremely high rates—they just can't wait around for fat.

Fat metabolism plays a major role in long races like the marathon, which are run at moderate paces, but it doesn't contribute much in the shorter, faster races of youth competition (800 to 5,000 meters). Figure 2.5 shows that the body uses more carbohydrates and less fat as running intensity increases; thus runners use more fat to fuel an 8-minute mile than the faster, more intense 5-minute mile.

The percentage of $\dot{V}O_2$max that runners can sustain in a distance race, which is reflected by the intensity or pace, determines how much fat and carbohydrate contribute to energy needs. Research on elite adult runners shows that they race distances up to 5,000 meters at approximately 100

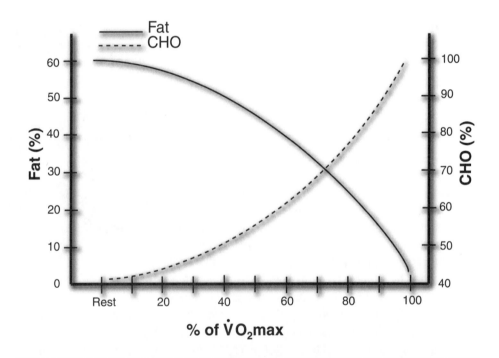

FIGURE 2.5   Contribution of carbohydrates and fat to energy needs at increasing running intensities, or percentages of $\dot{V}O_2$max.

Reprinted, by permission, from G.A. Brooks and J. Mercier, 1994, Balance of carbohydrate and lipid utilization during exercise: the "crossover" concept, *Journal of Applied Physiology* 76 (6): 2254.

percent of their $\dot{V}O_2$max. Few studies have been conducted to obtain this information on young runners; however, Cunningham (1990) found that outstanding high school male and female cross country runners raced 5,000 meters at around 90 percent of their $\dot{V}O_2$max. If they race 5,000 meters at this intensity, they surely race shorter distances at an even higher percentage of $\dot{V}O_2$max. At such high intensities it's likely that most of the young runner's ATP needs are met by the breakdown of carbohydrates, not fat. The heavy reliance on carbohydrates for fuel in competition underscores the need for young runners to eat a high-carbohydrate diet (more about that in the next chapter).

Now that we've ruled out aerobic lipolysis as a major energy pathway for any of the distance races in youth competition, we're left with anaerobic glycolysis and aerobic glycolysis to get you to the finish line in your quest for the mile record. Picture these two pathways as a fork in the metabolic road. It's an unusual fork because you're actually going to travel down both paths, taking each to different lengths—both energy pathways contribute to making ATP, but to different degrees. Table 2.1 shows estimates of the percentage contribution of the aerobic and anaerobic pathways when racing 800 to 5,000 meters. As the distance gets longer and race pace slows, runners use more aerobic energy. At 5,000 meters, for example, most of the energy (87 to 93 percent) comes from aerobic glycolysis. Even in the longer events, however, runners rely on some anaerobic energy for midrace surges, sprint finishes, and uphill running.

TABLE 2.1—Estimated Contribution of the Energy Pathways

Distance	PERCENT CONTRIBUTION TO GENERATING ATP	
	Aerobic pathway	Anaerobic pathway
800 m[a]	44-57	38-50
1,500 m-1 mi[b]	75-76	22-24
3,000 m	86-88	12-14
5,000 m	87-93	7-13

[a] Approximately 5-6% of the energy needs met by creatine phosphate.

[b] Approximately 1-2% of the energy needs met by creatine phosphate.

Data compiled from Martin and Coe (1997, page 185) and Newsholme, Leech, and Duester (1995, page 89). These data come from studies on adult runners; research has not been conducted to determine the contribution of each energy pathway in young runners. The contribution of aerobic metabolism is most likely greater in youths because their bodies are less effective at producing energy anaerobically.

Revving Up Your Metabolic Engine

In a physiological nutshell, the distance runner's basic challenge is to sustain the fastest pace that doesn't cause excessive fatigue and slowing. This challenge is met by relying as much as possible on the aerobic pathways. However, it takes a while for the oxygen-delivery system, the heart and blood vessels, to rev up, so a runner who starts a training session or a race without warming up properly will have to rely heavily on anaerobic metabolism to supply ATP until the heart begins pumping enough blood and the vasculature directs that blood to the working muscles. The main consequence of relying too heavily on anaerobic energy early in a race is lactic acid accumulation, which causes fatigue. In chapter 6 we cover how to warm up properly for training and racing.

Aerobic Fitness Makes the Difference

Two roads diverged in a wood, and I—
I took the one less traveled by,
And that has made all the difference.

—Robert Frost, "The Road Not Taken"

For the poet Robert Frost, taking the road less traveled made all the difference. For a distance runner at the fork in the metabolic road, aerobic fitness makes the difference. Early in an 800- to 5,000-meter race, if you lack aerobic fitness and you're running too fast, your muscles will be forced to rely heavily on anaerobic metabolism. While this pathway rapidly generates energy for high-intensity activity when the cardiovascular system can't supply the muscles with oxygen quickly enough, it has some major drawbacks. As we've already discussed, anaerobic glycolysis yields just two ATPs per glucose molecule. That's only five percent of the ATP produced through aerobic glycolysis. Not only is anaerobic glycolysis extremely inefficient because it burns huge amounts of energy for the small amount of ATP yielded, the only energy source that can be used for anaerobic glycolysis, glycogen, exists in very limited amounts in muscle cells. A girl weighing 50 kg (110 lb), for example, might have stores of only 200 to 250 grams of glycogen in her whole body. Several days of intense training without sufficient carbohydrate replacement in the diet can lead to glycogen depletion, a major cause of fatigue in distance running.

If you've gone out too fast and you're starting to fade 200 to 400 meters into a mile race, the culprit probably isn't glycogen depletion, unless you've been eating a very low-carbohydrate diet in the days leading up to the competition. Instead, the fatigue is likely caused by lactic acid accumulation, which is a natural product of anaerobic glycolysis. Lactic acid is produced during anaerobic glycolysis because without it, the muscles simply would be unable to contract. Lactic acid is thus essential for generating energy during high-intensity work, such as racing a mile. The problem with lactic acid, however, is that its acidic component—hydrogen ions, or protons, that dissociate from lactate molecules—lowers the body's pH, wreaking havoc in muscle cells. For example, it slows the rate of ATP production in the anaerobic pathway by breaking down the enzymes that catalyze the chemical reactions in metabolism, and it weakens muscle contractions by physically interfering with the overlapping protein myofilaments that enable muscles to generate tension.

Back at the fork in the metabolic road—200 meters into our attempt at the high school mile record—if you have a high level of aerobic fitness you'll be able to go farther down the aerobic pathway than the anaerobic pathway. In doing so, you'll avoid the two major causes of fatigue in races between 800 to 5,000 meters, lactic acid accumulation and glycogen depletion. Still, because the anaerobic pathway contributes a significant amount of energy, about 25 percent in a mile race, you'll also need a high level of anaerobic fitness, which we discuss later in the chapter.

Developing the Energy Pathways to Defy Fatigue

Two concepts define this chapter and underscore why successful coaches study exercise physiology: The body produces energy for distance running through three different energy pathways, and several different metabolic factors cause fatigue in distance races. These two concepts are fundamental to developing effective training programs for distance runners. They reveal, for example, that training must be comprehensive, stressing each energy pathway to the proper degree. This is determined by how much energy that pathway contributes to a given competitive event. A 5,000-meter runner, for example, will need to do more training to develop aerobic fitness than a 1,500-meter runner. And because lactic acid accumulation is a primary cause of muscle fatigue in 1,500-meter races, coaches must design sessions to train the 1,500-meter runner's body to hold off lactic acid accumulation and, when it inevitably starts to accumulate, to tolerate its effects.

In addition to the two key concepts, effective training is guided by the principle of specificity: Physiological adaptations are specific to the type, intensity, and duration of training. Let's say that you're designing a training session for a 5,000-meter runner and your objective is to improve maximal aerobic power. The athlete must run far and fast enough to stimulate the physiological changes that ultimately increase $\dot{V}O_2$max (see table 2.2 on page 33). If the training stimulus isn't sufficiently strong—that is, the athlete isn't running far and fast enough—the body simply won't adapt in the desired way. A common mistake is to run junk miles, or long, slow distance that doesn't push the aerobic energy system to a critical threshold. On the other hand, if the training stimulus is too strong—perhaps the athlete is running so fast that the anaerobic system dominates ATP production—the session won't last long enough to promote the intended adaptations. See part II for specific percentages of the total training load that runners should devote to developing aerobic and anaerobic fitness.

Improving Maximal Aerobic Power

The right training promotes substantial improvements in aerobic power. On average, $\dot{V}O_2$max in untrained adolescents is 35 to 45 milliliters per kilogram per minute for girls, 40 to 50 for boys. Following a moderate program, approximately 15 miles per week over two to three months, untrained adolescents will experience about a 15 percent increase in $\dot{V}O_2$max. With additional months and years of more intense training, young runners can boost their $\dot{V}O_2$max values to 50 to 60 (girls) and 60 to 70 (boys). The highest $\dot{V}O_2$max values recorded for elite adult distance runners are around 75 for women and 85 for men.

Training-induced increases in $\dot{V}O_2$max are caused by adaptations in the runner's heart, vasculature, and muscle cells (see table 2.2). In adults, studies show that training increases the dimensions of the heart's chambers, the thickness of its muscle wall, and the strength of its contractions. These changes enable the heart to pump more blood to the working muscles. Although there haven't been studies on the effects of training on heart size and contractility in adolescent runners, we assume that they adapt similarly because the functional outcome is the same for both groups: Training increases stroke volume, or the amount of blood that the heart can pump with each beat during maximal exercise. While training doesn't influence maximal heart rate (the highest number of heart beats per minute during the most intense exercise), it reduces heart rate during submaximal exercise and at rest. Well-trained distance runners

Using Heart Rate to Determine Optimal Training Intensity

To develop a specific energy pathway, training must stimulate physiological stress in a critical zone. Training below the zone's threshold won't result in desired adaptations, and neither will training too hard. How do you know whether you're training in the critical zones for developing the aerobic and anaerobic pathways? The most objective feedback comes from tests of oxygen consumption and blood lactic acid concentration in an exercise physiology lab. Such tests, however, are neither practical nor necessary for runners training in the real world. To obtain useful physiological data, all you need is a watch and some experience with taking your pulse. Heart rate is a useful measure of physiological processes because it increases in proportion to the muscles' oxygen demands.

Because specific ranges of heart rates are associated with adaptations of corresponding energy pathways, you have a great guide for determining optimal training intensities and paces. For example, research shows that $\dot{V}O_2$max increases in beginning runners who train at 65 to 75 percent of their maximal heart rate. So if Jenna has a maximal heart rate of 204 beats per minute, she should run continuously at a pace that raises her heart rate to between 133 to 153 beats per minute ($204 \times .65$ = 132.6 and $204 \times .75$ = 153) to increase her $\dot{V}O_2$max. In part II, we show you how to determine your maximal heart rate and calculate training paces for developing the energy pathways.

TABLE 2.2—Physiological Adaptations to Training

Energy pathways stressed by training	Physiological changes
Aerobic	↑ $\dot{V}O_2$max ↑ Maximal cardiac output ↓ Resting and submaximal heart rate ↑ Blood flow and oxygen delivery to working muscles ↑ Capillary density ↑ Lactic acid clearance from muscles ↑ Size and number of mitochondria ↑ Aerobic enzyme concentration and activity ↑ Capacity to metabolize fat
Anaerobic	↑ Anaerobic enzyme concentration and activity ↑ Maximal lactic acid production ↑ Capacity to buffer lactic acid

have resting heart rates as low as 35 to 45 beats per minute (bpm), much lower than normal rates of around 70 bpm.

Other responses to endurance training occur close to and within muscle cells. To handle the increased blood supply during high-intensity running, the vasculature adapts by channeling more blood flow to the working muscles and away from tissues and organs that don't require a large amount of oxygen. New capillaries are formed, enabling more oxygen to reach muscle cells and more lactic acid to be cleared from the muscles. Within muscle cells the most important adaptation to training is an increase in the number and size of mitochondria, the structures in which oxygen is used to generate ATP, and an increase in the number of mitochondrial enzymes that catalyze reactions in the aerobic energy pathways. These adaptations enable the runner to work at higher intensities without having to go farther down the anaerobic pathway, where the hazards of glycogen depletion and lactic acid accumulation lurk. As you'll see in chapters 6 and 7, the training methods for developing cardiovascular fitness and maximal aerobic power include continuous aerobic running, tempo running, and aerobic interval training.

Muscle Fibers for Endurance and Speed

When we said that aerobic fitness makes the difference for distance runners, we deliberately didn't say that it makes *all* the difference. That's because genetics are important, too. One of the most important genetic factors is muscle fiber type. We all inherit two major types of muscle fibers, Type I and Type II. Type I fibers are also called slow-twitch (ST) fibers because they generate contractile force slowly, resulting in low power output. ST fibers are built for endurance, containing many mitochondria and a large amount of a substance called myoglobin, which transports oxygen into the mitochondria. ST fibers support aerobic metabolism and resist fatigue during low- to moderate-intensity exercise.

In contrast, Type II fibers, also called fast-twitch (FT) fibers, contract rapidly and forcefully for speed and power, but they fatigue quicker than ST fibers. There are several subtypes of FT fibers, including fast-glycolytic (FG) and fast-oxidative-glycolytic (FOG) fibers. FG fibers rely exclusively on ATP generated through anaerobic metabolism, while FOG fibers can contract aerobically, meaning they combine characteristics of ST and FT fibers.

Table 2.3 shows the ratio of ST to FT muscle fibers in different groups of athletes. Individuals with a high percentage of ST fibers tend to excel in endurance activities, while individuals with a high percentage of FT fibers tend to excel in activities that demand short bursts of power and speed. According to leading exercise scientist Dr. Tim Noakes, an optimal ratio of ST to FT fibers for 800- to 1,500-meter runners is 50:50 (Noakes 2003). Let's say that you happen to have been born with a very high percentage, 75 percent, of FT fibers of the FG subtype, which are built for speed. If you're trying to break the U.S. high school record in the mile run, the first 300 to 400 meters will feel easy because you'll be running much slower than your maximum speed. However, your FG fibers aren't built for endurance. They have few mitochondria and a small amount of myoglobin, so they don't use oxygen to make ATP, relying instead on anaerobic glycolysis, which produces lactic acid. The genetic cards are

TABLE 2.3—Ratio of Slow-Twitch to Fast-Twitch Muscle Fibers in Different Groups of Athletes

Athlete group	ST fibers (%)	FT fibers (%)
Cyclists	50	50
Swimmers	50	50
Cross-country skiers	75	25
Sprinters (track and field)	26	74
Middle-distance runners	50	50
Long-distance runners	80	20

Data derived from Noakes (2003).

stacked against your going much farther than 300 or 400 meters in a mile race without fatiguing.

On the other hand, let's say that you were born with a very high percentage of ST fibers. It's possible that you might not even have the raw speed to reach 100 meters on pace for the U.S. high school mile record. One of the authors of this book, Russ Pate, was just that slow as a high school runner. For Russ, running 100 meters in 14.5 seconds was pretty close to a sprint. Russ's best time for the mile in high school was 4:44, which is good but far from record setting. By his late 20s, however, Russ was an international-class marathoner, with a PR (personal record) of 2:15. He also improved his mile PR to a respectable 4:17. In 1975, when he was 28 years old, Russ participated in a landmark exercise physiology study, in which runners such as Steve Prefontaine and Frank Shorter were assessed for measures such as $\dot{V}O_2$max and muscle fiber type. A biopsy of Russ's calf muscle showed that his ST fiber type composition was 90 percent, a major reason for his success at the longer races.

In general, athletes who have a high percentage of FT fibers are better suited for the middle-distance races (800 meters to the mile), while those with a high percentage of ST fibers will reach their potential in the longer races (3,000 to 5,000 meters). Genetics don't completely determine a distance runner's fate, however, as well-targeted training over many years can actually convert some muscle fibers from one type to another, allowing runners to compensate for weaknesses.

A Tightrope Walk Over a River of Lactic Acid

Getting back to our attempt at the high school mile record, let's suppose that you've got what it takes—an optimal ratio of ST to FT muscle fibers and supreme aerobic fitness—to reach 400 meters on pace, 58.0 seconds for boys and 68.4 seconds for girls. Although you're running comfortably and feeling strong, surviving the next two laps won't be easy. Even for world-class runners, the pace from 400 to 1,200 meters in a mile race is fast enough to recruit a large number of FT muscle fibers, so you'll certainly be traveling down the anaerobic pathway. Reaching the bell lap on target pace will be something like walking a tightrope strung over a river of lactic acid. Whether you successfully balance on the tightrope or fall into the river depends on a physiological balancing act.

When small amounts of lactic acid are produced, the substance is easily cleared through the bloodstream. Lactic acid is transported from the muscle cells where it was produced to other muscle cells, the liver, and the heart. All of these tissues use lactic acid to re-form ATP. This might seem puzzling if you've heard that lactic acid is like a poison that causes muscle fatigue. In recent years, exercise physiologists have learned that lactic acid is an extremely valuable energy source. It causes fatigue only when its production rate exceeds its clearance rate, a condition that leads to lactic acid accumulation in the muscles and blood. At slow running speeds, blood lactic acid levels remain low and constant, indicating that production and clearance rates are evenly matched. As running speed increases, however, lactic acid begins to accumulate rapidly and exponentially. Eventually a threshold is reached where lactic acid production exceeds its clearance.

Many training programs, such as *Daniels' Running Formula* (Daniels 1998) as well as our program in part II, emphasize training at speeds corresponding to the lactate threshold. One method of lactate threshold training involves continuous running for up to 35 or 40 minutes at 75 to 85 percent of maximal heart rate, or approximately 1 minute per mile slower than your PR for the mile. Over time, physiological adaptations to this training increase the lactate threshold, enabling runners to sustain faster paces before lactic acid begins to accumulate. One key adaptation is the development of new capillaries, tiny blood vessels that deliver oxygen to muscle cells, enabling them to make ATP aerobically and so avoid producing lactic acid. Capillaries also move lactic acid from muscle cells into the bloodstream.

Athletes can do training in which they work at their lactate threshold for extended periods of time, to increase the threshold and allow them to run longer and faster before lactic acid accumulates.

Sparing Energy Through Sound Technique

If you were walking a real tightrope over a raging river, a single wrong step or movement in your upper body might lead to a fall. Likewise, counterproductive movements in the running stride can topple you into the river of lactic acid. Consider a runner whose right arm crosses in front of his body, well past an imaginary midline that divides the two sides of his chest. As a result of this crossing action the runner's torso rotates to the left with every stride. To correct the imbalance, the runner will have to use muscles that aren't involved in a sound running stride. The extraneous muscle contractions use oxygen that could otherwise be used by the prime movers, the muscles that efficiently propel the runner's body upward and forward. If we measured this runner's oxygen consumption during a race, it would be higher than that of a competitor who is running at the same pace but has better form. Exercise physiologists refer to this as running economy. Poor running economy, which is linked to flawed technique and a lack of neuromuscular skill, taxes the aerobic system and causes runners to rely more heavily on anaerobic energy, which leads to early fatigue.

Bell Lap Physiology

The bell has just rung as we fast-forward to the 1,209-meter mark of the mile race. You've successfully survived the tightrope walk of the middle two laps. To make it interesting, imagine that you've slipped behind record pace by 2 seconds. Now you'll need to run the last 400 meters in 56 seconds (boys) or 66.4 seconds (girls). If the middle two laps are like walking a tightrope over a river of lactic acid, the last lap is like being immersed in that river and trying to stay afloat. To start your finishing kick you'll need to recruit more FT muscle fibers, which means that even more lactic acid will be produced. The challenge now is to swim or sink. In the muscles and bloodstream this challenge is met by clearing and buffering, or neutralizing, lactic acid.

The body's buffering system uses chemicals called bicarbonates, which are transported into the bloodstream from the liver and kidneys. Bicarbonates increase the body's pH, reducing its acidity. Remember that the acid part of lactic acid, which consists of hydrogen ions that dissociate from lactate molecules, causes muscle fatigue by destroying energy-catalyzing enzymes and interfering with the myofilaments that enable muscles to contract. As figure 2.6 shows, the chemical reaction for buffering lactic acid produces carbonic acid (H_2CO_3). The bloodstream transports the carbonic acid from the muscles to the lungs, where it breaks down into carbon dioxide and water. The carbon dioxide

University of North Carolina

Location: Chapel Hill, North Carolina

Coach: Michael Whittlesey

As a PhD candidate studying exercise physiology at the University of Connecticut, Michael Whittlesey spent his days conducting research and coaching the UCONN cross country and track teams.

"During graduate school I wanted to stay involved with the track team, and the more I stayed involved in coaching, the more I enjoyed combining my interests in coaching and research," Whittlesey says, and that's just what he's been doing since earning his PhD in 1997. In 1998, Whittlesey became the distance coach at the University of North Carolina at Chapel Hill, whose program he has guided to the highest ranks of competition. Every year from 1998 to 2003, the UNC-Chapel Hill women's cross country team qualified for the NCAA championships, placing sixth in 1999. During that time he also coached seven Tarheel runners to 23 All-American honors in cross country and track.

Discussing how he applies principles in exercise physiology to coaching, Whittlesey says, "We think about hitting every single aspect of fitness for running. So we do weight training and plyometrics because research shows that these types of training improve running economy. We do tempo running and long intervals to develop an aerobic base. And when we've built a base of aerobic and muscular strength, we add anaerobic work coordinated with weight training to emphasize speed."

Base training is a main feature of the UNC program, even for the 800-meter runners, who typically work up to 40 to 55 miles a week in the early phases of preparation for the track season. "An 800-meter race is 50-50," says Whittlesey, referring to the contribution of the aerobic and anaerobic energy systems. "To develop aerobic fitness our 800-meter runners do long intervals and run cross country, although they do only about half of the volume of our 5,000- and 10,000-meter specialists."

"Some 800 runners get nervous about losing their fast-twitch fibers and speed when they're doing base work," he explains. "But when we create the aerobic base and build muscular and tendon strength, we carry these aspects of fitness over to the anaerobic speed work. We're building speed—never losing speed."

The knowledge that Whittlesey has gained through research in exercise physiology influences the Tarheel program. But he is quick to mention the invaluable lessons that he has learned outside of the research lab, in daily coaching experiences. "The biggest thing I've learned," he says, "is that everybody is different in terms of the training that they can handle. So it's important to know the individual and to adapt the training according to their history."

Whittlesey stresses another lesson learned through his coaching experience: Even though supreme physiological fitness is essential for success, competitive ability and spirit are equally important. He says, "After races I don't talk with my runners about what time they ran or their splits. I talk with them about how they competed. Did they compete all the way to the finish line? Did they attack at critical points in the race?"

For high school runners who dream of competing in college, Whittlesey advises looking at their running career in the long-term, developing their competitive ability and progressively increasing their training volume and intensity every year.

stimulates ventilation, which explains why you're breathing so hard as you start your last lap kick.

$$H^+ + HCO_3^- \rightarrow H_2CO_3 \rightarrow H_2O + CO_2$$

FIGURE 2.6   The reaction that buffers lactic acid. Bicarbonates (HCO$_3$-) "mop up" hydrogen ions (H$^+$) to form carbonic acid (H$_2$CO$_3$), which is then transported to the lungs to form water and carbon dioxide.

Whether you're able to sustain the kick to the finish depends partly on how effectively your body produces and buffers lactic acid. Your body must generate lactic acid at high rates (because you need it to make ATP), buffer it, and then expel it as carbon dioxide. These capacities are developed through training that stresses the anaerobic pathway. Specifically, high-intensity interval training, which raises lactic acid to high levels and challenges the body to withstand its fatiguing effects, leads to increases in anaerobic enzymes and levels of bicarbonates (see table 2.2). You can find details on training methods for developing anaerobic fitness in chapter 7.

Overcoming Brain Fatigue

Our discussion of running physiology has focused on what happens in the muscles. That's where ATP is produced and where fatigue is observed as a decline in contractile force and power output. Muscles don't contract on their own, however—they respond to commands from the central nervous system (CNS), or neurons in the brain and the spinal cord. One of the hottest areas of research on endurance performance, the role of the brain in fatigue, has resulted in a new theory. This theory holds that muscles are unable to sustain high levels of contractile force during exhausting exercise because they get weak commands from a fatigued brain. Those who subscribe to this theory of CNS fatigue believe that certain byproducts of metabolism in the muscles reduce the strength of neural signals sent from the brain's motor cortex to the working muscles. Scientists don't yet understand the exact metabolic factors that cause CNS fatigue in events between 800 to 5,000 meters. Nevertheless, the theory offers interesting insights into the mind–body connection as well as clues for how runners can defy fatigue in its most extreme forms, such as during the last lap of a mile race.

Now you're on the backstretch of the bell lap, with 200 meters remaining in our imaginary mile. You've responded to the challenge of making up those 2 seconds that were lost in the middle two laps. Remember, for the final 400 meters boys have to run 56 seconds and girls have to run 66.4 seconds to break the record. Suddenly it seems as if someone has shackled five-pound weights to your legs and arms. Your brain is stridently commanding your body to lift your knees high, drive your arms powerfully, and "paw" the track with your spikes, but the communication lines are jammed with fatigue. You'll need supreme physiological fitness to maintain the sprint to the finish, but now more than ever sustaining the pace and holding form are matters of the mind. It'll take every scrap of your willpower, concentration, and courage to amplify the brain's commands to your muscles so that they keep generating powerful, efficient contractions and your technique remains sound.

As you round the last curve, now with 100 meters to go, you might find that the mental force you're exerting dissolves your perception of extreme physical fatigue. Suddenly the weights on your arms and legs are unshackled, and you've broken through to a new level of energy and speed. Have you noticed that at the end of world-class distance races, the winners cross the finish line looking as fresh as they did at the starting line, in jubilation, with ear-to-ear smiles on their faces? That's mind over matter! That's what we envision for you as you cross the finish line of our fantasy mile, setting a new U.S. high school record.

Striding Ahead

We've reached the finish line of our short course on running physiology. Along the way perhaps you've experienced the vicarious thrill of setting an American high school record in the mile run! The best reason for learning physiology is to apply it to training programs, which we do throughout part II. Before we get there, however, we extend our lesson in physiology to matters of nutrition. In the next chapter, you'll learn about optimal intakes of energy sources—carbohydrates, fats, and proteins—as well as nutrients such as water, vitamins, and minerals.

CHAPTER 3

Maximum Nutrition

Back in the 1960s and 1970s, when we were young distance runners, few athletes thought much about nutrition and diet. The prevailing attitude was that "if the oven is hot enough, anything will burn." Many runners ate whatever they liked, assuming that any kind of food would provide optimal fuel. The last few decades of research, however, have revealed that the types and amounts of foods that distance runners eat can strongly influence their performance and health. In this chapter we explain why nutrition matters for young runners and offer advice for creating an ideal diet. Along the way, we answer questions such as these:

- How much food should runners eat?
- What proportion of the diet should come from carbohydrates, fats, and proteins?
- Are vitamin and mineral supplements necessary?
- What's the best fare for prerace and postrace meals?
- Do runners need special sports drinks, or does water do the trick?
- What are the safest and most effective practices for gaining and losing weight?

Growing adolescents have considerable nutritional needs. Add to this the energy spent training, and you can see that nutrition needs to be a major focus for coaches, parents, sports medicine professionals, and young runners themselves. Yet studies show that junk foods make up one-third of the daily diet of up to 90 percent of American adolescents (Wahl 1999). Reports on the diets of young female distance runners reveal that 50 to 60 percent fall far short of daily requirements for caloric intake and vital nutrients such as calcium and iron (Loosli and Benson 1990).

It's a challenge for teenagers to maintain a well-balanced, nutritious diet given their hectic lifestyles, their access to junk food, and media-driven pressures to attain a certain body image as well as to buy foods and supplements that supposedly boost performance. To help you traverse the rocky landscape of fast foods, fad diets, and fantastic claims, we rely on the fundamentals of nutrition, which are derived from research and the advice of experts.

Diet and Performance

Ric's state cross country championship race started early—7:30 A.M. To get a little extra sleep, he skipped breakfast that morning. Ric ate his last meal, a cheeseburger and a chocolate shake, at 5:00 the night before the race. Feeling sapped right from the start, Ric wound up finishing almost a minute slower that he had expected to run on the 5K course.

Melinda usually takes a few sips from her water bottle between classes. But on the day of a big track meet, probably because she was nervous, Melinda forgot to bring her water bottle to school, and she didn't think to use the water fountains. At 400 meters into the 1,600-meter race, the clock showed 80 seconds, which was Melinda's goal pace, but her effort and building fatigue made the pace feel more like a 75 or 76. Physiologically, as a result of dehydration, Melinda was working way too hard.

Alicia had a great summer of training in preparation for her senior cross country season. From June through August she ran almost 500 miles, averaging about 40 miles a week. Over that time she also lost nine pounds, which she attributes to going on a vegetarian diet. Starting in mid-September, Alicia just didn't feel right. She was tired all the time, had trouble concentrating in school, and couldn't train—even an easy warm-up jog drained her energy.

Each of these stories has the same unfortunate ending: The runners fall short of their potential due to oversights in nutrition. For Ric, not eating enough before the competition resulted in hypoglycemia, or low blood glucose. Glucose is the form of carbohydrate that provides energy for the nerve cells in the brain and spinal cord. These cells transmit the neural signals that initiate muscle contractions. If nerve cells lack glucose, their signals decrease in intensity, resulting in less powerful muscle contractions. Glucose is released into the bloodstream from the liver, where it is stored in the form of glycogen. The liver can store only a small amount of glycogen, which is broken down to maintain blood glucose levels between meals, even during sleep. After an overnight fast, liver glycogen levels can be largely depleted and hypoglycemia can result, particularly if the meals of the days before weren't high in carbohydrates.

For Melinda, forgetting to drink water led to dehydration, which decreases the blood's volume. The main components of blood are plasma, which is mostly water, and red blood cells. When the body becomes dehydrated, the concentration of red blood cells increases. This thickening of the blood slows the transport of oxygenated red blood cells to the working muscles, forcing muscle cells to function anaerobically, which results in early fatigue. Dehydration also severely impairs the body's capacity to cool itself because it restricts sweating. Heat is a byproduct of nutrient metabolism, and if the body can't effectively dissipate this heat through sweat, ATP production diminishes greatly, in part because heat breaks down important metabolic enzymes.

The doctor's diagnosis for Alicia was iron-deficiency anemia. Along with this bad news came the order to stop running for at least three months—the rest of the cross country season—to allow her body's iron levels to return to normal. Iron plays an important role in forming hemoglobin, which transports oxygen in the blood, and myoglobin, which transports oxygen in the muscles. When iron levels fall, it becomes harder for the body to supply oxygen to muscle cells, which explains Alicia's general loss of energy and her inability to train without becoming exhausted. When Alicia started her vegetarian diet she eliminated the best sources of iron: red meat, chicken, and fish. A vegetarian diet doesn't automatically cause anemia, especially if it includes plant foods that contain iron (such as breads, grains, legumes, and certain vegetables and fruits) and iron supplements. Without these precautions, however,

Young runners need good nutrition, including a high-carbohydrate diet and the proper amounts of the other essential nutrients.

combining a vegetarian diet with heavy training loads certainly increases the risk for iron-deficiency anemia.

We could go on and on presenting cases of runners whose performance suffered due to oversights in nutrition. But, hoping that we've convinced you that nutrition matters, we'll now show you how to build an optimal diet for young distance runners. We begin by introducing the dietary foundation: macronutrients, or carbohydrates, fats, and proteins.

Carbohydrate Intake

In chapter 2 we discussed the role of carbohydrates as fuel for distance running. Let's review the main points:

▮ Carbohydrates are by far the main source of energy for ATP production in 800- to 5,000-meter events.

▮ The body's carbohydrate stores—blood glucose and liver and muscle glycogen—are very limited, especially in less mature youth.

▮ Muscle glycogen stores can be depleted over several days of intense training if they are not replaced through carbohydrate-rich foods, such as bread, cereal, pasta, legumes, fruits, and vegetables.

Carbohydrates are clearly a vital source of energy, so it's no surprise that experts recommend a high-carbohydrate diet for distance runners, following one of two guidelines. The first is based on the percentage of total daily caloric intake from carbohydrates, which should be between 55 and 70 percent. The other is based on the total grams of carbohydrates consumed, which should range between 7 and 9 grams per kilogram of body weight per day.

Table 3.1 outlines the estimates of total daily energy requirements. You can see from the fourth column that a 12-year-old girl who runs about 3 miles a day must consume approximately 2,200 calories per day to replace the calories that she burns, which is critical for maintaining health and a proper body weight. Of those 2,200 calories, approximately 1,210 to 1,540 should come from carbohydrates (2,200 calories per day × .55 = 1,210 calories from carbohydrates; 2,200 calories per day × .70 = 1,540 calories from carbohydrates) to meet the percentage recommendations for carbohydrate intake, as shown in the fifth column. The last column shows recommended carbohydrate intake based on the second set of guidelines, 7 to 9 grams of carbohydrates per kilogram of body weight per day. A 12-year-old girl who weighs 41.6 kilograms, or 91.6 pounds, should consume approximately 291 to 374 grams of carbohydrates per day (41.6 kg × 7 g per kg = 291.2 g; 41.6 kg × 9 g per kg = 374.4 g).

TABLE 3.1—Recommended Carbohydrate Intake for Young Runners

Age	Gender	Reference weight in kg (lb)	Total daily calories	ESTIMATED DAILY REQUIREMENTS	
				Carbohydrates (calories, based on 55%-70% of total caloric intake)	Carbohydrates (grams, based on 7-9 g per kg per day)
12	Girls	41.6 (91.6)	2,200	1,210-1,540	291-374
12	Boys	40.5 (89.2)	2,400	1,320-1,680	284-365
13	Girls	45.8 (100.9)	2,300	1,265-1,610	321-412
13	Boys	45.6 (100.4)	2,500	1,375-1,750	310-410
14	Girls	49.4 (108.8)	2,300	1,265-1,610	346-445
14	Boys	51.0 (112.3)	2,700	1,485-1,890	357-459
15	Girls	52.0 (114.5)	2,500	1,375-1,750	364-468
15	Boys	56.3 (124.0)	3,100	1,705-2,170	394-507
16	Girls	53.9 (118.7)	2,500	1,375-1,750	377-485
16	Boys	60.9 (134.1)	3,200	1,760-2,240	426-548
17	Girls	55.1 (121.4)	2,500	1,375-1,750	386-496
17	Boys	64.6 (142.3)	3,300	1,815-2,310	452-581
18	Girls	56.2 (123.8)	2,500	1,375-1,750	393-506
18	Boys	67.2 (148.0)	3,300	1,815-2,310	470-605

Estimates of the total daily caloric requirements were obtained by adding 300 calories (for 12- to 14-year-olds) and 500 calories (for 15- to 18-year-olds) to the estimated energy requirements of normally active teenagers. Estimated energy requirements derived from the Dietary Reference Intakes for Energy, Carbohydrates, Fiber, Fat, Protein and Amino Acids (published by the National Academy of Sciences, www.nal.usda.gov/fnic/etext/000105.html). The additional 300 and 500 calories roughly estimate the energy expended in running 3 and 5 miles per day.

Even though the values in table 3.1 are based on extensive research, they are only estimates. Your individual metabolic rate and energy expenditure in daily activities and training will determine your total caloric and carbohydrate intake. With the help of a registered dietitian or another certified nutritional counselor, you can determine your needs more precisely.

To know whether you're meeting your recommended daily intake of carbohydrates, you'll need to use nutrition information labels, which provide the number of grams of carbohydrate, fat, and protein per serving. Tables 3.2 and 3.3 list the carbohydrate contents of various foods in both grams and calories. Note that one gram of carbohydrate contains four calories. The foods are grouped by type of carbohydrate, complex or simple. Complex carbohydrates (table 3.2), named for their long chains of glucose molecules, are in starchy foods, grain products, and most vegetables. Simple carbohydrates (table 3.3) make up sugary foods and fruits. Both forms provide glucose for muscle activity; however, complex carbohydrates and fruits are usually healthiest because they are found in foods that contain high amounts of vitamins, minerals, and fiber. These nutrients are usually stripped away from processed foods like candy and donuts. For this reason experts recommend that no more than 10 percent of total caloric intake should come from highly processed sweets.

Using tables 3.2 and 3.3, let's add up the grams and calories of carbohydrates in a high-energy breakfast:

2 pancakes	=	28 grams (112 calories)
2 tablespoons syrup	=	30 grams (120 calories)
1 banana	=	28 grams (112 calories)
1 cup orange juice	=	26 grams (104 calories)
1 cup low-fat milk	=	12 grams (48 calories)
		124 grams (496 calories)

A 16-year-old girl who weighs 53.9 kg (118.7 lb) requires at least 1,375 calories from, or 377 grams of, carbohydrates each day. You can see from table 3.1 that this sample breakfast supplies roughly one-third of her daily carbohydrate requirement.

Fat Intake

As we discussed in chapter 2, the contribution of fat to total energy needs during running increases as the pace slows (see figure 2.5 on page 28). Fat thus plays a major role in fueling low- to moderate-intensity training runs and long races such as the marathon, but it provides only a small part of the young runner's energy in events from 800 to 5,000 meters. Nevertheless, some advantages exist for middle- and long-distance runners whose bodies are able to burn a large amount of fat. Fat is a highly concentrated source of energy; a gram of fat contains about nine calories, which far exceeds the energy in a gram of carbohydrate (four calories) and a gram of protein (also four calories). In addition, when the muscles burn fat, the body's limited stores of carbohydrate are spared. Carbohydrate sparing is important in distance running because it delays the fatigue caused by glycogen depletion. As we discussed in chapter 2, training improves the body's ability to use fat by increasing the rate of oxygen-rich blood flow to the muscles and by elevating levels of fat-burning enzymes.

TABLE 3.2—High-Carbohydrate Foods: Complex Carbohydrates

Food	Serving size	Grams of carbohydrate	Calories from carbohydrate
BREAD, CEREAL, PASTA, AND RICE			
Bread, whole wheat	1 slice	12	48
Bagel, cinnamon raisin	1 (3 1/2-in. diameter)	39	156
Flour tortilla	1 (8-in. diameter)	20	80
Pancake	1 (5-in. diameter)	14	56
Waffle, frozen, ready-to-heat	1	13	52
Cereal, ready to eat, Cheerios	1 cup	22	88
Cereal, ready to eat, Honey-Nut Cheerios	1 cup	46	184
Oatmeal, instant, maple and brown sugar	1 packet	31	124
Spaghetti or macaroni, cooked	1 cup	40	160
Rice, white, cooked	1 cup	45	180
VEGETABLES			
Broccoli, cooked	1/2 cup	4	16
Carrot, raw	1	7	28
Corn, frozen	1/2 cup	21	84
Lettuce, iceberg	1 cup	1	4
Peas, green, frozen	1/2 cup	11	44
Potato, baked	1	43	172
BEANS AND NUTS[a]			
Baked beans, canned	1/2 cup	26	104
Black beans, cooked	1/2 cup	20	80
Refried beans, canned	1/2 cup	19	76
Almonds, dry roasted	1 oz	6	24
Peanuts, dry roasted	1 oz	6	24
Sunflower seeds	1 oz	7	32
SNACKS[a]			
Popcorn	1 cup	6	24
Potato chips	1 oz	15	60
Tortilla chips	1 oz	18	72

[a]These foods are high in carbohydrates, but they can also be high in fat and sodium.

TABLE 3.3—High-Carbohydrate Foods: Simple Carbohydrates

Food	Serving size	Grams of carbohydrate	Calories from carbohydrate
FRUITS AND FRUIT JUICES			
Apple	1	21	84
Banana	1	28	112
Cherries	10	11	44
Grapes	10	9	36
Orange	1	15	60
Pear	1	25	100
Raisins	1/3 cup	38	152
Orange juice	1 cup	26	104
Grape juice	1 cup	38	152
Apple juice	1 cup	29	116
DAIRY PRODUCTS			
Milk, low fat (2%)	1 cup	12	48
Yogurt, plain	1 cup	16	64
Yogurt, fruit	1 cup	43	172
DRINKS			
Sport drinks	12 oz	16	64
Soft drinks	12 oz	38	152
BREAKFAST SWEETS			
Honey	1 Tbsp	17	68
Syrup, pancake	1 Tbsp	15	60
Jams and jellies	1 Tbsp	13	52
Table sugar	1 Tbsp	4	16
SWEET SNACKS			
Chocolate candy	1 bar (2 oz)	34	136
Chocolate chip cookies, store-bought	4	28	112
Doughnuts, glazed	1	27	108

Diet and Young Kenyan Distance Runners

Since the late 1960s Kenyan men have won an extraordinary number of medals in the Olympic Games and world championships in cross country and track. Over the last two decades women and juniors (age 19 and under) from Kenya have added to the overwhelming domination. The rest of the running world wants to know, "How do they do it?" Little scientific information exists about the training methods of the Kenyans, especially the juniors. But a study published in 2002 provided interesting insights into the young distance runners' diet. The subjects were 12 boys, average age 17.1 years, who were part of the Kalenjin ethnic group, which is famous for producing the world's best distance runners. Over a two-week period the researchers measured the runners' daily energy expenditure and diet composition. Here's a summary of the results:

- Daily energy expenditure: 3,155 calories
- Daily energy intake: 3,160 calories
- Energy intake from carbohydrate: 71 percent (8.7 grams per kilogram of body weight per day)
- Energy intake from protein: 13 percent (1.6 grams per kilogram of body weight per day)
- Energy intake from fat: 15 percent

The runners averaged 10K a day, and they participated in other activities, including stretching, strength training, and ball games such as soccer. Maize (corn) and kidney beans accounted for 81 percent of their diet. The Kenyan runners' carbohydrate and protein intake were very high compared to the recommendations of sports nutrition experts. In addition, these young Kenyan runners consumed much higher concentrations of carbohydrate and protein than are typically reported by distance runners from countries such as the United States, Canada, and Great Britain.

Source: Christensen, D.L., van Hall, G., and Hambraeus, L. 2002. Food and macronutrient intake of male adolescent Kalenjin runners in Kenya. *British Journal of Nutrition* 88:711-717.

Unlike carbohydrates, the body stores fat in abundant amounts. In healthy nonathletic teens, fat makes up 12 to 15 percent of body weight in boys and 21 to 25 percent in girls. On average, teenage distance runners have body-fat values of 8 to 12 percent for boys and 12 to 16 percent for girls (Butts 1982; Cunningham 1990; Sundberg and Elovanio 1982). A runner who weighs 60 kilograms (132 pounds) and whose body-fat content is only 12 percent has enough energy from fat stores to fuel approximately 600 miles of slow running. While fat plays a major role in energy production and numerous other physiological functions, an excess amount of body fat wastes energy because it's dead weight that makes the muscles work harder to transport the body. Sports nutrition experts recommend a diet in which only 20 to 25 percent of the total calories come from fat (but see the sidebar on page 51 for another view on fat intake).

Table 3.4 shows estimated requirements for daily fat intake in calories and grams (one gram of fat yields nine calories). By these estimates, a 14-year-old girl who runs 3 miles a day will need to eat about 460 to 575 calories from fat (51 to 64 grams) per day. Many teens have little problem meeting the requirements for fat intake. In fact, it's easy to eat too much fat if you enjoy foods like hot dogs, cheeseburgers, french fries, and pizza. Table 3.5 lists the fat content of some common foods.

As table 3.5 shows, dairy products such as cheese and ice cream have a high fat content. Runners who often get more than 25 percent of their calories from fat should consider switching to nonfat or low-fat dairy products. As for meat, even lean beef and pork contain a lot of fat. Low-fat alternatives are chicken and fish, but if these foods are

TABLE 3.4—Recommended Fat Intake for Young Runners

Age	Gender	Reference weight in kg (lb)	Total daily calories	Fat (calories, based on 20-25% of total caloric intake)	Fat (grams per day)
12	Girls	41.6 (91.6)	2,200	440-550	49-61
12	Boys	40.5 (89.2)	2,400	480-600	53-67
13	Girls	45.8 (100.9)	2,300	460-575	51-64
13	Boys	45.6 (100.4)	2,500	500-625	56-69
14	Girls	49.4 (108.8)	2,300	460-575	51-64
14	Boys	51.0 (112.3)	2,700	540-675	60-75
15	Girls	52.0 (114.5)	2,500	500-625	56-69
15	Boys	56.3 (124.0)	3,100	620-775	69-86
16	Girls	53.9 (118.7)	2,500	500-625	56-69
16	Boys	60.9 (134.1)	3,200	640-800	71-89
17	Girls	55.1 (121.4)	2,500	500-625	56-69
17	Boys	64.6 (142.3)	3,300	660-825	73-92
18	Girls	56.2 (123.8)	2,500	500-625	56-69
18	Boys	67.2 (148.0)	3,300	660-825	73-92

See the note at the end of table 3.1 on page 45 for an explanation of how we estimated total daily caloric requirements.

The High-Carbohydrate Versus High-Fat Diet Debate

A controversy has been brewing in sports nutrition since the mid-1990s, when research began to challenge the conventional notion that distance runners should eat a high-carbohydrate diet. These studies support the claim that the optimal diet is relatively high in fat (40 percent or more) and low in carbohydrates (around 40 percent). This view holds that because fat contains so much energy and spares glycogen, runners should eat more of it. By eating more fat runners will train their bodies to burn it as a preferred fuel. Some studies do support this argument; however, the studies are not applicable to young runners. Subjects in these studies were highly trained adult runners who performed tests at relatively low speeds for long durations, conditions under which fat contributes significantly to energy needs. The results suggest that a relatively high-fat diet might improve performance for highly trained, adult marathon runners. But young runners do not have the physiological capacities of elite marathoners, and because young runners compete at shorter distances and higher intensities, they burn less fat and more carbohydrates. Young athletes should avoid a high-fat diet because it won't improve performance, and, more importantly, because it is linked to heart disease.

cooked with butter or oil, their fat content skyrockets. For example, the fried fish sandwich with cheese that you can get at a fast food restaurant has around 29 grams of fat. The fish itself may have only 1 or 2 grams of fat, but the oil in which it's fried contains about 15 grams of fat per tablespoon. A source of hidden fat in carbohydrate-rich food is granola. The fat content of the cereals in table 3.5 range from 1 to 17 grams; many granola cereals are at the high end of this range. To make sure that you're not consuming unwanted fat, read the nutrition labels on cereal boxes carefully.

Like carbohydrates, fats come in different forms, some of which are healthier than others. Saturated fat and cholesterol are found primarily in animal products like beef, bacon, and dairy foods. Research shows that individuals who consume a lot of these fats are at high risk for heart disease. The cause of heart disease, the formation of fatty deposits on the inner linings of the coronary vessels, actually begins during childhood, so it is important for young runners to watch their saturated fat intake. According to nutrition experts, no more than 10 percent of daily fat should come from saturated sources. The rest should come from foods that are high in unsaturated fat, such as vegetable oils (canola, corn, safflower, and olive), soy, and fish. Eaten in moderation, these fats are good for your heart, other organs, and many physiological functions, including the immune system's response to disease.

TABLE 3.5—Fat Content in Common Foods

Food	Serving size	Grams of fat	Calories from fat
BREAD, CEREAL, PASTA, AND RICE			
Bread, whole wheat	1 slice	1	9
Bagel, cinnamon raisin	1 (3 1/2-in. diameter)	1	9
Cereal, ready to eat, frosted wheat squares	1 cup	1	9
Cereal, ready to eat, granola	1 cup	17	153
Oatmeal, instant, maple and brown sugar	1 packet	2	18
Spaghetti or macaroni	1 cup	1	9
Rice, white, cooked	1 cup	.5	4.5
DAIRY PRODUCTS			
Milk, 2%	1 cup	5	45
Milk, whole fat	1 cup	8	72
Yogurt, whole fat	1 cup	7	63
Yogurt, low fat	1 cup	3	27
Cheddar cheese	1 oz	9	81
Cream cheese	1 Tbsp	5	45
Butter	1 Tbsp	12	108
Ice cream	1/2 cup	12	108
MEAT, POULTRY, FISH, BEANS, NUTS, AND EGGS			
Ground beef, broiled (15% fat)	3 oz	16	166
Pork chop, broiled	3 oz	11	99
Chicken breast, skinless, broiled	4 oz	5	45
Fish, tuna, canned in water	3 oz	2	18
Fish, cod	3 oz	1	9
Baked beans, canned	1 cup	1	9
Almonds, dry roasted	1 oz	14	126
Peanuts, dry roasted	1 oz	14	126
Peanut butter	2 Tbsp	16	144
Eggs	1	5	45
SNACKS			
Popcorn, oil-popped	1 cup	3	27
Potato chips	1 oz	9	81
Tortilla chips	1 oz	7	63
Chocolate chip cookies, store-bought	4 cookies	10	90

Protein Intake

When you supply your body with enough carbohydrates and fats, it uses very little protein for fuel during running. Only in cases of extreme glycogen depletion and starvation does protein metabolism occur on a large scale. Nevertheless, the runner must replace proteins on a daily basis because they undergo a process of continuous deformation, or turnover, in the body. Protein is necessary for normal physiological functions, including energy metabolism and growth and repair of muscle tissue. As we discussed in chapter 2, muscle fibers are made of protein, so the athlete requires this nutrient to rebuild and strengthen tissue torn down in training. Protein also makes up hemoglobin and myoglobin, which are critical to endurance performance because they transport oxygen to muscle cells. Even the enzymes that spark reactions in the energy pathways are composed of protein.

Proteins are made up of compounds called amino acids. Twenty amino acids are required to build the proteins. Although the body can synthesize 11 of these by itself, the remaining 9, called the essential amino acids, must be consumed in the diet. The best protein sources are animal products such as lean meat, fish, poultry, eggs, and milk. Animal sources of protein are considered complete because they contain all of the essential amino acids. Many plant foods are good sources of protein, but they are incomplete, or lacking in one or two essential amino acids. Even so, vegetarian runners can get a complete supply of essential amino acids by combining proteins, or eating a variety of plant foods including beans, nuts, and whole-grain products such as corn, rice, wheat bread, and pasta.

For active adolescent boys and girls who aren't training, the recommended daily allowance (RDA) for protein is .85 to .95 grams per kilogram of body weight. An individual who weighs 59 kilograms (129.8 pounds) thus needs approximately 50 to 56 grams of protein per day. The RDA is a liberal standard that an athlete can easily meet on a diet that includes meat. One three-ounce serving of beef, chicken, or fish contains 20 to 24 grams of protein (see table 3.6). Add a serving of macaroni (7 grams) topped with an ounce of cheese (7 grams) along with a cup of milk (8 grams), and the total of 42 to 46 grams approaches the RDA for adolescents in just one meal.

Growing runners, who are constantly breaking down muscle tissue in training, need slightly more protein than their peers who don't train. The daily recommendation for endurance athletes is 1.2 to 1.6 grams per kilogram of body weight, so to figure out your recommended range for daily protein intake in grams, multiply your weight in kilograms by 1.2 and 1.6. Although runners have higher protein needs than normally active individuals, they don't need to take protein supplements. Runners can easily meet their extra protein needs by eating a well-balanced diet that contains enough calories to replace those burned in training.

TABLE 3.6—Protein Content in Common Foods

Food	Serving size	Grams of protein	Calories from protein
BREAD, CEREAL, PASTA, AND RICE			
Bread, whole wheat	1 slice	2	8
Bagel, cinnamon-raisin	1 (3 1/2-in. diameter)	7	28
Cereal, boxed, ready to eat, frosted wheat squares	1 cup	6	24
Cereal, boxed, ready to eat, crisp rice	1 cup	2	8
Oatmeal, instant, maple and brown sugar	1 packet	4	16
Spaghetti or macaroni	1 cup	7	28
Rice, white, cooked	1 cup	4	16
DAIRY PRODUCTS			
Milk, 2% fat	1 cup	8	32
Yogurt, whole milk	1 cup	8	32
Cheese, cheddar	1 oz	7	28
Cheese, cream	1 Tbsp	1	4
Ice cream	1/2 cup	3	12
MEAT, POULTRY, FISH, BEANS, NUTS, AND EGGS			
Ground beef, broiled (15% fat)	3 oz	22	88
Pork chop, broiled	3 oz	24	96
Chicken breast, skinless, broiled	3 oz	24	96
Fish, tuna, canned in water	3 oz	20	80
Fish, cod	3 oz	20	80
Baked beans, canned	1 cup	12	48
Black beans, canned	1 cup	15	60
Almonds, dry roasted	1 oz	6	24
Peanuts, dry roasted	1 oz	7	28
Peanut butter	2 Tbsp	8	32
Eggs	1	7	28
SNACKS			
Potato chips	1 oz	2	8
Tortilla chips	1 oz	2	8
Chocolate chip cookies, store-bought	4 cookies	2	8

Putting It All Together

To build an optimal diet for young runners we'll rely on the most widely accepted and highly recommended standard for proper nutrition—the Food Guide Pyramid, developed by nutrition scientists at the United States Department of Agriculture and the Department of Health and Human Services (see figure 3.1). The pyramid lists the recommended number of servings of food groups for a healthy diet. At the base of the pyramid are complex carbohydrates such as breads, cereals, and pasta. Nutrition experts recommend eating 6 to 11 servings of these foods per day. The next level contains vegetables (3 to 5 servings) and fruits (2 to 3 servings). The third level features dairy products such as milk, yogurt, and cheese (2 to 3 servings) along with sources rich in protein like meats, eggs, beans, and nuts (2 to 3 servings). At the top of the pyramid are fats, oils, and sweets, which should be eaten sparingly.

Normally active teens who eat a variety of foods from the first three levels of the food pyramid will meet their basic nutritional demands for good health. Runners, however, may need to increase the recommended number of food servings to replace the energy they use in training. The

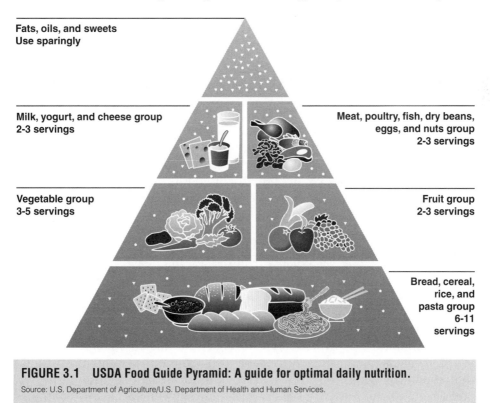

Fats, oils, and sweets
Use sparingly

Milk, yogurt, and cheese group
2-3 servings

Meat, poultry, fish, dry beans,
eggs, and nuts group
2-3 servings

Vegetable group
3-5 servings

Fruit group
2-3 servings

Bread, cereal,
rice, and
pasta group
6-11
servings

FIGURE 3.1 USDA Food Guide Pyramid: A guide for optimal daily nutrition.
Source: U.S. Department of Agriculture/U.S. Department of Health and Human Services.

Villanova University

Location: Villanova, Pennsylvania

Coach: Gina Procaccio

As a high school runner in Aston, Pennsylvania in the early 1980s, with PRs of 2:10 for 800 meters and 4:56 for the mile, Gina Procaccio was a self-described healthy eater. "I have to give credit to my mom," Procaccio says. "When you're in high school, you eat whatever Mom puts on the table. We ate a normal diet with meat and potatoes, and lots of pasta." Looking back on her stellar career as a distance runner—which includes a number-one ranking among American women for 3,000 meters in 1995—Procaccio attributes part of her success to her approach to nutrition. She now imparts her wisdom about healthy eating to the runners she coaches at Villanova University.

Procaccio has been the head women's track and cross country coach at Villanova since 2000, continuing a tradition that has established arguably the best distance running program in NCAA history. Between 1989 and 1998, the Villanova women won seven NCAA team cross country championships, with Procaccio serving as assistant coach for the 1994 and 1998 national championship teams. In her career as assistant and head coach at Villanova, eight of Procaccio's runners have earned All-American honors and three have won NCAA championships.

Procaccio believes that sharing her nutrition philosophy with her runners is part of her coaching responsibility. "When you're a coach, your athletes become like your own children. So the first thing that I tell my runners is that I don't care as much about their running as I care about their health and their life. And nutrition is a big part of that," she says. Her main concern is making sure that her athletes eat enough to replace the energy that they expend in training, which can include 50 to 60 miles a week when preparing for cross country and the longer races in track. "As long as my girls are eating three full and balanced meals a day, without junk food, they'll be at the right weight and they'll have the potential to perform their best," she says.

"But I don't want my runners to be too focused on food," Procaccio adds. "They shouldn't deprive themselves. After a meal, it's okay to have dessert. If you deprive yourself of something like dessert, you're just going to crave it even more."

While she understands the relationship between body weight and running performance, Procaccio is strongly against weight loss for the purpose of trying to run faster times. "We don't ever tell our runners that they need to lose weight. Instead, we give them guidance and advice on healthy nutrition and we answer their questions about the best foods to eat," she says.

Procaccio extends her philosophy on nutrition to young distance runners. "A teenage runner shouldn't deprive herself of food, thinking that she'll run faster times," says the coach. "Sure, she might feel a little lighter, but in the long run, it's not worth it, especially when you consider that eating disorders can impede normal growth and development. I want to see my girls running well and being healthy 10 years and longer down the road."

high end of the ranges—11 servings of complex carbohydrates, 5 servings of vegetables, 3 servings of fruits, and so forth—will supply about 2,800 calories per day. Looking at table 3.1 on page 45, you can see that this number of calories is more than sufficient for 12- to 18-year-old girls who average 3 to 5 miles per day. But for girls whose training is more extensive and for 12- to 18-year-old boys, the highest number of recommended servings might not meet energy needs. The best way to boost caloric intake is to start at the bottom of the pyramid and add servings of complex carbohydrates, fruits, and vegetables.

We've designed a sample menu on page 58 to meet the energy and nutrition requirements for a 17- to 18-year-old boy who runs 5 miles per day or who does other forms of training that demand as much energy. The total number of calories in the sample menu is 3,300, with 60 percent from carbohydrate, 15 percent from protein, and 25 percent from fat. This might seem like too much food, and it might be too much for younger runners who train less than 5 miles per day, but it's also possible that the sample menu provides too little energy for runners whose training is more extensive. It's not hard to tell if you're getting enough energy and nutrients—if you're maintaining a healthy body weight, you're in caloric balance, which means that you're replacing the energy burned in training.

Other Key Nutrients: Vitamins, Minerals, and Water

In addition to the three energy sources, food contains other important nutrients, namely vitamins, minerals, and water. These nutrients are not directly used to fuel muscle contraction. Instead, they perform vital physiological functions such as catalyzing reactions in the energy pathways, supporting nutrient and oxygen transport to the working muscles, promoting growth and healing, and protecting against disease. In this section, we examine these nutrients and their contribution to distance running performance.

Getting Your Vitamins and Minerals

Vitamins are organic compounds found in many meats, fruits, vegetables, and dairy products. It's essential for distance runners to get enough of these nutrients because they play a major role in energy metabolism; for example, niacin and several of the B-complex vitamins speed up the metabolism of carbohydrates and fats. Vitamins play other roles, too. Vitamin C, found in fruits and vegetables, strengthens bones and connective tissue. Research shows that this vitamin also protects the body against infections and common colds by boosting the immune system.

Sample Menu for a 17- to 18-Year-Old Male Runner

Total calories: 3,300 **Percent carbohydrate:** 60 **Percent fat**: 25 **Percent protein:** 15	
Breakfast	1 1/2 to 2 cups Cheerios (ready-to-eat cereal) 2 slices whole grain toast with 2 tsp margarine and 2 tsp jam 1 banana 12 oz orange juice 1 cup skim milk
Morning snack	1 bagel 1 apple (or other fruit) Water
Lunch	Chicken sandwich (3 oz skinless baked chicken breast, 2 slices whole grain bread, lettuce, mustard) 1 small bag of potato chips 1 slice of cantaloupe (or other fruit) 1 carrot 12 oz of a sports drink (e.g., Gatorade)
Afternoon snack	1/2 cup canned fruit or 1/4 cup dried fruit (e.g., raisins) 6 graham crackers (3-inch square) Water
Dinner	Cheeseburger (3 oz lean ground beef or turkey, whole wheat bun, tomato and lettuce slices, 1 slice cheese, ketchup, and mustard) 1/2 cup baked beans Large salad (2 cups lettuce or mixed greens, 1 cup mixed vegetables such as tomatoes, cucumbers, carrots, peppers, mushrooms, 2 tbsp low-fat salad dressing) Iced tea (decaffeinated)
After-dinner snack or dessert	1 cup low-fat fruit yogurt 6 vanilla wafers

Note: If breakfast and dinner meals are too much food for one sitting, you can substitute a sandwich, fruit, or vegetable for a snack.

Vitamin B_1 (thiamine), found in meats, grains, and nuts, helps form hemoglobin. Other vitamins are essential for young runners because they contribute to normal growth, such as vitamin D. This vitamin, found in dairy foods and eggs, promotes bone growth.

Minerals are inorganic elements found in water, vegetables, and animal foods. Minerals help build bones, form enzymes, transmit neural signals, and produce muscle contractions. For young runners, one of the most important minerals is calcium, which promotes bone growth and helps muscle contraction. Good sources of calcium include dairy products, vegetables, and whole-grain foods. Another important mineral for runners is iron, which is important in forming hemoglobin in red blood cells. Iron is found in red meats, green vegetables, eggs, nuts, and whole grains. If dietary intake of iron is insufficient, distance runners can easily suffer low iron and hemoglobin levels, because iron can be depleted through sweating and hemoglobin can be lost as red blood cells are broken down through the repetitive stress of the footstrike during the running stride. Adolescent girls lose iron through menstruation as well. Some studies show that more than 50 percent of young female runners do not consume the RDA for dietary iron, which is 15 milligrams per day for 14- to 18-year-old females (Loosli and Benson 1990). Extreme iron deficiency, like we saw earlier with Alicia, can result in anemia, a debilitating condition in which red blood cells and hemoglobin reach dangerously low levels.

Should Runners Take Vitamin and Mineral Supplements?

Because vitamins and minerals are critical to good health and athletic performance, many people think they should take supplements of these nutrients. However, most nutrition experts agree that young athletes do not need vitamin and mineral supplements if they eat a balanced diet, meaning they eat the required number of food servings from the food pyramid. If you're at all concerned that you're not getting enough of these nutrients, buy a generic multiple vitamin and mineral supplement that does not exceed 100 percent of the RDAs (the information labels on these products will tell you what percentage of the RDAs they offer).

No strong scientific evidence exists to prove that runners can improve performance by taking extra doses of vitamins and minerals. In fact, the body simply excretes excessive amounts of most vitamins and minerals. For example, vitamin C and the B-complex vitamins are transported in water in the body. These and other water-soluble vitamins are eliminated in the urine when the daily intake exceeds the body's requirements. In contrast, the fat-soluble vitamins—A, D, E, and K—are stored in body fat. These vitamins can be toxic when consumed in excessive amounts (several hundred percent of the RDA).

Staying Hydrated

As we saw in Melinda's case, runners who fail to match fluid intake with fluid loss suffer early fatigue because plasma volume decreases, thickening the blood and slowing the delivery of oxygen and nutrients to the muscles, and the body overheats. While fluid replacement is important for all distance runners, young runners have special needs. First, young runners are less efficient, so they generate more body heat than adult runners working at comparable intensities. Second, the adolescent's body doesn't cool itself as efficiently, in part due to lower sweating rates. Third, the adolescent body has a larger surface area to body weight ratio, which increases heat storage. Finally, evidence shows that if young athletes are not reminded to consume fluids, they do not drink enough to rehydrate the body.

Exercise scientists have not developed specific guidelines for fluid replacement in young runners. However, we've come up with the following recommendations based on research involving young athletes in other sports (Bar-Or and Unnithan 1994) and adult endurance athletes (American College of Sports Medicine 2000). Coaches should insist on even more fluid intake if runners show signs of dehydration, including dry lips, sunken eyes, and muscle cramps. Runners should increase their fluid intake if they notice that they are urinating infrequently and if their urine is dark yellow.

▌ Two hours before training and competition: Drink 1 to 2 cups (8 to 16 ounces) of water or a sports drink.

▌ During training: Drink 4 to 6 ounces of water or a sports drink every 15 to 20 minutes.

▌ During competition: In 800- to 5,000-meter races, runners do not need to drink fluids if they are sufficiently hydrated before the start.

▌ After training and competition: Drink 16 to 20 ounces of water or a sports drink for every pound of weight lost.

▌ Runners should avoid drinking caffeinated beverages such as soda and iced tea because they promote urination and water loss.

Water is often the best drink for young runners, but in some cases sports drinks that contain a 4 to 8 percent solution of carbohydrates and electrolytes are better. For example, runners who lose their appetite for solid foods after intense workouts and races can begin to replace their glycogen stores with a sports drink. In addition, runners who don't enjoy drinking water typically don't rehydrate their bodies adequately. These runners drink more fluid when it's in the form of flavored sports drinks.

Energy for Competition:
Prerace and Postrace Meals

It's an unfortunate but fairly common occurrence for runners to race poorly because of what they have or have not eaten in the hours before competition. Like Ric, athletes who skip a meal on race day may experience hypoglycemia, general exhaustion, and muscle fatigue, even before the race starts. In addition, eating too soon before a race or eating the wrong kinds of foods can cause an upset stomach.

In general, distance runners should eat a high-energy meal about two to four hours before competing, in which approximately 60 percent of the calories come from carbohydrates. For morning races, breakfast foods—cereal with milk, toast and jelly, and pancakes or waffles with syrup—can be ideal. It's okay to include small amounts of fat and protein, such as butter and bacon, for taste. For afternoon or evening races, some runners prefer a plate of pasta because it has a high carbohydrate content and digests easily. Research clearly shows that the optimal prerace meal is high in carbohydrates. Beyond this guideline, perhaps the best advice is to go with what works best for you. Take note of the foods that you ate before the races in which you felt and performed best. Then, stick with those foods for your prerace meal in the future.

Diet composition plays an important role in recovery, especially after longer races (3,000 to 5,000 meters). The primary goal of the postrace meal is to replenish depleted glycogen, so it should be high in carbohydrates. In addition, the postrace meal should include protein to rebuild damaged muscle and to re-form enzymes in the energy pathways. The normal runner's diet, which we discussed earlier, is generally sufficient for the postrace meal, but some experts contend that the timing is critical. They cite research evidence that glycogen resynthesis occurs faster when athletes eat a high-carbohydrate meal within two hours of exhausting training or competition.

Body Weight and Composition

You can see simply by looking that a slight, lean build is characteristic of many elite runners. Some athletes would certainly reach a higher competitive level if they had the "ideal" runner's body. However, while it's possible to alter body weight and composition by changing dietary and training practices, doing so haphazardly usually damages performance and health. Consider the case of Jackie, a 16-year-old girl who has increased her weekly mileage during the summer from 30 to 50 to prepare for the upcoming cross country season. In addition to increasing her mileage so drastically, Jackie has decided to cut 300 calories per day from her normal diet in order to lose 10 pounds over the summer. Jackie's body will be operating under a condition called negative caloric balance, where energy intake is less than energy expenditure.

As a result of this energy drain, Jackie faces detrimental health and performance consequences. A severe negative caloric balance is linked to menstrual dysfunction, specifically conditions called oligomenorrhea (irregular and infrequent menstrual periods) and amenorrhea (absence of menstrual periods). As we discussed in chapter 1, these conditions prevent proper bone development and can even lead to significant bone loss. Research shows that athletes with menstrual disturbances are two times more likely to suffer stress fractures than athletes with normal menstrual function (Brukner and Bennell 1997). In addition, adolescent girls who experience abnormal menstrual cycles are at high risk for osteoporosis later in life. Even if Jackie's energy drain isn't severe enough to disrupt her normal menstrual periods, it will likely hurt her running by failing to restore nutrients used to fuel her training, especially glycogen, protein, vitamins, and minerals.

Jackie's case is one of many that demonstrate the negative effects of drastic measures for altering body weight and composition. Strategies for losing and gaining weight go beyond the scope of this book, so when young runners want to lose or gain weight, parents and coaches should consult physicians and certified nutrition specialists. Under no circumstances should coaches and parents ever pressure runners to lose weight. Even well-intended comments such as, "If you lost a few pounds, you'd run a lot faster," can lead to very serious consequences.

Striding Ahead

An understanding of the connection between nutrition and endurance performance is vital to success in developing young runners. Before moving on to the psychological side of running in the following chapter, let's recap the main connections in this relationship:

▍ Because carbohydrates are the primary source of energy in events from 800 to 5,000 meters, they should make up a large part of the young runner's diet, approximately 55 to 70 percent or 7 to 9 grams per kilogram of body weight.

▍ As long as runners eat enough of a variety of foods from the food pyramid, they don't need to supplement nutrition with vitamin and mineral pills.

▋ Coaches must encourage runners to drink enough water or sports drink before, during, and after training sessions.

▋ The ideal prerace meal, which runners should eat about two to four hours before competition, is high in carbohydrates. Runners should eat a high-carbohydrate meal soon after competitions.

▋ Drastic measures to change weight and body composition can negatively affect performance and health. Parents and coaches should consult a physician or professional nutrition expert for sound strategies and should closely supervise runners who want to lose or gain weight.

CHAPTER 4

Champion Psyche

In chapter 2 we covered the physiology of distance running while leading you through an imaginary attempt at the U.S. high school record in the mile run. We're going back to the starting line of that race, this time to examine the psychology of distance running and how emotions, beliefs, and thoughts interact with physiological processes and thereby influence running performance. We focus on the most important qualities of mental fitness for runners—willpower and motivation, confidence, concentration, and tactical skill—and discuss how they influence performance and how runners can develop them through targeted training. Keep two things in mind throughout this chapter: First, all young runners, if only because of their lack of experience, have plenty to gain by developing mental fitness, and second, with the right methods, the qualities of mental fitness are highly trainable.

Understanding the Mind–Body Connection

Recall the scenario from our fantasy mile race: It's a perfect day for going after the high school record in the mile run—great weather, a fast track, a first-rate field, and a packed stadium abuzz with excitement and anticipation. The announcer has just introduced the field, and the starter has called you to the line. Picture yourself there, imagining your emotions and the thoughts running through your mind. Maybe you're just a little nervous, which is understandable and probably good for your performance. On the other hand, maybe you're so nervous that you're literally shaking in your spikes. Perhaps doubts are creeping into your mind as you question whether you've trained right and are physically prepared for the challenge. Trying desperately to cast your doubts aside, you remind yourself to concentrate. In fact, you're concentrating so hard on concentrating that you've forgotten your race strategy. You've gone from psyched up to psyched out. Although you're still standing on the starting line with your competitors, you might as well be 100 meters behind before the starting pistol even fires.

Don't underestimate the influence of mental state on running performance. When you're nervous or afraid, your heart and breathing rates increase, your blood vessels widen, and the body releases hormones such as epinephrine, or adrenaline, that speed up the metabolism of stored carbohydrates and fats. These fight-or-flight responses prepare the body to launch into an extremely intense burst of physical activity, which is ideal if, say, you're hiking in the wilderness and you cross paths with a mountain lion. If, on the other hand, you're about to run a 5K race, extreme nervousness can waste valuable energy while you're standing still, energy that should ideally be conserved for your muscles during the race.

Wasting energy isn't the only negative effect of nervousness and fear. Another is tension in muscles that aren't prime movers in the running stride, such as the shoulder muscles. This muscle tension can harm technique and cause fatigue by increasing oxygen consumption. Muscle tension also constricts blood vessels, denying muscle cells of oxygen and forcing them to rely on anaerobic metabolism, which leads to lactic acid accumulation. But physiological fatigue pales in comparison to the pure psychological effects of the self-doubt that so often accompanies nervousness. The tiniest bit of self-doubt opens the door to a flood of negative thoughts at critical points, such as when the pack you're in is breaking up or when a steep hill is coming up. Just let a thought like *I can't possibly cover this break* or *Oh no, I always get dropped on hills* run through your mind, and before you know it you're fatigued and slowing down.

We have to admit a tinge of regret for setting such a negative scene, spoiling your fantasy run for the mile record before it even begins. Unfortunately, the scene is common for many young runners who are in fine physical condition but fall short of their potential because they lack mental fitness. Also too common is the misconception that a champion psyche is simply nature's gift—runners either possess mental fitness or they don't. Research and our experience tell us that this is far from true.

Boosting Willpower and Motivation

In their bag of tests for assessing fitness in distance runners, exercise physiologists measure fractional utilization, which is the percentage of $\dot{V}O_2$max that runners can sustain throughout a race. In world-class marathon runners, for example, fractional utilization is typically around 85 percent, which means that over the marathon distance their muscles consume oxygen at close to the maximum rate. In contrast, in recreational marathon runners fractional utilization might be only 70 percent. An exercise physiologist would explain the difference by saying that the elite marathoner has a higher level of aerobic fitness due to a greater cardiac output, a denser network of capillaries, and more mitochondria in muscle cells. A sports psychologist, however, might have a different explanation: Elite marathon runners have a higher fractional utilization because they possess more willpower to push themselves harder, nearly to their limit.

The bottom line is that to be an elite distance runner, you must be willing to push yourself and to endure strong signals of discomfort and fatigue, which the body sends to the brain to slow you down in order to avoid extreme physical stress. You must also have the willpower to lead a strictly disciplined life in which conserving energy for training is a priority. For young runners, this means resisting some normal and enjoyable activities of youth, such as eating junk food, or staying up late to hang out with friends rather than getting a few extra hours of sleep to prepare for an early morning run. The willpower to endure physical discomfort and to be so disciplined results from an uncommon depth and breadth of motivation.

In any group of young runners motivation varies widely. On one end of the scale are runners who can cut huge chunks of time from their PRs with even a little boost in motivation. On the other end are extremely motivated runners, so much so that their single-minded dedication might hurt their performance. To optimally motivate young runners, coaches must first understand each individual's reasons for participating, and then tailor their coaching style and the training program accordingly. Another challenge for coaches and parents alike is to inspire values that motivate young runners to participate for the best reasons: self-improvement and the satisfaction that comes from dedication and hard work. Becoming a great motivator takes considerable experience, which evolves over time through trial and error. To help coaches and parents who are new to working with young distance runners, we offer some tips for boosting willpower and motivation on page 68.

Building Confidence

Obviously a great degree of self-confidence is essential for peak distance running performance. But what factors determine a runner's self-confidence, and how can runners develop it? One important source of confidence is consistent competitive success, or an unbroken series of races in which the runner accomplishes his goals. Confidence will snowball with each successful race. With this in mind, coaches should design training programs to ensure gradual improvement so that runners peak at the end of the competitive season when championship meets are held. Also, early-season goals should be relatively easy to achieve. The first few competitions of each

Boosting Willpower and Motivation: Tips for Parents and Coaches

1. Be mindful of individual motives for participation.

In any group of young runners, reasons for participating will vary. Because some runners participate for fun and to be around friends, a sure way to decrease their motivation is to put too much emphasis on competitive success. In contrast, coaches should encourage runners who are motivated mainly by successful performance to shoot for the stars.

2. Set goals for racing and training.

Goals help runners focus their mental and physical energy on a purpose, whether it's to win the state championship or to break 6:30 in the mile. Runners should have goals both for races and for every training session. Regardless of the outcomes, racing and training goals can boost motivation. When runners accomplish their goals, they're inspired by feelings of satisfaction and success. When they fall short of their goals, the challenges of overcoming disappointment, figuring out what went wrong, and preparing for future success are often the best sources of motivation, although young runners need coaches and parents to help them view failure in this light. See chapter 8 for more on setting racing and training goals.

3. Push 'em, but not too hard.

In chapter 1 we emphasized potential health risks of distance running for children and adolescents. We also recognized that most young runners will slow down or stop long before they reach their physical limit. For many young athletes, though, major psychological breakthroughs come from finding out just how far they can push themselves. It's okay to encourage young runners to put more effort into demanding training sessions and races, as long as coaches and parents watch closely to see that runners don't push themselves too hard.

4. Inspire values of dedication, hard work, and self-improvement.

Without question, the most powerful motivation comes from the feelings of satisfaction and accomplishment that young runners experience as a result of hard work and self-improvement. These feelings develop intrinsic, or internal, motivation, which sports psychologists emphasize as a key to mental fitness. Parents and coaches play a major role in boosting intrinsic motivation by challenging athletes to work hard and by regularly drawing their attention to the connection between hard work and success. One other hint to inspire these values: Praise the young runner's good efforts frequently.

5. Reward with awards.

Sports psychologists tell us that extrinsic awards, like trophies, ribbons, and other material prizes, are usually less effective at increasing motivation than intrinsic rewards. Nevertheless, when they accompany intrinsic rewards, prizes motivate athletes by reminding them of the satisfaction that comes with success. A T-shirt for completing a summer training program, a letter jacket for making the varsity team, or a new CD for setting a PR are great extrinsic sources of motivation.

season, for example, should be devoted to accomplishing technical and tactical goals. As the season progresses, runners should view each race as a stepping stone to the ultimate goal of a PR or a high finish in championship meets. The confidence gained from performing well at the end of the season will carry over to the next season.

Successful training sessions also boost confidence. Young runners must learn that successful training doesn't mean finishing ahead of teammates in an interval session, or setting a new PR for a 5-mile course every time. Successful training means running at the assigned pace and effort to accomplish specified training objectives for a given day. For this to happen, coaches must clearly communicate the objectives and how to meet them. Let's say that you've planned an easy 3-mile run for your athletes on Tuesday, with the objective of promoting recovery from a demanding interval session the day before. You must communicate to your athletes that if they push themselves and run too fast on the recovery run, they will not be successful in accomplishing the training objective. The confidence your athletes might gain from running hard in the recovery session may be short-lived, because if they don't recover properly, they won't have the energy to successfully complete upcoming workouts in which the objective will be to push hard and run fast.

Coaches should provide plenty of feedback during and after workouts so that runners can tell whether they've accomplished the training objectives. This feedback includes times run in interval sessions, videos of running technique, and charts that show athletes' training progression over time.

One more key to boosting confidence involves the "significant others" in the runner's life. Even when everything is going well, confidence can be shaken by criticism from coaches, parents, and even friends. Runners also need coaches, parents, and friends to help repair the emotional wounds when training and racing aren't going so well. Runners can regain lost confidence with reminders that a bad race is just a temporary setback and encouragement to focus on future success.

Perfecting Concentration

A major aim of mental training is to gain control over your thoughts by focusing your attention, or concentrating. Coaches instruct runners to concentrate all the time, but this is easier said than done because so many cues compete for your attention in competition. We can categorize these cues by whether they are outside (external cues) or inside (internal cues) the body (see table 4.1). If you focus only on external cues—your competitors, upcoming hills and turns, or instructions from the coach—you'll overlook what's going on internally. If you focus only on internal

TABLE 4.1—Focusing Attention

Internal cues	External cues
Technique	Other competitors
Feelings of fatigue and muscle tightness	Coach's instructions
Sense of pace and effort	Demands of the course
Thoughts about strategy	Spectators' cheers

cues—running form, thoughts about pacing and strategy, or feelings of fatigue—you'll lose sight of what's going on around you.

The key to concentrating effectively is to focus on the right cues at the right moment. Think of this skill as adjusting the focus on a beam of light that can be varied in direction and width. Runners vary the direction of attention by focusing on internal or external cues, and they vary the width of attention by focusing narrowly on a few cues or broadly on many cues. A runner with a narrow-internal attention style might concentrate on her technique, excluding other internal and external cues. In contrast, a runner with a broad-external attention style might open her focus to include other competitors, the coach's instructions, and the encouragement of spectators.

The ability to quickly adjust the direction and width of the attention beam is critical to successful racing. Sometimes the focus has to be internal and narrow. For example, when approaching a steep hill in a cross country race you should concentrate on good technique, so you might focus on pushing more forcefully off the ground with the driving leg. After establishing good hill-running technique, you must shift your focus to include external factors such as the competition. If you're concentrating only on your technique, you might miss a competitor breaking away and surging up the hill.

Concentration is greatly influenced by how psyched up, or mentally energized, you are. When mental energy is low and you're not psyched up, the attention beam widens and it becomes difficult to focus on important cues. In contrast, when mental energy is too high, the attention beam narrows and can't easily change direction, causing you to overlook important cues as the race unfolds. By mastering the skills of adjusting your energy level and concentrating on the right cues at the right moments, you'll find yourself mentally absorbed in the race without being overwhelmed by negative thoughts and fatigue.

Coaches should plan some workouts just for developing concentration skills. One strategy is to practice running in a pack, which demands shifting your focus from your own movement and positioning (to avoid tripping on someone's feet and running too wide on turns) to cues coming from your competitors. For example, by listening to the breathing rate of other runners in the pack, you can tell whether they're having trouble with the pace. Practicing pack running also helps you learn to relax and go with the flow without being distracted. As you may have observed in elite adult races, a pack offers a tremendous advantage because runners work together, creating an intangible energy that pulls everyone along. It takes considerable skill in focusing attention and maintaining relaxation to gain this advantage, so practice running in a pack with your teammates to help you develop this skill.

You also need to be able to concentrate when you're running alone. When you're in a race and you find yourself alone behind a pack, you're challenged to stay in mental contact, which means feeling that you're still in the hunt and having the confidence to bridge the gap. If you practice running alone you can develop this aspect of mental fitness. In interval training sessions coaches can stagger runners every 10 seconds or so, with instructions to include the runners ahead in their visual and mental focus. Some sessions should allow the trailing runners to catch up.

Avoiding Anxiety and Fear

Negative emotions such as anxiety and fear hurt performance by wasting energy, increasing fatigue, and limiting concentration. One way to avoid these emotions is to put failure into perspective. The most mentally fit runners don't fear failure because they know that it can be the foundation for success. After a bad race they think about what went wrong in their preparation or tactics. When they identify the reasons, they make the necessary adjustments for future races, and they're more motivated than ever to succeed. Above all, when runners don't fear failure they are willing to take chances, which often leads to major breakthroughs.

Visualize Success

For many runners, uncertainty about performance outcomes is a source of anxiety and fear. Visualization, where athletes mentally rehearse competition, is often very useful for reducing uncertainty and boosting confidence. Here's how to perform visualization: In a quiet setting, close your eyes and imagine yourself in an upcoming competition. See, hear, and feel yourself moving through each stage of the race, as if you were actually running the race. The idea is to visualize positive outcomes and ways to achieve them. For example, see yourself running with good form, hear the split times you're shooting for, and feel the effortless movement. Or, you can visualize your best races from the past. By practicing visualization several days a week for only five minutes at a time, you can replace uncertainty about performance with positive expectations.

Mental fitness includes being able to concentrate, or knowing when to focus on external factors and when to focus on internal factors.

Relax

Another key to eliminating anxiety and fear is relaxation. Like concentration, relaxation is critical in distance running, but it's difficult to master. Coaches often direct runners to relax, but this seems contradictory—the physical basis of running, after all, is to generate tension in the form of muscle contractions. The goal during training and racing is to relax not the whole body, but specific muscles that aren't the prime movers. Runners should focus on detecting and reducing tension in the shoulders, hands, and face. Coaches can help by analyzing the runner's technique and expression for tightness and strain. The coach's cues to relax should be specific to the body part that looks tight, such as "relax your shoulders" or "loosen your hands." Before each training session and race, runners should relax by doing quiet, enjoyable activities such as reading, listening to music, talking with friends, or watching TV.

Know the Course

This cross country strategy is to become familiar with race courses by training on them. When courses are too far from home to train on regularly, you should run on and study the course the day before the race. Knowing the course helps you anticipate changes in attention focus as the race unfolds. If, for example, you know that a steep 400-meter hill is close to the finish line, you'll be prepared to gather your strength and concentrate on your best technique when the time comes. When you know the course you can prepare by visualizing your performance on it.

Develop a Familiar Prerace Routine

A consistent warm-up will help you focus your attention and avoid worrying. The routine might include a specific duration of jogging, sequence of stretching exercises, number of strides, and so forth. You can make the routine familiar by performing it regularly before training sessions, especially those that simulate the physical and mental demands of competition.

Racing Tactics

Stacy is an elite runner whose only plan for racing is to lead the pack from the start. Front running works perfectly in small dual meets where Stacy is superior to her competitors. She opens up a huge lead and holds on to win, even though she slows in the final stages. In championship races against runners of comparable ability and fitness, however, the strategy often backfires. Try as she might, Stacy can't break away from her competitors. The pack's jostling, an unfamiliar experience, distracts her and weakens her concentration. When she can't shake the other runners as the race progresses, she begins to doubt her ability to win. Finally, when the pack begins to kick, Stacy can't respond—she doesn't have a finishing kick because she never practiced one.

In contrast, runners with a repertoire of well-tested and effective strategies usually have high levels of motivation and confidence. Moreover, they know how to concentrate on the right strategic cues as the race unfolds. Successful racing means using the best tactics for a given situation, taking into account your fitness level, your goals, the ability and tactical approaches of your competitors, the weather, the course conditions (in cross country), and so on. Runners should train to master various tactics, including racing for time, front running, surging, and kicking.

Racing for Time

This tactic involves setting and adjusting your pace to reach intermediate distances on target for a final goal time. It's a tactic that all young runners should practice from the time they start training. Beginners need to learn to run their own races rather than blindly following someone else's plan. Moreover, racing for time emphasizes pacing skill, which helps beginners avoid starting too fast or too slow. Finally, runners who master this tactic experience a boost in mental fitness. When the stopwatch shows

Smoky Hill High School

Location: Aurora, Colorado

Coach: Greg Weich

For the distance runners at Smoky Hill High School, training for mental fitness begins with communication. "Every day we start practice with a team meeting," says Smoky Hill coach Greg Weich. "I begin the meeting by asking my kids how they feel. I know that they've had a full day of school with the stresses of exams, homework, and their social lives. So, while I have a general workout in mind for the day, I individualize training based on each kid's mental state. I trust my kids to tell me if they're not able to handle a workout on any given day. This approach is a major key to keeping high school kids motivated to run their best."

Weich's approach to developing mental fitness in high school runners has paid big. Since 1993, the Smoky Hill boys' and girls' cross country and track teams have consistently been among the top in Colorado, winning several state championships along the way. In 2002 the girls' cross country team was ranked fifth in the nation, and in 2003, it was ranked second.

Explaining the mental factors that are fundamental to his team's success, Weich says, "We run a low-stress program, avoiding big psychological buildups to competitions by keeping the kids on an even keel. We don't even talk about racing until the day before a meet. Our kids are competitive enough—they don't need me to get them pumped up with pep talks. All we ask is that our kids run 100 percent. As far as I'm concerned, there is no 101 percent."

Goal setting and pace-oriented training also motivate the Smoky Hill runners. Before the start of each cross country and track season, Weich asks his runners to write down their goals on an index card. They list their performance goals for the upcoming season and their running careers, as well as their academic and personal goals. "If a kid wants to run 16:30 for 5K, and we determine that it's a realistic goal, we set workouts up to get him ready to run that pace," Weich explains. "We're very conscious of pace. Once we've built a base, we'll jump right into doing 500- to 1,000-meter repeats at race pace. In cross country season we might do 15 percent of our training at 5K pace, which is a lot."

By teaching his runners to focus on pace and strategy, Weich builds both their concentration and their confidence. "Hard, consistent training sessions mentally callous runners and build their confidence," he says. "By the time we've done 120 days of consistent training, we've built a lot of confidence. But to keep our kids focused in training, we don't encourage them to think about racing results and winning state championships. Instead, we talk about improving some aspect of their running, whether it's their technique, pacing, hill running, or whatever they need to work on. Say that we have a kid who is falling behind on the hills in early cross country races. We'll take that runner aside and have him do special hill workouts so that by the state championships, hill running is second nature for him, and he's a very confident hill runner."

that you've achieved your time goal or that you've set a new PR, you gain confidence and motivation for future races.

To race for time, the coach and athlete decide on a goal time that is challenging but achievable considering the athlete's current fitness, the point in the competitive season, and the weather. Let's say that Michelle's goal is to run 5:24 for 1,600 meters, which calls for averaging 81 seconds for each 400-meter split. If Michelle were to run at an even pace her splits would be 81 (400), 2:42 (800), and 4:03 (1,200). Physiologically, even-paced running is advantageous because it restrains runners from going out too fast and fatiguing from lactic acid accumulation. However, especially in events from 800 to 3,000 meters, the energy and excitement at the start of a race often make it difficult to run the first lap on even pace, so Michelle might set her splits in these ranges: 79 to 80 (400), 2:41 to 2:43 (800), and 4:03 to 4:04 (1,200). If the leaders set out at a pace of 74 seconds for the first 400, Michelle will have to let them go. If Michelle's early pace is on target but faster than her competitors', she'll have to run in front. Most important, she'll have to concentrate on running her own race while staying aware of what her competitors are doing.

Another approach to racing for time is to run negative splits, which means covering the last half of the race faster than the first half. Physiologically, this tactic works well because it helps runners avoid early fatigue. Psychologically, negative-split running is a knockout strategy every time. In youth races, most of the runners slow markedly in the last half. If you run negative splits, you'll be passing your competitors rather than getting passed. With every runner you pass, your confidence will climb a notch.

Most record-setting performances by elite adult distance runners are characterized by a combination of even-pacing and negative splits. Figure 4.1 shows an example, Haile Gebrselassie's 1-kilometer splits in his world record for 10,000 meters (26:22.75), set in 1998. If Gebrselassie had run evenly for the entire race, he would have averaged 2:38.3 per kilometer. After a fast first kilometer (2:35.8), kilometers 2 though 9 were very close to the average pace; the widest range in kilometer splits was only 3.2 seconds. The amazing last kilometer was covered in 2:31.2, which is close to 4:00-mile pace. Gebrselassie's 5K splits were almost perfectly even: 13:11.7 for the first half and 13:11.05 for the second.

There's one important caveat to racing for time: Runners must be flexible, even to the point of abandoning the plan midway through a race. We're thinking of a scenario where you're on perfect pace early in the race, running with the leaders, and feeling better than ever. The leaders begin to surge, and you have to decide whether to stay on goal pace or to cover the break. If you completely ignore the competition and focus only on your planned splits, you might miss a great opportunity to challenge yourself for a major breakthrough. When you're feeling good in the

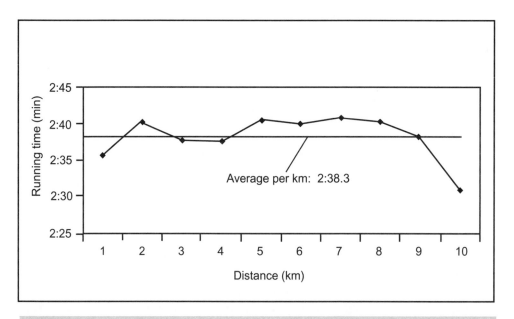

FIGURE 4.1 Haile Gebrselassie's 1-kilometer splits for his world-record 10,000-meter race (26:22.75), set on June 1, 1998, in Hengelo, Netherlands.

middle of a race, you might experiment with forgetting about split times and focusing on competing. Keep in mind, though, that most of the time runners feel strongest in the late stages of the race when they have paced themselves early on.

Young runners won't learn pacing skills by themselves. Coaches must teach these skills and provide training experiences to reinforce them. As a first step, runners should learn the splits required to achieve their time goals. Coaches can hand out pacing charts such as table 4.2 and quiz athletes to make sure that they've memorized their splits. In addition, in chapter 8 we'll show you how to integrate methods for developing pacing and tactical skills into race-specific sessions such as aerobic and anaerobic interval training.

Racing for Place

Racing for time and maintaining an even pace aren't always useful strategies, especially in cross country. Instead, sometimes the best tactic is to aim for a certain finish place. Let's say Brad's goal is to place in the top 25 of a cross country race. Brad has to know the demands of the course and plan how much effort to put into different segments of the race. During the race, he has to gauge his success by his position relative to his competitors. If Brad finds himself running with the lead pack and the pace

TABLE 4.2—Pacing Chart

METERS									
100	**200**	**400**	**800**	**1,000**	**1,500**	**1,600**	**3,000**	**3,200**	**5,000**
:15	:30	1:00	2:00	2:30	3:45	4:00	7:30	8:00	12:30
:15.5	:31	1:02	2:04	2:35	3:52.5	4:08	7:45	8:16	12:55
:16	:32	1:04	2:08	2:40	4:00	4:16	8:00	8:32	13:20
:16.5	:33	1:06	2:12	2:45	4:07.5	4:24	8:15	8:48	13:45
:17	:34	1:08	2:16	2:50	4:15	4:32	8:30	9:04	14:10
:17.5	:35	1:10	2:20	2:55	4:22.5	4:40	8:45	9:20	14:35
:18	:36	1:12	2:24	3:00	4:30	4:48	9:00	9:36	15:00
:18.5	:37	1:14	2:28	3:05	4:37.5	4:56	9:15	9:52	15:25
:19	:38	1:16	2:32	3:10	4:45	5:04	9:30	10:08	15:50
:19.5	:39	1:18	2:36	3:15	4:52.5	5:12	9:45	10:24	16:15
:20	:40	1:20	2:40	3:20	5:00	5:20	10:00	10:40	16:40
:20.5	:41	1:22	2:44	3:25	5:07.5	5:28	10:15	10:56	17:05
:21	:42	1:24	2:48	3:30	5:15	5:36	10:30	11:12	17:30
:21.5	:43	1:26	2:52	3:35	5:22.5	5:44	10:45	11:28	17:55
:22	:44	1:28	2:56	3:40	5:30	5:52	11:00	11:44	18:20
:22.5	:45	1:30	3:00	3:45	5:37.5	6:00	11:15	12:00	18:45
:23	:46	1:32	3:04	3:50	5:45	6:08	11:30	12:16	19:10
:23.5	:47	1:34	3:08	3:55	5:52.5	6:16	11:45	12:32	19:35
:24	:48	1:36	3:12	4:00	6:00	6:24	12:00	12:48	20:00
:24.5	:49	1:38	3:16	4:05	6:07.5	6:32	12:15	13:04	20:25
:25	:50	1:40	3:20	4:10	6:15	6:40	12:30	13:20	20:50
:25.5	:51	1:42	3:24	4:15	6:22.5	6:48	12:45	13:36	21:15
:26	:52	1:44	3:28	4:20	6:30	6:56	13:00	13:52	21:40
:26.5	:53	1:46	3:32	4:25	6:37.5	7:04	13:15	14:08	22:05
:27	:54	1:48	3:36	4:30	6:45	7:12	13:30	14:24	22:30
:27.5	:55	1:50	3:40	4:35	6:52.5	7:20	13:45	14:40	22:55
:28	:56	1:52	3:44	4:40	7:00	7:28	14:00	14:56	23:20
:28.5	:57	1:54	3:48	4:45	7:07.5	7:36	14:15	15:12	23:45
:29	:58	1:56	3:52	4:50	7:15	7:44	14:30	15:28	24:10
:29.5	:59	1:58	3:56	4:55	7:22.5	7:52	14:45	15:44	24:35
:30	:60	2:00	4:00	5:00	7:30	8:00	15:00	16:00	25:00

Rows show minutes and seconds for even-paced running across standard track distances.

feels too fast, he'll have to slow down. Or, if Brad isn't even in the top 50 by the middle of the race and he's feeling good, he'll have to pick up the pace. With feedback from the coach about his place as the race unfolds, Brad will be able to make the right adjustments so that he doesn't wind up at the finish line with too much or too little energy left.

Racing for First Place

If your goal is to finish in first place, you might use one of several strategies including front running, surging, and kicking. The first strategy, front running, is a double-edged sword—it can cut your competitors by breaking their spirit and shaking their confidence, but it can cut you if you wield it improperly. Front runners must be supremely fit and confident that they can cover the distance alone.

Front runners can also use a surging tactic, in which they speed up over segments of the race in order to shake competitors and break their confidence. The surge should be planned to catch the competition off-guard and to convince them that you're in control of the race. To learn this strategy, watch the world-class Kenyan athletes, who have used surging to dominate the endurance events in international competitions such as the Olympic Games.

When learning to pace, runners must develop the self-control to keep on pace even when the pack around them surges. But they must also be able to judge when it would benefit them to surge with the pack.

Another strategy for winning races is kicking. Kickers feed off the energy and momentum of the other runners by tucking themselves in the pack in the early stages of the race. Then, in the final stages they use their fitness and speed to sprint away from competitors. Runners should practice starting their kicks from different distances. For example, a runner who lacks basic speed might experiment with a long, controlled sprint 400 to 600 meters out. Runners with good speed might wait until the last 100 to 200 meters to start an explosive sprint.

Experimentation is the key to mastering racing strategies. Runners who can't adapt tactics to different competitive situations limit themselves to performing well only when the conditions suit them. In addition, using the same plan race after race can get boring and limit motivation. Runners who are skilled at many different racing strategies have the potential for superior performance every time they toe the starting line. And it's fun to try different approaches on a regular basis.

Striding Ahead

In this chapter we've stressed that distance runners must be mentally fit to reach their potential. The elements of mental fitness are willpower and motivation, self-confidence, a flexible attention style, and pacing and tactical skill. The most important point, though, is that mental fitness can be improved with training. This improvement depends on carefully planned training and racing experiences that go beyond simply conditioning the body's physiological systems. Indeed, every training session should be geared toward developing mental as well as physical fitness. When we discuss the details of training design in part II, we suggest ways to integrate methods for developing mental fitness. Before we get to training methods, however, we'll cover one last scientific foundation: the biomechanics of running.

CHAPTER 5

Optimal Technique

Athletes in most sports devote a great deal of training to improving technique, or the proper form for carrying out movement skills. Right-handed golfers work on keeping a straight left arm during the swing, basketball players spend hours perfecting the follow-through of the jump shot, and high jumpers practice their over-the-bar technique by performing specialized drills. Technique is important for distance runners, too, though many don't realize it. In this chapter we discuss proper technique and ways coaches can design effective technique training and offer advice for improvement. We first consider the influence of running technique on performance and injury prevention, and then we present 10 "tech tips" to help you diagnose strengths and weaknesses.

Technique and Performance

The basic objective in distance running is to move the body at the fastest speed that doesn't cause excessive fatigue and slowing. In other words, the goal is to run fast without running out of energy. As we discussed in earlier chapters, one of the most consistent findings in research on young runners is that they're inefficient relative to adult runners—they use more oxygen to sustain submaximal paces. One reason for the higher oxygen cost is deficient technique. Flaws in technique limit performance potential by increasing the energy cost of running, which speeds up the physiological processes that cause fatigue, such as glycogen depletion and lactic acid accumulation. Consider the consequences of poor stride timing. Running speed is the product of stride frequency (the number of strides in a given period of time) and stride length (the distance covered in two successive landings of the same foot). While these characteristics vary among runners, research shows that for each individual a range exists in which energy costs are lowest. If a runner's stride frequency is too low or too high, or if his stride length is too short or too long, the energy required to sustain a given pace increases, and fatigue occurs sooner than it otherwise would.

A common problem among novice runners is a low stride frequency, which means that the duration of the stride cycle—the time, for example, between successive right-foot landings—is relatively long. A low stride frequency can increase energy costs, measured as oxygen consumption, in a few ways. For one, it can reduce the body's forward momentum because the runner's foot tends to stay on the ground too long. If the body's momentum stalls with every footstrike, the leg muscles have to generate extra contractile force to reaccelerate the body and push off the ground. It's like a bouncing ball that's deflated and has to be pumped up every time it lands. This stalling and reaccelerating rapidly uses oxygen and energy.

In addition, if the foot spends too much time on the ground the runner won't be able to take advantage of stored elastic energy, a major energy-saving mechanism. As we discussed in chapter 1, elastic energy is stored in certain leg muscles and tendons as they stretch when the runner's foot hits the ground. As the muscles and tendons recoil, the elastic energy can help propel the body upward and forward, but the timing of the elastic stretch and shortening of the muscles and tendons is critical. If too much time passes after the stretching action, as often occurs in runners whose stride frequency is low, the energy stored in the muscles and tendons will dissipate.

Now consider the runner whose stride frequency is too high. This runner takes short, rapid steps, leaving his foot on the ground for a short duration. Upon footstrike the runner's support leg has to generate a relatively large amount of propulsive force in an instant. Researchers have theorized that this condition can impair distance running performance by forcing the body to recruit extra FT muscle fibers. Recall from chapter 2 that these muscle fibers generate a great amount of force rapidly, so they are well-suited for runners with a high stride frequency. However, FT muscle fibers are also subject to rapid fatigue because they rely on ATP generated through anaerobic glycolysis, the energy pathway that produces lactic acid. At a given speed—say, mile race pace—the runner who takes excessively short, rapid strides will accumulate more lactic acid and fatigue sooner than if he took longer, slower strides (presumably recruiting a greater amount of ST muscle fibers).

Research shows that well-trained and highly experienced runners self-select an optimal stride frequency and stride length. That is, these runners naturally choose the stride pattern that requires the least amount of energy. Most experts recommend letting this self-optimizing process occur naturally, rather than purposefully trying to adjust stride frequency and length. One problem involving stride frequency and length does call for purposeful correction, though. This problem, called overstriding, occurs when the foot strikes the ground far in front of the center of gravity (the most concentrated point through which gravity acts to pull the body to the ground), which is just above the center of the pelvis when running. In overstriding the front leg strikes the ground in a propping or braking position (see figure 5.1). This action greatly reduces the runner's forward momentum and costs the muscles extra energy to reaccelerate the body to push off the ground.

FIGURE 5.1   Overstriding: an energy-wasting technical flaw.

Technique and Injury Prevention

In addition to improving running economy and performance, good technique is essential for injury prevention. With every footstrike the runner's body is subjected to forces two to three times its weight. Given the repetitive nature of the running stride, a flawed movement pattern can unduly stress muscles, bones, tendons, and ligaments. The risk of injury is especially high when poor technique is coupled with structural abnormalities, most notably misalignment of the foot, shin, thigh, and pelvis. When the leg is not vertically aligned, the muscles and joints bear more stress on one side than the other. Elite runners usually have relatively straight legs, and not surprisingly, they tend to have fewer injuries than nonelite runners. For all runners, a technically sound stride helps to assure that no one muscle group or joint structure is overloaded.

To illustrate how structural abnormalities and flaws in technique can cause injuries, we'll look at the biomechanics of the foot and lower leg upon footstrike (see figure 5.2). In a normal landing the foot hits the ground and pronates, or rolls inward at the ankle joint (see figure 5.2a). Slight pronation is beneficial because it lowers the whole foot to the ground and helps cushion the impact. Excessive pronation, however, pulls the foot out of alignment with the lower leg (see figure 5.2b). This stresses the arch, Achilles tendon, and connective tissue supporting the ankle and knee joints. Runners with flat feet or low arches, knock-knees, and weak ankles tend to overpronate and as a result are at risk for injuries such as stress fractures of the foot and shin, plantar fasciitis (arch pain), Achilles tendinitis, and runner's knee.

Another biomechanical problem that can occur during footstrike is excessive supination, or outward rolling of the foot. Supination, which follows pronation in a normal landing, puts the foot into position for a forceful push-off. Upon landing, some runners supinate without allowing the foot to pronate and absorb impact forces (see figure 5.2c). This causes undue stress on the lateral side of the ankle, knee, and hip joints. Runners who supinate excessively suffer injuries such as iliotibial band syndrome (lateral knee and hip pain), Achilles tendinitis, and calf muscle strains.

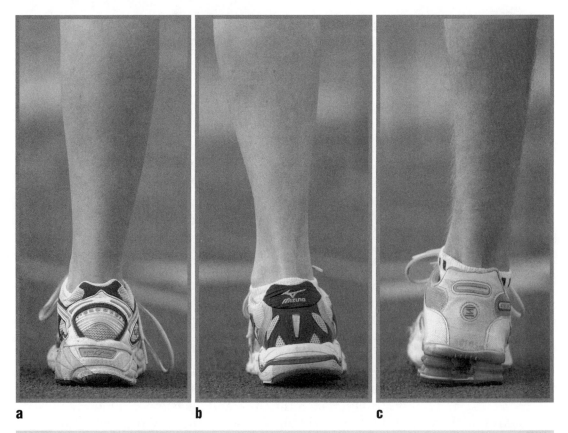

a   b   c

FIGURE 5.2 Footstrike positions: normal *(a)*, excessive pronation *(b)*, and excessive supination *(c)*.

Choosing the Right Shoes

The right pair of training shoes can help to correct technical flaws and prevent the injuries they cause, especially for runners with mobile (unstable) ankle and knee joints. With so many brands and models to choose from, however, it can be hard to find the perfect pair. You should shop for shoes at running stores with experts on staff who will take the time to analyze your limb structure and technique before recommending a shoe. It'll help to know a little about shoe design as well as what questions to ask the experts, so here's a quick primer for running-shoe novices:

How durable is the outersole?
Does it have good traction for the surfaces you run on?

The outersole is the material that covers the bottom of the shoe. It can have shallow ripples, best for running on the road, or it can have deep grooves or a waffle pattern, best for cross country and trail running. If you usually wear through the outersole of your running shoes, ask for the most durable material available.

How cushioned is the midsole?
How many miles can you expect before the midsole loses its shock absorption?

The midsole, which lies between the outersole and the upper part of the shoe, is made from various materials depending on the brand and model, including ethylene vinyl acetate (EVA), gel, and air. The softness of the midsole can vary greatly, so it's important to choose a shoe that has the right amount of cushioning and spring for you. Generally, runners with mobile lower limb joints—for example, runners who pronate excessively—need a harder midsole, which restricts rolling at the ankle joint. Runners with rigid lower limbs are typically better off with a more cushioned shoe for mobility and shock absorption. The material of the midsole usually determines how long a shoe will last. Depending on the runner's weight, technique, and training surfaces, the better running shoes should last between 400 and 600 miles before shock absorption is seriously impaired.

How much motion control is built into the shoe?

The design of a running shoe is characterized by its last, which refers to two features: (1) how the outersole and midsole are attached to the upper part of the shoe and (2) the basic form or shape of the shoe. The shoe's last influences its stability, or motion control. In a board-lasted shoe, a firm board connects the outersole to the upper material on the instep, adding support that reduces pronation. Runners with a neutral landing are better off with a slip-lasted shoe, which forgoes the extra support in order to allow more motion at the ankle joint. The last is also characterized by its straightness. A straight-lasted shoe has a relatively straight inner edge running along the instep, which means that the midsole and outersole material extend medially, under the arch. Straight-lasted shoes are optimal for runners with flat feet, because they need extra arch support. In contrast, in a curve-lasted shoe the extra material is cut out, which is optimal for runners who have high arches and who toe in.

Genes play a major role in determining an individual's bone and joint structure. For runners with structural abnormalities, improving technique isn't a simple matter of adjusting limb movements. Instead, technique must be altered through other means. Excessive pronation, for example, can be corrected with a running shoe that is designed to prevent the foot from rolling inward. For extreme cases of pronation runners might need orthotics, which are shoe inserts made from shock-absorbing materials that guide the foot through its most efficient and least stressful movement pattern. Runners whose legs aren't perfectly aligned can improve their technique and reduce their injury risk by performing special stretching and strengthening exercises. We describe some of these exercises in the next chapter, but we recommend that any runner with structural misalignment and joint instability consult a sports doctor to determine whether orthotics are necessary and to get a program of stretching and strengthening exercises that best addresses individual needs.

Technique Tips

Because vast differences in size, strength, flexibility, coordination, and bone and joint structure characterize any group of young runners, it's a bad idea to try to change one runner's technique to match another's. No single ideal form exists for distance runners. Even so, the study of biomechanics reveals certain characteristics of sound form that all runners should work to acquire in order to conserve energy, improve performance, and prevent injuries. We highlight these features in 10 tech tips that will help you identify strengths and weaknesses in young runners' form. First, however, to help you focus on the most important aspects of technique, we'll break down the running stride into its successive segments, or phases.

Using Video to Evaluate Technique

Evaluating strengths and weaknesses in running technique is a challenge because running involves so many body parts moving rapidly at the same time. It's difficult to see flaws such as overstriding and insufficient ankle extension because they occur so quickly. The solution to this problem is a video camera, which you can use to film technique sessions, interval training, and races. During the recovery periods in an interval session, for example, the coach and runner can view the tape in slow motion, freezing it at critical points in the stride cycle. This way you can identify problems and experiment with adjustments as a workout progresses.

The two major phases of the stride are called stance and swing. The stance phase consists of the actions that occur while the foot is in contact with the ground, whereas the swing phase consists of the actions that occur when both feet are off the ground and the body is aerial. To guide our description of these two phases, we'll refer to the sequence of four photos in figure 5.3, which shows a runner moving through half of a stride cycle, beginning with the right-foot landing and ending with the left-foot takeoff.

a

b

c

d

FIGURE 5.3 **The phases of a stride cycle.**

The stance phase begins when the foot contacts the ground and ends with the pushing-off action that propels the body into flight. The sub-phases of stance are landing (see figure 5.3a), midsupport, and takeoff (see figure 5.3b). When you're watching a runner in the landing subphase, focus on foot position as well as the extent of flexion, or bending, of the ankle, knee, and hip joints. When evaluating foot position, check for whether the runner has a neutral landing or whether she pronates or supinates (you'll need to video the runner from behind to check this). From the side, check foot placement to determine whether the runner is overstriding. In a separate evaluation of the landing subphase, watch how much the leg joints flex immediately upon footstrike to check for excessive lowering of the hips on landing, a common flaw in young runners' technique.

An instant after landing, the hips pass over the foot and the takeoff subphase begins. The body is propelled upward and forward as the driving leg pushes against the ground, exerting force in a backward, downward direction (see figure 5.2b). You should direct your attention to the ankle, knee, and hip joints during this subphase to assess the degree of extension, or straightening. As running speed increases, these joints should extend to a greater degree, reflecting a more forceful pushing-off action.

After pushing off the ground, the leg begins the swing phase, preparing for another landing in a sequence of three subphases: follow-through, forward-swing, and foot-descent. Figure 5.3c illustrates the follow-through of the right leg after it pushes off the ground. Soon after takeoff, the extended leg should bend at the knee so that the foot remains close to the body, creating a shorter lever in the trailing leg. In the forward-swing phase (see figure 5.3, c and d), the foot should move forward and up toward the buttocks. At the end of forward-swing, the knee should lift to a height that depends on the running speed. A higher knee lift assists faster running by allowing stride length to increase. After the knee reaches its peak height, the foot-descent subphase begins. This action should be a rapid lowering of the thigh with little movement at the knee joint.

Now that you're familiar with the phases of the running stride, you're ready for the 10 tech tips for sound form.

Relax muscles that aren't active in the running movement. While baseball coaches issue the command to keep an eye on the ball, and golf coaches advise their athletes to keep the head down, distance coaches are famous for telling runners to relax. But when coaches don't specify what they mean, tired runners can easily mistake "relax" for "slow down." They may loosen muscles all over the body, including the arm and leg muscles that generate propelling force. If runners relax everything, they reduce the contractile force produced by the leg muscles, shorten their stride, decrease their stride frequency, and slow down. As we discussed in chapter 4, it's critical for runners to eliminate tension in the muscles that don't contribute to the running movement, because tension in these muscles is counterproductive. At the same time runners must maintain a high level of contractile force in the prime movers. If you're cuing runners to relax, then, be specific about the part of the body that looks tense, such as the shoulders or hands.

Keep your body in an almost upright position, squaring your shoulders and holding your head level.   Good form is characterized by stable, straight posture of the upper body, without energy-wasting turning and swaying motions. In correct posture, the upper body leans forward slightly and shoulders are squared so that the arms can swing freely to counteract hip rotation. The head is level without turning or bobbing, and the eyes are focused 20 to 30 meters ahead. One of the most important factors for maintaining good body position is core strength, or strength in the abdominal and back muscles that support the hips and spine. In addition, good posture requires a conscious effort to avoid slouching and excessive upper-body movement. You can help runners focus on posture by cuing them to pull their shoulders back if they're slouching, to run tall, and to imagine being pulled upward by a rope attached to the top of the head.

Drive your arms and legs in the direction that you want your body to go.   Arm movements should be coordinated with the legs to balance the body and counteract rotational forces. Figure 5.4 illustrates the importance of good arm action. As the runner's right knee lifts in front of the body, the hips naturally rotate right to left. To offset the turning action of the hips caused by lifting the right knee, the left arm moves forward, stabilizing the upper body. The runner maintains balance when the left arm moves in sync with the right leg and vice versa. When evaluating arm action, focus on where the movement occurs. To minimize unnecessary motion of the upper body, the arms should swing naturally at the shoulder joint rather than opening and closing at the elbow joint, which should be kept at about a 90-degree angle. Focus also on the direction and range of arm movements.

FIGURE 5.4   Efficient upper-body posture and arm action.

While the hands may pass slightly in front of the body, they should not cross over an imaginary vertical line that divides the body into right and left halves. The best range of arm movement varies with running speed. At fast paces, the arms should move vigorously, with the hands passing the hips on the downswing and coming up even with the shoulders on the upswing.

Upon striking the ground and during the takeoff subphase, the foot should point straight ahead rather than turn inward or outward. Runners who have a natural toe-in or toe-out may have difficulty positioning their feet straight. Trying to change these athletes' foot placement isn't a good idea because it might cause a painful twisting at the knee and hip joints. In any situation where changes in technique cause joint pain, it's best to let the runner use the style that feels most comfortable.

Settle into your own natural stride length and frequency. As we discussed earlier, if stride length and frequency are not in optimal ranges, the energy demands of running increase and performance suffers. Without laboratory testing, it's difficult to tell whether a runner needs to adjust stride length or frequency. Unless runners are obviously overstriding or taking short, choppy steps, they should not consciously alter their strides when running at a constant pace. With training and experience most runners naturally choose a stride length and frequency that optimize performance. Coaches should, however, watch for how runners pick up the pace in midrace surges and sprint finishes. For the distances over which young runners race, the best strategy for speeding up is to consciously increase stride length by generating greater propulsive force in the takeoff subphase. Mastering this technique requires training to enhance strength and flexibility.

Minimize downward sinking and upward bouncing. When the runner's foot contacts the ground and as the body moves over the foot, keep an eye on the head and hips. Do they stay at the same height throughout the stance phase, or do they drop like an anchor? Sinking of the hips reflects a major technique flaw, excessive flexion at the knee and ankle joints. When the hips sink and the leg joints collapse immediately upon footstrike, the muscles have to expend considerable energy just to correct the downward movement and raise the body. The causes of this sinking are leg weakness, poor neuromuscular skill, or a combination of both. Correcting this problem involves strength training, such as circuit training and weight training, as well as technique drills that isolate the action of the leg upon footstrike, promoting rapid and forceful extension. Coaches should cue runners with this flaw to stiffen their knee and ankle joints upon footstrike.

Also watch the head and hips for excessive bouncing. This occurs during the takeoff subphase when runners exert too much vertical force against the ground. Bouncy runners will benefit from technique drills that promote pushing off the ground in a more backward than downward direction. In one such drill the runner tows the coach, who pulls him backward with a harness attached to the hips.

When running at fast speeds, land on and push off from your midfoot or forefoot. An effective stride begins with foot positioning upon landing. The part of the foot that touches the ground first depends on running speed. As the speed gets faster footstrike should occur closer to the ball of the foot for a more efficient pushing-off action. In races and fast interval sessions, the best technique is to strike first on the ball of the foot. The whole foot is then naturally lowered to the ground for an instant, allowing for slight pronation and shock absorption. During the takeoff subphase you should also push off from the front of the foot.

The best runners tend to be midfoot and forefoot strikers. That's why you often hear coaches cuing their runners to get up on their toes. Heel strikers typically spend too long on the ground, losing forward momentum when they have to roll into position for push-off. The arch, ankle joint, and Achilles tendon must be able to withstand considerable force, so heel strikers who want to convert to midfoot or forefoot will have to improve their strength and flexibility first. Some runners, particularly those with flat feet, will have great difficulty landing on the front part of the foot. Again, because of the risk of injury, never force runners to

Since a runner gains propulsive force from the combined movements of the ankle, knee, and hip, good extension of these three joints must be present for an efficient stride.

Eisenhower High School

Location: Yakima, Washington

Coach: Phil English

At a recent summer running camp, Phil English, the distance coach at Eisenhower High School in Yakima, Washington, conducted an informal experiment to test a theory about the influence of lower-body strength and balance on running performance. He asked a group of runners to try balancing while standing on a bocce ball, which is about the size of a softball (bocce is a lawn bowling game that is popular in Italy). "It's not an easy thing to do," he says. "But the kids who were better runners had less difficulty and were able to balance longer." Now, bocce-ball balancing is one of many unique exercises that the Eisenhower runners do for developing lower-extremity strength and balance, which English believes are essential for improving running technique.

English views technique training as the solution to two problems for young runners: temporary performance setbacks due to nonlinear patterns of growth, especially for girls, and poor performance due to inefficient form. "Girl runners usually don't progress linearly from their freshman to senior years," says English. "They go through ups and downs with growth and maturation. But our girls run their fastest times as seniors. One of the reasons for this [successful long-term development] is that we give them a good solid technique base."

Many high school runners, both boys and girls, have inefficient form. "Overstriding is incredibly common," English observes. "They have difficulty negotiating hills. They don't effectively use the ankle joint for a powerful takeoff phase in the running stride. There's also a settling of the center of gravity." He believes that the major causes of poor technique are lack of strength and conditioning, explaining, "Before starting to train, the typical young runner lacks general body strength. She can't do many pull-ups and push-ups, and she can't generate a lot of force with her leg muscles." Technique training at Eisenhower includes exercises for developing strength, balance, and coordination. The athletes do circuit training, weight training, medicine ball work, and an effective form of core strength training called Pilates. They also focus on strengthening the feet and ankles with barefoot running on grass and various drills. Prior to interval training sessions, for example, the Eisenhower runners do, among three or four other drills, an arms and toes drill, in which they take small steps by forcefully opening and closing the ankle joint, keeping their knees straight without dropping their center of gravity. "We do these lower-extremity drills so that late in a race, the kids are able to get on the balls of their feet to generate force," says English.

The technique training has clearly paid off for the Eisenhower runners. Since 1986, when English began coaching at the school, the girls' and boys' cross country teams have won eight state championships. The girls have qualified for the state meet every year but one, amassing a dual-meet record of 207 wins and 5 losses. English was named National Coach of the Year for girls' cross country in 2001.

alter their technique if the change doesn't suit their body structure or if it causes pain.

Avoid overstriding and passive landings—land with your foot close to your hips and moving backward. In an effort to increase stride length, some runners make the mistake of swinging the lower leg forward in a kicking action just before landing. You can detect this flaw because the foot appears to be reaching out to the ground. Often the result is over-striding, which we've defined as foot placement well in front of the hips, where the center of gravity is located. For a smooth and efficient style, the foot should land only slightly in front of the hips, as shown in figure 5.3a (page 87).

Overstriding is linked to another technical flaw: forward movement or lack of movement of the foot at the instant it strikes the ground. If the foot is moving forward upon landing, the ground returns force to the body in a backward direction, slowing the runner down. This is called a passive landing. In contrast, if the foot is already moving backward as it lands, the ground reaction force will help propel the body forward. This technique is called an active landing. A runner can develop the active landing skill through drills and conscious effort to paw the track, or bring the foot toward the body in the foot-descent subphase.

In the takeoff phase, extend your joints, especially your ankle. You can imagine how little propulsive power runners would generate if they used only one joint in the takeoff phase. An effective stride requires the coordinated extension of the three major leg joints—ankle, knee, and hip. You can tell if runners are achieving good ankle extension by whether their toes point downward as their feet leave the ground. For good knee and hip extension during fast running, you should be able to draw a diagonal line from the ankle joint to the hip joint when looking at the runner from the side. At slower speeds, however, runners do not need to completely straighten their leg joints.

Lift your knees to increase stride length and running speed. In the forward-swing subphase, knee flexion lifts the foot off the ground and hip flexion brings the knee up in front of the body. Especially during fast running, lifting the knee high is critical because it brings the foot into proper position for the next landing and push-off. Runners who have poor knee-lift tend to drop the foot to the ground too quickly after push-off. This shortens stride length by limiting the amount of time over which force can be produced by the opposite driving leg. Several of the drills in chapter 6 are designed to increase knee lift.

Alter your posture and stride mechanics for proper uphill and downhill form. On tough cross country courses, hill-running technique plays a major role. Going uphill, runners should try to maintain their rhythm and pace without straining. The main technical adjustment for uphill running is to lean slightly forward and to more forcefully extend the drive leg as it pushes off the ground. Arm action should also be more vigorous going uphill. Finally, the eyes should focus 20 to 30 meters ahead. When runners' eyes turn to the ground, it's a sure sign that the hill has defeated them.

Downhill sections allow runners to relax and maintain pace with relatively little effort. Runners should lean backward slightly and allow their strides to increase in length. The action should be controlled rather than reckless to avoid jarring that causes injury. Good downhill runners have the strength and technique to use the hill to pick up speed and pass competitors.

Striding Ahead

To advise runners about what they should keep doing as well as what adjustments to make in their form, coaches must know how to diagnose strengths and weaknesses in technique. The features to watch for include

- a stable upper body,
- efficient arm movement,
- placement of the foot under the hips upon landing (avoiding overstriding),
- fairly stiff leg joints upon landing (avoiding excessive flexion, or sinking, of the ankle, knee, and hips),
- sufficient knee-lift to match running speed,
- an active landing, and
- sufficient extension of the leg joints in the takeoff subphase.

Training to correct flaws in technique involves increasing flexibility with stretching exercises, improving joint stability with strength exercises, and refining movement patterns with technique drills. We discuss these methods in the following chapter.

PART II

TRAINING AND RACING PROGRAMS

Now that we've covered the scientific basis of distance running, let's talk training! We begin in chapters 6 and 7 by introducing training methods for developing physical and mental fitness. We devote chapter 6 to methods for building a base of conditioning, focusing on four general fitness capacities: flexibility and mobility, strength endurance, technical skill, and cardiovascular fitness. Then, chapter 7 covers methods for developing four fitness capacities that prepare runners for competition: aerobic fitness, anaerobic fitness, race-specific fitness, and mental fitness. In these two chapters we describe a total of 17 training methods for developing the eight general and specific fitness capacities. For each method we discuss the dose—the appropriate intensity, volume (distance or duration), and frequency of training—and we illustrate sample sessions for runners of different developmental levels.

Our goal for chapters 6 and 7 is to simply introduce the training methods. In chapters 8 through 10 we show you how they fit into a comprehensive, long-term program, walking you through a five-step process for designing training programs:

❚ **Step 1:** Assess initial fitness and training, racing, and health history (chapter 8).

❚ **Step 2:** Set goals for racing and training (chapter 8).

❚ **Step 3:** Map out macrocycles, or seasons of training and competition (chapter 9).

❚ **Step 4:** Plan and implement training sessions (chapter 9).

❚ **Step 5:** Evaluate and revise the program as necessary (chapter 10).

In these chapters you'll learn about a formal method for designing training programs called periodization. Using periodization within our five-step process will enable you to select the best training methods for individual runners based on their fitness, experience, and competitive goals. In addition, this approach will help you design long-range training programs that safely and progressively guide young runners to their ultimate potential.

CHAPTER 6

Training Foundation

Watching elite runners performing at their peak, you have to be impressed by the sheer intensity of their effort. Great runners are able to maintain fast paces over long distances because they train at fast paces. It's simple: to race fast you have to train fast. But consider that the potential height of your racing peak is determined by the strength and depth of your fitness foundation, which is built with capacities such as flexibility, mobility, strength endurance, technique, and cardiovascular endurance. In this chapter we describe nine training methods for developing a strong foundation, or base, for distance running (see figure 6.1). We refer to these methods as general because they don't simulate the exact movements or the specific physiological and psychological demands of cross country and track racing, nor do they necessarily require the high-intensity effort that racing demands. Instead they lay a foundation of fitness to support more advanced, race-specific training, which we cover in the following chapter. A strong base boosts the runner's potential to develop high levels of race-specific fitness and reduces injury risk. Because the general methods prepare runners for race-specific training, they are used more in the early phases of preparation and less as the racing season draws near. (See chapter 9 for details on how much general and race-specific training runners should do as a season progresses.)

The sample sessions presented in this and the next chapter are appropriate for most runners. Individuals are different, however, and we intend for these sessions to present general, flexible guidelines. It's likely that some individuals will find the sessions too easy and some will find them too difficult, so coaches should adapt the doses of these workouts to meet the specific abilities, needs, and training responses of individual athletes.

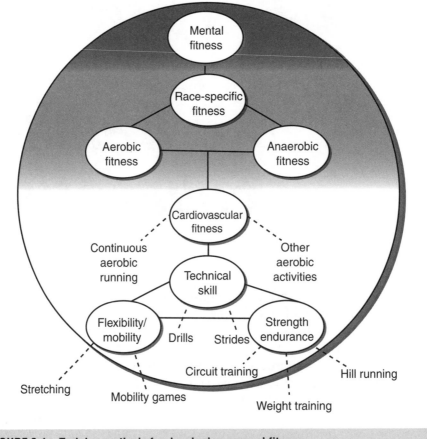

FIGURE 6.1 Training methods for developing general fitness.

Developing Flexibility and Mobility

Flexibility is the capacity to move the limbs through a range of motion for optimally performing a particular activity. Mobility is the capacity to make coordinated, goal-directed movements in different planes (forward, sideways, and diagonally). Because running doesn't demand the extensive flexibility of sports such as gymnastics or figure skating, and because the limbs move mostly in one plane, many distance coaches don't include training for flexibility and mobility, which is a mistake for several reasons.

Distance running strengthens and tightens particular muscle groups, causing imbalances in muscles on opposing sides of limbs and joints. For example, runners tend to have tight hamstring muscles. Runners don't lift their knees very high when covering long distances at relatively slow speeds, which means their hamstrings don't stretch much. Repetitive movement of such a limited range of motion can tighten the hamstrings, causing strains and tears when runners extend their stride for faster running in workouts and races. In addition, the calf muscles can become tight, increasing the risk of calf strains and tears, as well as Achilles tendon injuries.

A number of recent studies have presented contradictory findings on the effects of stretching. On one side is research supporting the conventional view that stretching prevents injuries and enables the muscles to contract more forcefully and efficiently. On the other side are studies that show no effect on injury prevention and athletic performance. A new theory even suggests that distance runners who stretch could perform *worse* because flexible muscles are like loose springs—they can't generate sufficient elastic energy to aid in propulsion in the running stride.

Weighing the conflicting research and considering the practices of sports medicine experts as well as elite distance runners, we take the side supporting regular stretching. Our main reason is that distance running causes imbalances in muscle strength and flexibility that limit performance and increase injury risks, and stretching can correct these imbalances. The stretching exercises on pages 100 to 104 emphasize muscle groups, such as the hamstrings, calves, and hip flexors, that are typically tight in distance runners. Individual differences in flexibility exist, however, so developing stretching routines for individual runners requires diagnostic tests for muscle imbalances in strength and flexibility. This sort of testing is done by athletic trainers, sports physicians, physical therapists, and other health professionals who specialize in sports medicine.

Dynamic and Static Stretching

Pages 100 through 104 illustrate a routine of 13 stretching exercises for flexibility. Figures 6.2a through 6.2g show dynamic stretches, which involve continuous movement of the limbs through sweeping ranges of motion. Figures 6.2h through 6.2n show static stretching exercises, which involve holding the position without movement.

FIGURE 6.2a
Arm reach and swing
Extend the arms above the head and then swing them downward in a wide, sweeping action.

FIGURE 6.2b
Head rolls
Slowly roll the head in a circle, gently stretching the neck muscles. Complete repetitions in the clockwise direction and then switch to the counterclockwise direction.

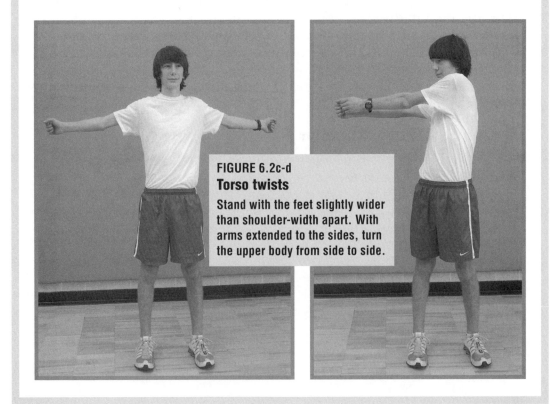

FIGURE 6.2c-d
Torso twists
Stand with the feet slightly wider than shoulder-width apart. With arms extended to the sides, turn the upper body from side to side.

Dynamic Stretches (continued)

FIGURE 6.2e
Hip circles

Make a slow circling action with the hips, gently stretching the groin and hip muscles. Complete repetitions in the clockwise direction and then switch to the counterclockwise direction.

FIGURE 6.2f
Leg swing

With the left foot firmly planted and the left leg straight, gently swing the right leg from the hip. Keep the right leg as straight as possible. Finish repetitions for the right leg and then repeat with the left leg.

FIGURE 6.2g
Ankle swing

Pointing the foot downward, make a slow circling motion, gently stretching the muscles and connective tissue around the ankle. Repeat with the other foot.

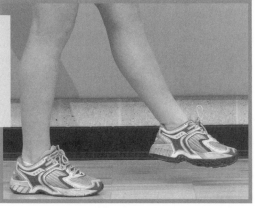

FIGURE 6.2h
Iliotibial-band stretch

With the left hand against a support, place the left leg behind the right leg, with the left foot 8 to 12 inches to the outside of the right hip. Gently lower the left hip, stretching the lateral side of the left thigh, where the iliotibial band runs from the hip to the knee. Repeat for the right leg.

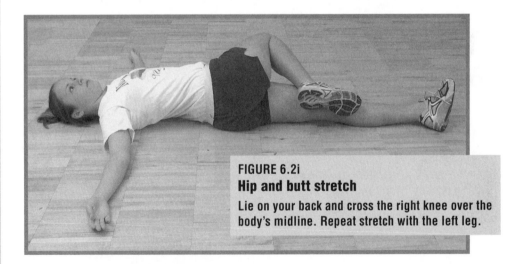

FIGURE 6.2i
Hip and butt stretch

Lie on your back and cross the right knee over the body's midline. Repeat stretch with the left leg.

Static Stretches (continued)

FIGURE 6.2j
Groin stretch
Sit with the soles of the feet together and use the elbows to press down on the inner thighs.

FIGURE 6.2k
Hamstring stretch
Reach forward, keeping the legs straight. Don't strain to touch the toes.

FIGURE 6.2l
Back stretch
On all fours, tighten the abdominal muscles and arch the back, like a cat.

(continued)

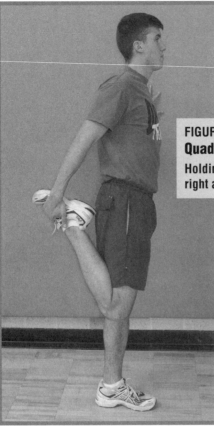

FIGURE 6.2m
Quad stretch
Holding onto a support with the left hand, pull the right ankle up and back. Repeat for the left leg.

FIGURE 6.2n
Calf and Achilles tendon stretch
Plant the left foot firmly behind the right foot and bend at the left ankle by pushing downward with the shin. Repeat on the right leg.

Follow these guidelines for performing the stretching exercises:

▌ Always warm up the muscles by jogging for 5 to 15 minutes before stretching.

▌ Perform dynamic stretches before static stretches. We recommend performing the exercises on pages 100 to 104 in the order that they appear. The dynamic stretching exercises loosen up the joints and prepare the muscles for static stretching. The movements in dynamic stretching should be slow and gentle rather than fast and ballistic. Do 10 to 15 repetitions of each dynamic exercise.

▌ When performing static stretching, hold the position for 20 to 60 seconds, without rocking or bouncing. Stretching should never be so vigorous that it causes quivering or pain in the muscles.

▌ Use the same stretching routine for both training and racing. A familiar stretching routine will help you stay comfortable and relaxed during the prerace warm-up, when competitive anxiety can make it difficult to concentrate on proper preparation. Spend at least 10 to 15 minutes stretching, never rushing the routine.

▌ Stretch before and after training. Many runners only think of stretching as a pretraining and prerace activity, but stretching after training and racing is essential for maintaining flexibility and preventing injuries.

Games for Improving Mobility

The main reasons for training to improve mobility are to strengthen the muscles and connective tissue that surround the joints and to prevent injuries. Runners who lack mobility are at risk for ankle and knee sprains when training and racing on uneven surfaces. Poor mobility can also lead to injury when the primary muscles used for running become fatigued, activating weak, untrained supplemental muscle groups. Mobility training is a way to condition these supplemental muscles.

Formal drills, such as side shuffles, backward running, and cariocas, can improve mobility. For young runners, however, the best mobility training is playing games such as basketball, soccer, flag football, and keep-away. Games are best because they not only involve running and jumping movements in different planes, they're also fun. One of our favorite mobility games is ultimate Frisbee, which is a mixture of rugby and American football without the tackling. A 15- to 20-minute session of ultimate Frisbee once or twice a week during the early phases of preparation is a great way to improve mobility while developing a base of endurance and speed.

How to Play Ultimate Frisbee

Ultimate Frisbee, or ultimate for short, is a noncontact game that two teams play on grass. In official games, each team has seven players. For purposes of training and fun, simply pick sides among the runners on your team. The object of the game is to score goals by throwing a Frisbee to teammates and advancing it across the opposing team's goal line. You can advance the Frisbee only by passing it, so the player who catches it is not allowed to take any steps, but the game still has plenty of running and movement in different planes as players try to get clear of defenders to catch the Frisbee. If the defense intercepts the Frisbee, they become the offense and try to score. The Frisbee also changes direction if an offensive player drops it, or if it hits the ground on an incomplete pass.

An official field is 70 by 40 yards (64 by 36.5 meters), but you can adjust the field according to the number of players and your training objectives. A longer and wider field will challenge runners to cover more distance and can even promote the development of anaerobic fitness.

To prevent injuries, coaches should stress that ultimate is a noncontact game.

Developing Strength Endurance

The term *strength* refers to the ability to exert maximum muscular force, as you would do if you were bench pressing a heavy barbell one time. Your strength is largely determined by the cross-sectional area and mass of your muscles. The importance of absolute strength in athletics depends on the sport. Offensive linemen in football obviously need large muscles and extraordinary strength to successfully block defensive opponents. In contrast, distance runners don't need extraordinary strength because they don't exert maximum force in the running stride. Runners don't need large, bulky muscles to be successful; instead they need a combination of strength and endurance (or strength endurance) to produce moderately high levels of muscular force over long periods of time. This capacity is essential for delaying fatigue, maintaining good running form, and preventing injuries.

Strength endurance training requires working the muscles against greater loads than they normally have to resist. Since the objective is to gain a combination of strength and endurance, the training dose is critical. Runners develop strength endurance using light resistive loads and a large number of repetitions. The combination of low resistance and high repetitions allows you to perform the exercise for a long duration of time to gain endurance in addition to strength, as opposed to the high resistance–low repetitions method used to develop maximum strength and gain muscle mass. We suggest three methods of strength endurance training for distance runners: circuit training, weight training, and hill running.

Warming Up and Cooling Down

Several of the training methods in this chapter are best applied as parts of warm-up and cool-down routines for training sessions and races. Here is a sample 30-minute routine for warming up that incorporates stretching, technique drills, and strides:

▪ 10 to 15 minutes of easy jogging

▪ Dynamic stretching (using the exercises in figures 6.2a to 6.2g on pages 100 to 101)

▪ 5 × 100 meter strides (working down from 5,000-meter race pace to 800-meter race pace)

▪ Static stretching (using the exercises in figures 6.2h to 6.2n on pages 102 to 104)

▪ Technique drills (using the drills in figures 6.5a to 6.5f on pages 128 to 129)

This warm-up routine serves several important physiological functions that prepare the runner for training and racing. The jogging revs up the body's aerobic machinery by increasing heart rate and blood supply to the muscles, the stretching loosens the joints and muscles for optimal stride mechanics, and the 100-meter strides and technique drills prime the neuromuscular pathways for the upcoming fast running. Warming up is also an important part of psychological preparation for races because it helps runners focus their attention on a familiar routine rather than worrying about the competition.

The sample warm-up has elements that runners can also use for cooling down after races and intense training sessions. Cool-downs should include 10 to 15 minutes of easy jogging followed by dynamic and static stretching.

Circuit Training

Circuit training consists of a series of strength endurance exercises organized in a sequential pattern that is called a circuit. You can arrange the stations of a circuit on the infield of a track, in a gymnasium, at a park, or wherever space permits. On page 108, we present sample circuit training sessions for runners of different developmental levels in the preparation period or at the very start of training for an upcoming competitive season. The sample sessions in this part of the book present guidelines for training during the early phases of the preparation period, or when training first begins at the start of a season. We illustrate developmental progression over the years by showing sample sessions for beginners, intermediate runners, and advanced runners. We don't, however, provide detailed guidelines for progression *within* a single season, from the preparation period to the competition period. We'll briefly address such within-season progression for each method in this chapter. In chapter 9 we present more detailed guidelines on how to organize training in specific phases of the preparation and competition periods within a season.

The exercises for the sample circuit training sessions are illustrated in figures 6.3a to 6.3n on pages 109 to 114. As you read the instructions, keep in mind that proper technique is essential in circuit training because although the exercises are intended to prevent injuries, they can actually cause injuries if performed incorrectly.

For the sample circuit training sessions, we've selected exercises that stress the main muscle groups used in running. Each station includes an exercise for the arms, body core (abdomen and back), and legs. Exercises for the arms, core, and legs are ordered sequentially, allowing time for recovery before the athlete works the same body part again at the next station. If you use the same muscle groups consecutively at a station, excessive localized fatigue can result. This fatigue reduces the number of repetitions you are able to perform, limiting the desired gain in endurance.

Sample Sessions: Circuit Training

Duration of session: 15-60 minutes
Intensity: Controlled movement rate; >70% HRmax
Frequency: 10-30 repetitions per exercise
Recovery: 20-30 seconds between exercises; 3-5 minutes between circuits

SAMPLE SESSIONS FOR THE EARLY PREPARATION PERIOD

	NUMBER OF REPETITIONS		
Exercise	**Beginner** $CA^a = 12\text{-}14$ $TA^b = 0\text{-}2$	**Intermediate** $CA = 14\text{-}16$ $TA = 2\text{-}4$	**Advanced** $CA = 16\text{-}18$ $TA = 4\text{-}6$
Station 1			
• Push-ups	10-12	14-16	18-20
• Curl-ups	18-20	22-24	26-28
• Squats	18-20	22-24	26-28
Station 2			
• Assisted chin-ups	10-12	12-14	14-16
• Back extensions	10-12	14-16	18-20
• Heel raisers	18-20	22-24	26-28
Station 3			
• Assisted dips	6-8	10-12	14-16
• Leg extensions	18-20	22-24	26-28
• Medicine-ball step-ups	10-12 (each leg)	14-16 (each leg)	18-20 (each leg)
Station 4			
• Medicine-ball chest passes	10-12	14-16	18-20
• Superman arm and leg raisers	10-12 (each side)	14-16 (each side)	18-20 (each side)
• Lunges	10-12	14-16	18-20

[a]CA = chronological age in years.
[b]TA = training age in years.

Strength Endurance Exercises

FIGURE 6.3a
Push-up (station 1)
With the back and legs straight, lower the body to the ground and then push up to starting position.

FIGURE 6.3b
Curl-up (station 1)
Begin with the back flat on the ground and the fingertips a few inches from the edge of a mat. Keeping the chin tucked to the chest and tensing the abdominal muscles, slowly raise the body by curling the trunk. Stop the curling movement when the fingertips are a few inches off the mat, then gently lower the back to the ground.

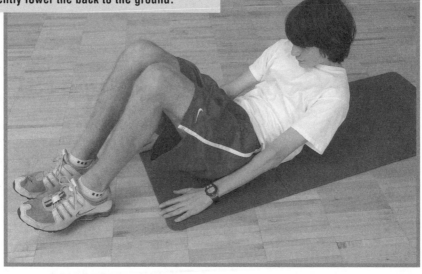

(continued)

FIGURE 6.3c
Squat (station 1)

Begin by standing tall with the feet placed slightly wider than shoulder-width apart and the arms outstretched in front. Slowly bend at the knees, hips, and ankles. Keep the back straight by tensing the abdominal and back muscles. Keep the chin up, parallel to the ground. At the end of the lowering movement, the angle formed by the lower and upper legs (behind the knee) should be 120 to 140 degrees. Hold a medicine ball or dumbbells in outstretched arms for extra resistance.

FIGURE 6.3d
Partner-assisted chin-up (station 2)

With help from a partner, lift the body so that the chin rises slightly over the top of the bar. Slowly lower the body back to the starting position. The partner should provide enough help so that at least 12 repetitions can be performed before fatigue.

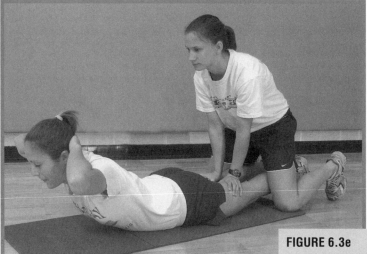

FIGURE 6.3e
Back extension (station 2)
Lying facedown, hands behind the head, slowly raise the head and torso off the ground. Slowly lower the body to the starting position.

FIGURE 6.3f
Heel raiser (station 2)
Starting with the heels flat on the ground and the balls of the feet on a two-by-four block of wood (or on the edge of a curb), raise the heels by standing on tiptoes. Lower the heels to return to the starting position.

(continued)

FIGURE 6.3g
Partner-assisted dip (station 3)

With help from a partner, raise and lower the body by bending at the elbows. Keep the back straight by tensing the abdominal and back muscles. The partner should provide enough help so that at least 12 repetitions can be performed.

FIGURE 6.3h-i
Leg extension (station 3)

Lie on your back, tensing the abdominal muscles. Slowly bring both knees to the chest, grasping them with the hands. Then, extend the legs straight out and hold them a few inches off the ground for five seconds. Slowly lower the legs to the ground and repeat.

FIGURE 6.3j-k
Step-up with medicine ball (station 3)

Begin with the right foot on top of a step or wooden box, high enough so that the thigh is parallel (but not beyond parallel) to the ground. Hold the medicine ball directly in front of the chest, arms fully outstretched. Keeping the back straight, step up onto the step or box, and then step down. Switch sides after completing the assigned repetitions with the right leg.

FIGURE 6.3l
Medicine-ball chest pass (station 4)

Throw the medicine ball as in a basketball chest pass, keeping the elbows out and extending the arms directly in front of the body. For stability, take one step forward just prior to releasing the medicine ball. Partners should stand six to eight feet apart. The throwing action should be fast but controlled.

(continued)

FIGURE 6.3m
Superman arm and leg raiser (station 4)

Lying face down with arms and legs outstretched and chin touching the ground, lift the right arm and the left leg three to five inches off the ground and hold for three seconds. Lower the right arm and left leg, and then do the exercise with the left arm and right leg.

FIGURE 6.3n
Lunge (station 4)

With the right leg supporting the body, slowly raise the left knee, extend the left leg, and gently lunge forward. The left shin should be perpendicular, or just slightly beyond, in relation to the ground. From this position, raise the body, and repeat the movement by lunging with the right leg. Use dumbbells or a weighted vest for extra resistance.

Most young runners enjoy circuit training because it adds variety to daily workouts, it's physically challenging, and it produces visible results, including enhanced muscle tone, improved posture, and a more powerful stride. Even so, it's important to be creative and change the circuit exercises over time. While there should be 8 to 12 exercises in a circuit, the exercises themselves can vary as long as they stress muscles used for postural support, driving the arms, absorbing impact forces, and propulsion. For example, to develop the calves, you can replace heel raises with rope jumping. Instead of doing curl-ups for the abdominal muscles you can do crossover sit-ups or crunches. For alternative exercises for the abdominal and back muscles, we suggest Pilates, which is an excellent form of exercise for developing core strength and good posture.

Depending on the type of exercise and the athlete's developmental level, the number of repetitions will range between 10 and 30, performed at a controlled rate. Going too fast can result in sloppy technique, increasing the risk of injury. Include a 20- to 30-second recovery period in between exercises at each station, which is short enough to keep your heart rate elevated, thereby ensuring an endurance training effect. If you do the exercises properly and keep the recovery period short, circuit training will elevate your heart rate to at least 70 percent of maximum throughout the session. To further promote the endurance effect, coaches can arrange the stations several hundred meters apart so when athletes complete the exercises at one station they have to run to the next station.

One complete circuit should take 15 to 20 minutes. At the start of a training season, runners should perform only one circuit per session. Over time you can work up to performing two to three circuits. This type of training can be quite lengthy—if you do three circuits with a five-minute recovery between circuits, the session can take up to an hour or more. These workouts are demanding on the cardiovascular system and the muscles performing the resistance exercises, but they are extremely valuable in building a fitness base.

Many exercises that use the body weight as resistance are sufficient for developing strength endurance. However, conditioned intermediate or advanced runners can increase the intensity by doing circuit exercises with added resistance in the form of medicine balls, dumbbells, sand bags, ankle weights, or any other objects that create an extra load. The added resistance should be light enough to allow the athlete to perform at least 15 repetitions with good technique before fatiguing.

Training Terminology

In this and the following chapter, we present sample training sessions that apply the methods under discussion. We use the following terms to describe the training dose:

▌ *Volume* refers to the distance or duration of all or part of a training session. Volume can be expressed as the number of miles, kilometers, or minutes covered in a run or a strength endurance session.

▌ *Frequency* refers to the number of times a repetition is performed in a training session. The frequency of repetitions must be noted when planning circuit training, weight training, and interval running. For example, an athlete might do four repetitions of a 600-meter run, a session that is written as 4 × 600 meters.

▌ *Intensity* refers to the amount of effort required to complete a repetition or a training session. When we describe training methods involving running, we'll define intensity by running time, pace per mile or kilometer, or percentage of maximal heart rate. The session above might be further developed as 4 × 600 meters at 2:00 for each 6:00. When we describe strength endurance training methods (circuit and weight training), we'll define intensity by the load lifted. Athletes can increase training intensity by exerting more effort or by decreasing the recovery interval between repetitions during interval workouts.

▌ *Recovery* refers to the length of time between repetitions during interval training. We can add a recovery interval to complete our sample session: 4 × 600 meters at 2:00 with a 2:00 jog recovery. In this session, the athlete would jog for two minutes after each 600-meter repetition. Recovery can also be expressed in a ratio, relative to the duration of a repetition. For a session of 4 × 600 meters at 2:00, a 1:1 recovery period would last 2:00. Or, a 1:0.5 recovery period would last 1:00 and a 1:1.5 recovery period would last 3:00.

Weight Training

As in circuit training, the objective of weight training for distance runners is to build strength endurance in order to improve performance and prevent injuries, so most of the same principles and guidelines for circuit training also apply to weight training. For example, the weight training dose should be low in intensity and high in repetitions to develop muscular strength and endurance rather than pure strength.

For intermediate and advanced runners, weight training can supplement circuit training as the training season progresses, but first make sure that the weight training equipment is the appropriate size for youths. Weight machines in gyms and fitness clubs are usually sized for adults, and free weights on long bars may be too cumbersome and difficult for smaller athletes to control. If you don't have access to appropriately sized equipment, circuit training with added resistance, such as medicine balls and dumbbells, is an excellent means of developing strength endurance.

If properly sized, weight machines offer the advantage of isolating specific muscle groups. They also minimize the risk of injury because the path over which the movement occurs is controlled by pulleys and other mechanical devices. In contrast, free weights require considerable balance and technique to isolate key muscles and stabilize the movement. Because the technical demands are much greater for free weights, experts recommend starting out on machines and progressing to free weights over time.

The sample weight training sessions on page 118 include exercises using both machines and free weights (see the exercises and instructions in figures 6.4a to 6.4l on pages 119 to 123). As in circuit training, weight training should stress the leg and arm muscles involved in the running movement and the core muscles that stabilize the torso. The exercise order should allow for recovery of a given muscle group before it is stressed again, so the sample sessions alternate exercises for the arms, body core, and legs. It's best to stress large muscles first, then small muscles. For variety, you can substitute the exercises in our sample sessions with others that stress the same muscle groups. (For alternative circuit and weight training exercises, we refer you to *Strength Training for Young Athletes* by William Kraemer and Steven Fleck. This book features illustrations and detailed instructions for performing numerous circuit and weight training exercises.)

Like circuit training, weight training can prevent injuries; however, injuries can occur if coaches don't supervise the exercises closely, providing instruction and feedback on technique. Several free weight exercises require spotters to help position the bar and to assist athletes if they have difficulty lifting the weights.

A concept called repetition maximum, or RM, guides coaches in determining the appropriate dose of weight training for each individual. For example, a 12 RM is the amount of weight that an athlete can lift 12, but not 13, times without excessive straining and loss of form. To develop strength endurance, distance runners should perform 8 to 15 repetitions of each weight training exercise using a 10- to 15-RM load. To determine how much weight to lift for, say, a 12 RM, start with a very light load that can be lifted at least 20 times. After resting for several minutes, increase the weight by 10 to 15 percent and perform the repetitions until fatigue sets in. Repeat this process, with sufficient rest periods, until 12 repetitions is the maximum number that you can perform.

Sample Sessions: Weight Training

Duration: 20-60 minutes
Intensity: 10-15 repetition maximum; controlled rate of movement
Frequency: 8-15 repetitions per exercise
Recovery: 1-2 minutes between exercises

SAMPLE SESSIONS FOR THE EARLY PREPARATION PERIOD

Exercise	Intermediate CA^a = 14-16 TA^b = 2-4	Advanced CA = 16-18 TA = 4-6
Bench press	12-15 reps at 15RM[c]	10-12 reps at 12RM
Abdominal crunches	10-12 reps at 15RM	12-15 reps at 15RM
Barbell squats	12-15 reps at 15RM	10-12 reps at 12RM
Overhead press	10-12 reps at 12RM	8-10 reps at 10RM
Good mornings	10-12 reps at 12RM	8-10 reps at 10RM
Knee extensions	12-15 reps at 15RM	10-12 reps at 12RM
Knee curls	10-12 reps at 12RM	8-10 reps at 10RM
Dumbbell arm pumps	12-15 reps at 15RM	10-12 reps at 12RM
Barbell heel raisers	12-15 reps at 15RM	10-12 reps at 12RM
Lat pulldown	12-15 reps at 15RM	10-12 reps at 12RM

No sample workout is given for beginners because we recommend that runners with a training age of less than two years use circuit training rather than weight training.
[a]CA = chronological age in years.
[b]TA = training age in years.
[c]RM = repetition maximum (see text for explanation).

FIGURE 6.4a-b
Bench press

Lying on a bench with the feet flat on the floor, grip the bar so the hands are shoulder-width apart. Lower the bar to the upper chest in a controlled manner. Press the bar upward to the starting position. Do not raise the back or buttocks off the bench.

FIGURE 6.4c-d
Abdominal crunch

Bend forward at the waist by contracting the abdominal muscles, avoiding a jerking action. Slowly return to starting position.

(continued)

FIGURE 6.4e
Barbell squat

Stand with the bar resting on the shoulder blades, hands and feet spaced slightly greater than shoulder-width apart. Keeping the back as upright as possible, lower the body by bending at the hips, knees, and ankles. At the end of the lowering movement, the angle formed by the lower and upper legs (behind the knee) should be 120 to 140 degrees. Lift the body to the starting position, keeping the feet flat on the floor.

FIGURE 6.4f
Overhead press

Beginning in the same position as in barbell squats, press the bar above the head until the arms are straight. Lower the bar slowly to the starting position. During the lowering and lifting movements, keep the feet flat on the floor.

Weight Training Exercises (continued)

FIGURE 6.4g
Good morning

Beginning in the same position as in barbell squats, with the knees slightly bent, bend forward at the waist until the torso is almost parallel to the floor. Slowly raise the body back to the starting position. During the lowering and lifting movements, keep the back straight.

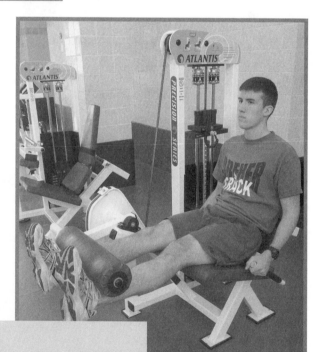

FIGURE 6.4h
Knee extension

Sit in the machine as in a chair and lift the weight by straightening the legs. Hold for two seconds. Slowly lower the weight to the starting position. During the lifting and lowering movement, keep the back flat against the seat.

(continued)

FIGURE 6.4i
Knee curl

Lie facedown on the machine bench with the knees hanging slightly over the edge and the heels under the pads. Lift the weight by slowly pulling the heels to the buttocks. To lower the weight, straighten the legs in a controlled manner.

FIGURE 6.4j
Dumbbell arm pump

Standing with one foot propped up on a bench or chair, pump the arms rapidly using the same motion as in the running stride. Stand tall and keep the supporting leg straight, avoiding a sitting position of the hips.

FIGURE 6.4k
Barbell heel raiser

Beginning in the same position as in barbell squats and making sure the feet point straight ahead, raise the heels by extending at the ankles and pushing down with the toes. Lower the heels to return to the starting position.

FIGURE 6.4l
Lat pulldown

Keeping the back straight and shoulders squared, lower the bar, avoiding a jerking action. After bringing the bar under the chin, slowly extend the arms, allowing the bar to return to the starting position.

The lower end of the repetition range allows athletes to refine their lifting technique without becoming too fatigued. For example, if you perform 10 to 12 repetitions of barbell squats with 15-RM loads, you won't strain during the last few lifts. Athletes should never do exercises that involve many different joints and require coordinating the whole body, such as barbell squats, under conditions that compromise good technique. When form breaks down, the risk of injury increases, so it's best to reduce the number of repetitions when you are still perfecting technique or if you experience excessive fatigue.

The year-to-year progression of weight training involves increasing the intensity, or the load lifted, by reducing the RM load over time. For intermediate runners, 15-RM loads are appropriate because they are light enough to allow mastery of technique, yet heavy enough to increase strength endurance. The light load also reduces stress on growing bones in individuals who are still maturing. Advanced runners who are more physically mature and have learned the proper technique will benefit from heavier weights such as 10- or 12-RM loads.

We recommend that runners do not begin weight training in a season until they have done 6 to 10 circuit training sessions over a period of three to four weeks. Circuit training helps build a strength endurance base to prepare athletes for more intense weight training. In the beginning, the weight training session should include only one set. As the training season progresses, athletes may perform two or three sets. As the competitive season draws near and race-specific methods begin to be emphasized, the contribution of weight training to the total training load should decrease. Consider an intermediate-level runner who builds up to three sets of our sample weight training session twice a week by the end of the preparation period. Throughout the racing season, she might do only one set on two days per week, which will maintain her strength endurance base. The RM loads will have to increase periodically as athletes gain strength endurance. It's important to keep detailed records of weight training workouts so that athletes can systematically increase their RM loads.

Hill Running

Several of the training methods described in this chapter have crossover effects—they develop more than one general fitness capacity. For example, circuit training builds both strength endurance and cardiovascular fitness because the prolonged, continuous nature of circuit training stresses the skeletal muscles as well as the heart and vasculature. One of the most complete crossover methods is hill running, which develops strength endurance, cardiovascular fitness, and technique. We focus on uphill running for developing strength endurance because running uphill places an extra load on the leg muscles and requires more vigorous arm action than running on level ground.

As shown in the sample sessions that follow, hill running to develop strength endurance is a form of interval training because it involves repetitions separated by recovery periods. The slope of the hill should be steep enough to force runners to alter their technique by using more vigorous muscle force than they would when running on level ground. The hill should not be so steep that it causes runners to strain and lose proper form. The distance of the hill should be fairly short, 200 to 400 meters. The session will still promote muscular endurance if runners take a short recovery between repetitions by jogging back down the hill. Even a short early-season session for a beginner, 6 × 200 meters, totals 2,400 meters of running when the downhill jog recoveries are included. You might even extend the repetitions another 50 to 100 meters on the flat, after the hill crests. In cross country, inexperienced runners tend to ease up when they get to the top of a hill, so if they practice holding the pace they'll gain a competitive advantage. Because the main objective of hill running is to develop strength endurance, the intensity should not highly stress the anaerobic system and cause fatigue from lactic acid accumulation. A guideline for intensity is to run at a pace that corresponds to 3,000- to 5,000-meter race pace.

At the start of the preparation period, we recommend a low number of hill repetitions (five or six), even for advanced runners. The year-to-year progression for hill training in the sample sessions features an increase in the distance of each repetition. Younger, less fit runners may have difficulty holding efficient form on long hills, so you can intensify the dose by increasing the number of repetitions instead. A 16-year-old with three years of training experience might start a new season by doing 5 × 400-meter hills, and over the course of the preparation period his session might progress to 10 × 400 meters.

Sample Sessions: Hill Running

Duration of repetitions: 200-400 meters

Intensity: Fast but controlled

Frequency: 5-10 repetitions

Recovery: Jog back to starting position

Total volume per session: 1,000-4,000 meters

SAMPLE SESSIONS FOR THE EARLY PREPARATION PERIOD

Beginner *CA[a] = 12-14* *TA[b] = 0-2*	*Intermediate* *CA = 14-16* *TA = 2-4*	*Advanced* *CA = 16-18* *TA = 4-6*
5-6 × 200 m	5-6 × 300-400 m	5-6 × 400-500 m

[a]CA = chronological age in years.
[b]TA = training age in years.

Developing Technical Skill

We've emphasized the importance of sound running technique and its role in improving running economy, conserving energy, and preventing injuries. Two methods of technique training that help young runners learn the best postures and patterns of movement in the running stride are drills and strides. Technique drills and strides also help break bad habits before they become permanent.

Technique training typically fits into daily sessions as part of a warm-up or by complementing other methods. For example, an early-season training session emphasizing general training methods might feature a warm-up that includes the technique drills that we describe in the next section, followed by 8 to 10 100-meter strides, and ending with a 20-minute game of ultimate Frisbee. A critical aspect of any technique session is feedback from the coach. Too often young athletes perform technique drills incorrectly, reinforcing inefficient movement patterns. If possible, coaches should videotape technique sessions to give feedback on strengths and weaknesses.

Technique Drills

The sample sessions that follow include four technique drills for distance runners, which are illustrated in figures 6.5a to 6.5f on pages 128 to 129. These drills train the neuromuscular system to help runners develop the following characteristics of sound technique: correct posture of the upper body, high knee lift, powerful extension of the driving leg in the takeoff phase of the stride, correct pattern of dorsiflexion (closing) and extension (opening) at the ankle joint, and efficient arm action.

In each drill the upper body should be squared at the shoulders and bent very slightly forward at the hips. The core muscles should support the torso in a way that makes you feel tall. With your chin parallel to the ground, your eyes should focus straight ahead. Practicing this posture helps you avoid turning movements of the upper body, flailing of the arms, and the inefficient stride mechanics that occur when the body slouches or leans too far forward or backward. Each drill also emphasizes a coordinated and vigorous pumping of the arms, in which the hands move up and down without crossing too far in front of the body.

Two of the drills in particular—high-knee marching (see figure 6.5a) and high-knee running (see figure 6.5f)—emphasize extending the driving leg during the takeoff phase of the stride and lifting the knees. These biomechanical features increase stride length, which as we discussed in chapter 5 is the most efficient way to surge or kick in middle- and long-distance races. If you can generate a great amount of propulsive force by extending the driving leg, and if you can keep your leading foot off the ground by raising your knee high, your stride will naturally lengthen. Runners who are unable to quicken the pace by extending their stride length are at a great disadvantage.

The basic skipping drill (see figure 6.5, b to d) develops optimal biomechanics of the lower leg and foot. The basic skipping drill isolates the action at the ankle joint, which helps correct the common flaw of lack of movement at that joint, especially as the foot leaves the ground on takeoff. It is also important because, as we discussed in the last chapter, much of the propulsive force in an optimal running stride comes from extending the ankle joint. In the basic skipping exercise the athlete keeps the knees fairly straight, forcing the muscles that extend the ankle to do all the propulsive work.

Sample Sessions: Technique Drills

Duration of repetitions: 10-100 meters
Intensity: Fast but controlled
Frequency: 3-6 repetitions per drill
Recovery: Walk or jog back to starting position

SAMPLE SESSIONS FOR THE EARLY PREPARATION PERIOD

Drill	Beginner CA^a = 12-14 TA^b = 0-2	Intermediate CA = 14-16 TA = 2-4	Advanced CA = 16-18 TA = 4-6
High-knee marching	3 × 20 m	3 × 30 m	3 × 40 m
Basic skipping	3 × 40 m	3 × 60 m	3 × 80 m
Butt kicks	3 × 20 m	3 × 30 m	3 × 40 m
High-knee running	3 × 30 m	3 × 40 m	3 × 50 m

[a]CA = chronological age in years.
[b]TA = training age in years.

Technique Drills

FIGURE 6.5a
High-knee marching

This drill exaggerates walking (because both legs don't leave the ground at the same time) by demanding high knee lift and an extended driving action of the leg on takeoff. Begin by vigorously raising the right knee to bring the thigh parallel to the ground. The right foot should be dorsiflexed, which means that the toe should be pulled toward the shin. The left leg should be straight, contacting the ground only with the ball of the foot and the toes. Keeping the right foot dorsiflexed, lower the leg, bringing the foot under the hip as the forefoot contacts the ground. The shoulders should be squared and the upper body should lean forward only slightly at the hips. The arms, kept at a 90- to 120-degree angle, should swing vigorously (as the right knee comes up, the left arm moves forward). Make sure that the arms don't cross in front of the body. Continue the cyclic marching movement.

FIGURE 6.5b-d
Basic skipping

Just as a child skips, land on the heel and quickly roll off the ball of the foot, accentuating the pushing-off action. The knees should be fairly straight but not rigid. After pushing off and extending fully at the ankle joint, quickly pull the toe to the shin prior to landing. Swing the arms vigorously without crossing them in front of the body.

FIGURE 6.5e
Butt kicks

Make a running motion with an exaggerated follow-through action in which the heel lightly touches the buttocks. The action occurs by bending the knee. Instead of lifting the knee in front of the body as in a normal stride, the knee and thigh remain vertical throughout the drill.

FIGURE 6.5f
High-knee running

This drill is very similar to the high-knee marching drill, except this drill features running movement rather than marching movement. Because most of the generated force is vertical, the objective is not to move forward quickly, but to take many rapid, short strides.

Technique Strides

In this method of technique training, the athlete runs repeated strides over short distances (100 to 150 meters) at race pace and faster. During these sessions, the coach identifies any areas for improvement in the runner's form and gives instructions for making corrections. To show you how technique strides can be used in individualized training, let's consider the runner who overstrides, has a passive landing, and brings his arms across the front of his body, causing rotation of the torso. A session for this athlete might involve 15 repetitions of a 150-meter stride with complete recovery between repetitions. To work on each flaw, the session can be divided as follows:

▌ 5 × 150 meters at 1,500-meter race pace, with the focus on correcting the overstride by planting the foot closer to the body

▌ 5 × 150 meters at 800-meter race pace, with the focus on an active landing

▌ 5 × 150 meters at a controlled sprint, with the focus on driving the arms in a straight line without crossing over the body's midline

As with drills, athletes should do technique strides when they are rested. Fatigue limits the ability to perform and thereby learn the correct motor patterns. Coaches should pay special attention to runners' technique during training sessions that are designed to cause fatigue, especially race-specific sessions (see chapter 7). After all, the objective of technique training is to apply it to racing situations when fatigue occurs. To keep runners focused on form during high-intensity training sessions and races, coaches should use the verbal cues we recommended in the technique tips in chapter 5.

Developing Cardiovascular Fitness

Cardiovascular fitness refers to the capacity of the heart and vasculature to supply the working muscles with a high rate of oxygen-rich blood flow. Cardiovascular fitness largely determines one's endurance, or the ability to sustain moderate physical activity for a long duration without fatiguing. In this section we describe two training methods for developing cardiovascular fitness: continuous aerobic running and nonrunning aerobic activities.

Continuous Aerobic Running

Traditionally, coaches and runners have used the term *long slow distance,* or LSD, to describe the main method for developing cardiovascular fitness. We'll replace this outdated term with *continuous aerobic running,* or CAR, because the *slow* in LSD gives the impression that runners can improve their aerobic conditioning simply by jogging. The pace required to reach the threshold for improving cardiovascular endurance will not necessarily feel fast, but neither will it feel like a jog.

CAR is probably the simplest of all training methods. All you need are the right clothes for the conditions, a good pair of shoes, a stopwatch, and a course. As often as possible, runs should be on soft surfaces rather than asphalt or concrete to avoid excessive jarring. You should also vary training courses to make this method more enjoyable. If you live close to grassy rolling hills, mountain trails, beaches, dirt roads, or other interesting settings, do your continuous aerobic running in these natural environments.

Depending on the runner's developmental level and event specialty, as well as the phase of preparation for competition, the duration of CAR varies from 20 to 70 minutes, or approximately 3 to 10 miles (5 to 16 kilometers). In the sample CAR sessions that follow, we've expressed the duration of training in minutes rather than miles or kilometers. If you run for time rather than distance, you don't have to measure all your running courses. You're also free to venture and explore new areas without having to worry about running too short or too long. The low end of the range, 20 minutes, is suitable for beginners at the start of the season. The high end of the range, 70 minutes, is appropriate for advanced runners who specialize in 3,000- and 5,000-meter races and have gradually built up to this volume.

The pace should elevate the heart rate to roughly 65 to 75 percent of the maximum (see the sidebar on heart rate on page 133). It should be fast enough that runners don't feel they're simply jogging, but slow

Sample Sessions: Continuous Aerobic Running

Duration: 20-70 minutes
Intensity: 65-75% of HRmax
Frequency: 1 repetition
Recovery: None

SAMPLE SESSIONS FOR THE EARLY PREPARATION PERIOD

Beginner *CA[a] = 12-14* *TA[b] = 0-2*	Intermediate *CA = 14-16* *TA = 2-4*	Advanced *CA = 16-18* *TA = 4-6*
20-25 min at 65% of HRmax	25-35 min at 70% of HRmax	35-45 min at 75% of HRmax

[a]CA = chronological age in years.
[b]TA = training age in years.

enough that they can converse with training partners. To ensure that they are within the target intensity range, runners should stop to take their heart rate 10 to 15 minutes into the run. If their heart rate is outside of the target range, runners should adjust their pace accordingly. For runs over 40 minutes, it's a good idea to check heart rate again at the halfway point.

Keep individual differences in mind when planning CAR sessions. Beginners who have been training for less than one year may need to run at an 8:00- to 8:30-mile pace (5:00 to 5:20 per kilometer) for optimal intensity. In contrast, advanced runners (training age of four years) may need to run at a 6:30- to 7:00-mile pace (4:00 to 4:20 per kilometer). If beginners try to keep up with advanced runners, their effort may exceed the threshold for aerobic conditioning, in which case anaerobic metabolism will kick in and fatigue will rapidly follow. If runners have to slow down or stop, they won't achieve the beneficial cardiovascular effects.

The duration of CAR should increase year to year. As shown in the sample sessions, the advanced cross country runner's session (45 minutes) is more than twice as long as the beginner's (20 minutes), and the advanced runner works at the higher end of the intensity range. Even though a 13-year-old with one year of training experience might be able to handle 45 minutes or more, actually running that much could backfire. If the 13-year-old has the potential and desire to excel several years down the road, his training volume has to increase over the years to experience continued improvement. By age 16 or 17, he might need to run for 90 or 100 minutes to enhance aerobic fitness. Such extensive training, which is more suitable for elite adult runners, exposes the young runner to injury and burnout.

The duration of CAR should also increase over the course of a single training season. For example, over the first two months of the preparation period, beginning cross country runners might increase the duration of a run from 20 to 35 minutes. At the same time, these runners will have to quicken their pace because their aerobic conditioning will improve. Over a single training season, the pace required to keep their heart rate within 65 to 75 percent of maximum might be lowered by as much as 30 seconds per mile.

Nonrunning Aerobic Activities

Because the focus of cardiovascular fitness is the heart and vasculature rather than the prime mover muscles, any continuous, rhythmic activity that uses large muscle groups is a suitable training method. As long as they're elevating their heart rate to 65 to 75 percent of maximum, young runners can improve their cardiovascular fitness by cycling, swimming, cross-country skiing, in-line skating, and so on. It's a good idea to include

Using Heart Rate to Guide Training Intensity

Heart rate is an excellent measure of physiological responses to training and the intensity of training because it increases in proportion to the muscles' need for oxygen. On average, maximal heart rate (HRmax) for adolescents is 190 to 210 beats per minute (bpm). Runners can precisely determine HRmax by counting their heart beats immediately after completing an all-out three- to five-minute run at an even pace. The HRmax from this test can be used to gauge the training intensity for continuous aerobic running and for other running methods that we describe in chapter 7.

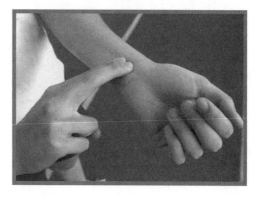

The two photos on this page show how to take your pulse, which is an echo of the heartbeat. The pulse can be felt in the wrist (radial artery) and the neck (carotid artery). To take your pulse at the wrist, place your right hand in your left palm, with the fingertips of your right hand on your left thumb. Slowly slide the first two fingertips along the edge of the thumb toward your wrist. Once your fingertips are on your wrist, feel for the pulse, count the number of beats for 15 seconds, and multiply by four. To take your pulse at your neck, place the first two fingers of your right hand on your neck, level with your Adam's apple. Slide your fingers back until they are in the groove between your Adam's apple and the large muscle running down the front and side of your neck. Press gently to feel the pulse, count the number of beats for 15 seconds, and multiply by four.

Another way to measure heart rate is to use a monitor that straps to the chest and digitally records the number of beats per minute on a wristwatch. Advancements in technology have made heart rate monitors relatively inexpensive and easy to use.

Flathead High School

Location: Kalispell, Montana

Coach: Paul Jorgensen

Books, magazine articles, and lectures at coaching clinics shape training programs for distance runners. In special places, however, training is also influenced by the natural environment. One of these places is Kalispell, Montana, located in the northwestern part of the state in the shadow of Glacier National Park. Hundreds of miles of trails traverse Kalispell's Flathead Valley and the bordering Rocky Mountains, including grown-over logging trails, horse trails, bike trails, and hiking trails.

Early on summer mornings, accompanied by their coach, Paul Jorgensen, the Flathead High School distance runners head for these trails to build endurance and strength. In early June, the runners start their summer training program, running about 40 minutes three days a week. By summer's end they're up to an hour or so, resulting in a 50- to 60-mile training week. "It sure beats running downtown and dodging cars," says Jorgensen. "The trails go in all directions, so we can go for weeks without covering the same ground. We see deer, elk, and sometimes bears. A lot of my kids' enjoyment and motivation for running comes from being together in this environment."

Trail running poses unique coaching challenges for Jorgensen, who follows the pack on a mountain bike. One day several years back, a few members of the girls' team returned from a run, jogging along with handfuls of wildflowers. "Now I encourage my kids to run faster than 'flower-picking' pace," says Jorgensen. "I challenge them to go at a fairly fast pace for the distance. I don't want them jogging because that's not going to do them any good, and sometimes it's harder to run slow than to run fast."

Jorgensen views trail running as a means for developing many of the physical qualities essential for successful racing, especially in cross country. He says, "My kids develop leg strength from surging up hills and agility from going around turns and going over uneven terrain. There are tree roots and rocks, so the kids have to be alert and pick up their feet. Trail running gets us ready for the changing paces of cross country racing." An added benefit is the mental toughness that trail running develops. Once every few weeks during the summer, the Flathead runners do a hard 10-mile run on the rugged trails in the Swan Mountain Range, climbing 1,000 feet during the workout.

While trail running is the backbone of the summer training program at Flathead, other methods contribute to building a strong base. Two or three days a week, often after their morning trail run, the athletes lift weights. A typical session incorporates 10 to 12 exercises, including bench presses, clean-and-jerk lifts, biceps curls, hamstring curls, and several exercises for strengthening the abdominal and back muscles. The emphasis is on strength endurance rather than pure strength, so the runners do 12-15 repetitions with lighter weights.

One of the longest trails in Kalispell is the trail of success that Jorgensen has built. Since he started coaching the boys in 1970 and the girls in 1979, Jorgensen's cross country teams have won 20 state titles, 11 for girls and 9 for boys.

these supplementary activities throughout the season for beginners and in the early phases of preparation for all runners. Too much continuous running can be boring, and nonrunning methods add variety, making training fun and enhancing motivation. Supplementary activities that stress many different muscle groups also help young runners develop fitness in a well-rounded way, which is important because whole-body fitness reduces the risk of injury from the repetitive stress of running. Finally, in the unfortunate event of injury, experience with nonrunning activities pays dividends. Injured runners who are familiar with training on a bicycle or in the pool are able to use these methods immediately to maintain aerobic fitness while their injuries heal.

Striding Ahead

General training methods build a foundation of all-around fitness that includes the heart and vasculature, muscles and connective tissue, and neuromuscular system. Developing general fitness is the most important training objective for beginners and for runners of all developmental levels in the early phases of preparation for an upcoming racing season. A strong fitness base gives runners the strength and endurance to successfully handle heavy loads of high-intensity, race-specific training methods. But the advantages go well beyond just preparing runners for more demanding training within a season. General training can influence a runner's entire career. Based on scientific principles and anecdotal evidence, we're convinced that runners who incorporate methods such as circuit training, weight training, and technique drills have longer and more successful careers than runners whose training is just based on running. Runners who use the methods described in this chapter avoid injuries—especially injuries due to muscle imbalances—and are ultimately able to train at higher intensities because their bodies can withstand the stress. We move on to discuss race-specific training methods in the following chapter, but don't lose sight of their relationship to the general methods we've covered here.

CHAPTER 7

Race-Specific Training

The general training methods are sometimes described as "training to train" because they build a fitness base from which you begin race-specific training. In this chapter we move on to the more advanced, race-specific methods, which you might think of as "training to race." The race-specific methods—tempo running, aerobic intervals, anaerobic intervals, race-specific intervals, time trials, and pacing and tactical exercises—simulate the physiological and psychological demands of competition (see figure 7.1). They develop the energy pathways, muscle fibers, motor patterns, and tactical skills needed for peak performance in races from 800 to 5,000 meters.

Race-specific training methods are guided by the principle of specificity: Physiological adaptations to training are specific to the methods that runners use. While general training methods such as continuous aerobic running build a foundation of aerobic fitness, they don't stress the body enough to cause the physiological changes that increase $\dot{V}O_2$max and the lactate threshold to their highest levels. In addition, the general methods don't condition the body to withstand the fatiguing effects of anaerobic metabolism, such as lactic acid accumulation. In other words, the general methods don't completely prepare runners for the physiological demands of racing. Complete preparation includes race-specific methods, which stress and condition the aerobic and anaerobic energy systems as well as the mind, at very high levels.

To race fast, runners have to train fast. However, this means that although race-specific methods greatly improve fitness for racing, they can also lead to injury and burnout. When using these methods you must increase the training dose gradually over time. Beginners, especially those who have not yet reached puberty, should start out with very low doses of the race-specific methods and slowly increase the dose. For runners of all levels, the use of race-specific methods should increase

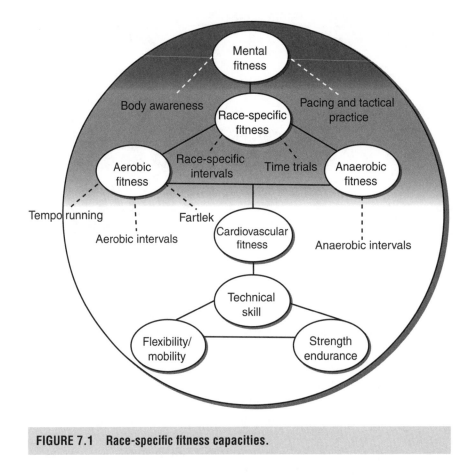

FIGURE 7.1 Race-specific fitness capacities.

gradually through each successive phase of preparation. As you'll see in chapter 9, where we present guidelines for incorporating general and race-specific methods into the training program, we don't recommend eliminating race-specific training from early phases. You should include some form of high-intensity running in the training program year-round. It's critical for young runners to keep their ability to recruit FT muscle fibers and to experience the vigorous movements of fast running. This will ensure a smooth transition from general to race-specific methods, reducing the risk of injuries that can occur with sudden changes in training intensity.

Developing Aerobic Fitness

The most important physiological determinant of distance running performance is aerobic fitness, or the body's capacity to deliver oxygen to the working muscles and process it rapidly to form ATP. The higher your aerobic fitness, the less you'll rely on the anaerobic energy system, delaying fatigue caused by glycogen depletion and lactic acid accumulation. To improve aerobic fitness you must raise the lactate threshold and increase $\dot{V}O_2$max. In this section we describe three methods—tempo running, aerobic interval training, and fartlek—that bring about these physiological adaptations while also developing qualities of mental fitness such as willpower and pacing skill.

Tempo Running

One way to improve aerobic fitness is to increase the threshold at which lactic acid production begins to exceed its clearance in the muscles. Research shows that in young runners this threshold typically occurs at a pace that corresponds to 75 to 85 percent of HRmax. At this intensity runners can sustain the pace for a fairly long time before fatigue sets in. A highly fit 18-year-old, for example, might be able to sustain running at 85 percent of HRmax for up to 40 minutes or more. Coaches often refer to running at this intensity as tempo running. There are two versions: interval tempo running and continuous tempo running.

Sample sessions for interval and continuous tempo running are shown on page 140. The following guidelines will help you set the intensity, or pace:

▮ The pace should result in a heart rate of 75 to 85 percent of maximum. To make sure that heart rate is in the target range, runners can stop to check their pulse about one-fourth of the way through the run. With experience, runners should be able to judge the right pace without having to stop for a pulse check. Heart rate monitors are helpful because athletes can look at their watches for pulse readouts without having to stop.

▮ The pace should stimulate vigorous but not labored breathing, so that runners find it difficult to talk.

▮ The pace should feel mentally and physically challenging, but at the end of the session, runners should be able to sustain the pace for another 6 to 10 minutes before having to slow down.

▮ For many runners the optimal pace is approximately one minute per mile slower than their current race pace for the mile run and 30 seconds slower than their pace per mile for 5,000 meters.

When you use heart rate to determine the right intensity along with a stopwatch to check your pace, you can do tempo running anywhere, from flat dirt roads to rolling grassy hills to a 400-meter track. Coaches should stress the importance of maintaining a pace that keeps the heart rate at 75 to 85 percent of maximum. Beginners should train at the lower end of the range and advanced runners should train at the higher end. Because tempo training involves fast but not all-out running, it's tempting to push the pace and compete with teammates. Two ways to keep teammates from racing during tempo sessions are to group runners of similar ability or have them start at staged intervals and run alone.

Sample Sessions: Interval Tempo Running

Duration of repetitions: 3-10 minutes per repetition
Intensity: 75-85% of HRmax; approximately 1 minute per mile slower than mile race pace
Frequency: 2-10 repetitions
Recovery: 30-90 seconds of brisk jogging
Total volume per session: Approximately 2-6 miles (3,200-10,000 meters)

SAMPLE SESSIONS FOR THE EARLY PREPARATION PERIOD

Beginner CA[a] = 12-14 TA[b] = 0-2	Intermediate CA = 14-16 TA = 2-4	Advanced CA = 16-18 TA = 4-6
4 × 3 min with 60 s recovery, or 3 × 5 min with 90 s recovery	4 × 4 min with 60 s recovery, or 3 × 6 min, with 90 s recovery	4 × 6 min with 30 s recovery, or 3 × 8 min, with 60 s recovery

[a]CA = chronological age in years.
[b]TA = training age in years.

Sample Sessions: Continuous Tempo Running

Duration: 12-40 minutes
Intensity: 75-85% of HRmax; approximately 1 minute per mile slower than mile race pace
Frequency: 1 repetition
Recovery: None
Total volume per session: Approximately 2-6 miles (3,200-10,000 meters)

SAMPLE SESSIONS FOR THE EARLY PREPARATION PERIOD

Beginner CA[a] = 12-14 TA[b] = 0-2	Intermediate CA = 14-16 TA = 2-4	Advanced CA = 16-18 TA = 4-6
12-14 min at 75% of HRmax	14-18 min at 80% of HRmax	18-24 min at 85% of HRmax

[a]CA = chronological age in years.
[b]TA = training age in years.

Interval Tempo Running

A session of interval training involves 2 to 10 repetitions ranging from 3 to 10 minutes each. Short rest periods of 30 to 90 seconds of brisk jogging separate the repetitions. The rest periods are a mental break for runners to refocus their attention on maintaining pace and holding form. The interval method, which is less physically and mentally demanding than the continuous method, works well at the start of the training season, when runners lack the fitness, especially the mental fitness, to sustain fast-paced running without a break. Interval tempo running is also best for beginners who need to develop pacing and concentration skills.

Continuous Tempo Running

Once they're ready, runners benefit greatly from continuous tempo running because, in addition to developing aerobic fitness, it hones pacing skills and concentration. Interval training isn't as good for developing these mental qualities because during a repetition runners might anticipate the upcoming recovery period and let up mentally.

We recommend 12 to 40 minutes of running, depending on the athlete's development and event specialty. Of course, beginners should start at the low end of the range. More advanced runners who specialize in the shorter distances, particularly 800 meters, don't need to do as much tempo running as 5,000-meter runners. For example, the longest continuous tempo run for an 18-year-old 800-meter runner might be around 25 minutes, whereas if he were a 5,000-meter specialist, he might run for 40 minutes.

From season to season and year to year, increase the volume (time or distance) and elevate the intensity of the sessions. In the sample sessions for continuous tempo running the advanced athlete runs up to 12 minutes longer than the beginner and works at a considerably higher intensity. Because tempo running improves aerobic fitness by increasing the lactate threshold, target paces will naturally get faster over time. For example, at a training age of two years, runners may require a pace between 7:00 to 7:30 per mile (around 4:20 to 4:40 per kilometer) to elevate their heart rate to 80 percent of maximum. After three or four years of training the

Adding Variety to Interval Training Sessions

Many of the sample interval training sessions throughout the book have repetitions of a single duration or distance such as 4 × 2 minutes or 6 × 300 meters. We use the same repetitions for simplicity, but you can alter the duration and distance of repetitions to add variety. For example, an interval tempo session of 4 × 2 minutes might be changed to 1 × 3 minutes, 1 × 2 minutes, and 1 × 3 minutes. The total duration is the same (8 minutes), and so is the physiological result.

required pace may decrease to 6:00 to 6:30 per mile (around 3:45 to 4:00 per kilometer).

The duration and speed of tempo running should also increase gradually throughout a single preparation phase leading up to competitions. For example, over a four- to six-week period in which a tempo session is held once per week, a 16-year-old training for cross country might progress from an interval session of 3 × 4 minutes to 3 × 7 minutes. Within a training season, once the runner is able to handle long repetitions (i.e., over 6 minutes), it's often best to move from interval tempo running to the more demanding continuous tempo running.

Aerobic Intervals

Even though interval and continuous tempo running are fairly intense methods essential for boosting aerobic and mental fitness, they don't maximally stress the aerobic system. To develop aerobic fitness to its fullest potential you have to train at paces at which the muscles consume oxygen at a near-maximum rate. The best method for meeting this objective is aerobic interval training. Interval training offers a physiological advantage over continuous running by allowing the body to experience an intense training stimulus for a longer duration. Let's say that a 16-year-old runner with a training age of 4 years runs continuously at a pace that maximally stresses his aerobic system, eliciting $\dot{V}O_2$max. He might last for 8 to 10 minutes before slowing due to fatigue, and he might cover between 2,500 and 3,000 meters. If he did repeated 3-minute runs at the same pace, taking a 3-minute recovery interval between each repetition, he'd be able to run considerably longer than 8 to 10 minutes. He might be able to do six or more 3-minute repetitions before fatiguing, subjecting his body to $\dot{V}O_2$max for 18 minutes and covering closer to 5,000 meters. The interval method extends the duration of running at high intensities because the recovery period allows lactic acid to clear from the muscles. This type of training stimulates the physiological adaptations that increase $\dot{V}O_2$max.

The ideal venue for aerobic interval training is one that simulates the racing venue. When training for cross country, you should do intervals on courses similar to your race courses. When training for track races, you should do intervals on a track or on a flat, soft surface such as a dirt road or golf course fairway.

As shown in the following sample sessions for aerobic interval training, the intensity of running should match 3,000- to 5,000-meter race pace, eliciting a heart rate at 85 to 95 percent of HRmax. Many different combinations of duration and frequency can have the desired training effect. Even numerous repetitions of very short runs, such as 20 × 100 meters with a brisk 50-meter jog recovery, can raise oxygen consumption to maximum levels for a long period of time. Our recommendation for aerobic interval training for distance runners, however, is to cover longer repetitions—600 meters to 1 mile—to promote pacing skill and a sense of rhythm. At the start of the preparation period for track season, for example, intermediate 3,200-meter runners might do 800 to 1,000 meter repeats. The total volume of a session should range between 1,200 meters for beginners and 8,000 meters for advanced runners who specialize in the longer races.

The intervals are often expressed as a ratio of the run duration relative to the recovery duration. For a 1:1 run-to-recovery ratio, the recovery period lasts precisely as long as the repetition. If a runner finishes a mile repeat in 5:42, he should take 5:42 to recover before the next mile repeat. We recommend ratios of 1:0.5, 1:1, and 1:1.5 for aerobic interval training. If runners are so fatigued that they fail to achieve the goal pace on a repetition, the coach should lengthen the recovery period. While recovering between repetitions runners should jog rather than walk or stand still. Jogging speeds recovery because the light muscle contractions push lactic acid from the muscles into the bloodstream.

The progression of aerobic interval training is similar to that of tempo running. The first step is to gradually increase the duration of repetitions and the total volume per session. The second is to the lower the pace over a single season, from season to season, and from year to year. The third is to gradually increase the intensity of repetitions over time. For example, beginners should set their target paces at 5,000-meter race pace, while advanced runners set a target closer to 3,000-meter race pace. See chapter 9 for examples of how aerobic interval sessions progress over the course of a season.

Sample Sessions: Aerobic Interval Training

Duration of repetitions: 600 meters-1 mile

Intensity: 85-95% of HRmax; 3,000-5,000-meter race pace

Frequency: 2-10 repetitions

Recovery: Run-to-recovery ratios of 1:0.5, 1:1, or 1:1.5

Total volume per session: Approximately .75-5 miles (1,200-8,000 meters)

SAMPLE SESSIONS FOR THE EARLY PREPARATION PERIOD

Beginner CA[a] = 12-14 TA[b] = 0-2	Intermediate CA = 14-16 TA = 2-4	Advanced CA = 16-18 TA = 4-6
2 × 600 m with a 1:1 recovery, or 2 × 800 m with a 1:1.5 recovery	4 × 800 m with a 1:1 recovery, or 3 × 1,000 m with a 1:1.5 recovery	4 × 1,000 m with a 1:1 recovery, or 3 × 1,200 m with a 1:1 recovery

[a]CA = chronological age in years.

[b]TA = training age in years.

Fartlek

The last training method for developing aerobic fitness is fartlek, which is the Swedish word for speed play. In fartlek training you run continuously in a natural setting, such as a forest area or park, changing the pace at will. If you feel like sprinting from one tree to the next, that's what you do. If, after the sprint, you're in the mood for a long, controlled effort covering one mile, go for it. This lack of structure has benefits and drawbacks. When the duration of a fartlek session exceeds 15 minutes or so, and the surges are sufficiently fast (at least 5,000-meter race pace) the training stimulus can lead to marked gains in aerobic fitness. In addition, fartlek can be a lot of fun because it's about running playfully. A team of runners can take turns leading the surges without announcing when they'll begin to surge and how long the surge will last. Fartlek develops varied pacing skills and the mental toughness required to cover surges in races. The drawback is because fartlek is unstructured, the coach can't control the training dose for each individual, so it's possible for runners to work too easy, or worse, too hard.

To regulate the training dose, coaches can apply a more controlled method of fartlek, which we've adapted from the book *Better Training for Distance Runners* by Martin and Coe (1997). In this method, the coach dictates the duration of surges and recovery intervals by blowing a whistle. For example, during a continuous run of 20 to 30 minutes, one sharp blast of the whistle cues the runners to begin a surge at 1-mile race pace and to hold the pace until the next whistle sounds. Two sharp blasts signal

Race-specific training needs to be planned carefully so that it doesn't lead to injury and burnout.

surging at 3,000-meter race pace, and three sharp blasts signal 5,000-meter race pace. When the runners have surged long enough, the coach blows the whistle again to signal a recovery jog.

Developing Anaerobic Fitness

Races between 800 to 5,000 meters can max out the aerobic energy system, creating a significant demand for anaerobic energy. In an 800-meter race, for example, up to 50 percent of the ATP may be supplied through anaerobic glycolysis (see table 2.1 on page 29). As we discussed in chapter 2, to some degree all distance races engage the anaerobic pathway to fuel midrace surges, uphill climbs, and finishing sprints. Under these conditions lactic acid accumulates rapidly, and unless the runner has trained her body to clear and buffer the lactic acid, she will fatigue and slow at critical points in races.

Anaerobic interval training is the main training method for conditioning the body to defy the fatigue associated with lactic acid accumulation. In this method you run at maximum intensity, forcing the body to generate a large amount of ATP anaerobically and deal with lactic acid accumulation. Anaerobic intervals are sometimes called speed endurance training because they emphasize running fast when you're tired. Sessions usually take place on the track, which ensure level ground and smooth footing.

As the sample sessions on page 146 show, repetitions range from 200 to 800 meters, depending on the athlete's development and event specialty. Our guideline for intensity is to run each repetition 5 to 15 percent faster than race pace for 1,500 to 1,600 meters, eliciting 100 percent of maximal heart rate. If a runner's goal for 1,600 meters is 5:28 (an average of 82 seconds per 400 meters), he should run his 400-meter repetitions in 70 to 78 seconds. In addition to training the body to withstand anaerobic fatigue, this method develops a psychological sense of reserve speed, which makes race pace feel relatively easy. Another intensity guideline is to run each repetition as fast as possible, knowing that it has to be repeated the prescribed number of times. The number of repetitions ranges from two to eight. The total volume of an anaerobic interval training session is relatively short, ranging between 600 to 3,200 meters.

Each repetition should exhaust the runner so that continuing for another 100 meters at the assigned speed would be extremely difficult, if not impossible. Between repetitions you should spend as much time recovering as you need in order to run the next repetition at the prescribed pace. The run-to-recovery ratio should range from 1:2 to 1:4. For example, in a session of 4 × 400 meters in which the runner covers each 400 in 70 seconds, the recovery period should last between 2:20 (1:2) and 4:40 (1:4). Although the repetitions should be exhausting, the intensity should not be so high that the runner's form falls apart. To prevent injury, coaches should increase the recovery period to allow complete rest, or stop the session if the runner drastically loses form. The best activity during the recovery period is jogging, although the repetitions might be so exhausting that runners need to walk for a short time. If runners need four minutes to recover between 400-meter repetitions in a session of 4 × 400 meters, they might walk the first two minutes of the interval and jog the last two minutes.

The sample sessions show how anaerobic interval training progresses over time. From season to season and year to year, repetition distance and session volume should increase gradually. The most important element of progression is to run the repetitions at faster speeds. For example, at a training age of 3 years, a 15-year-old boy might be able to run 3 × 400 meters with 5 minutes recovery in an average of 68 seconds. At age 17, the same athlete might improve his average to 61 to 62 seconds.

Anaerobic fitness training progresses within a season as the number of repetitions and total volume of sessions increase. For example, intermediate 3,200-meter runners might start out with a session of 4 × 400 meters. As the competition period approaches, they might be able to handle 6 or 7 × 400 meters.

Sample Sessions: Anaerobic Interval Training

Duration of repetitions: 200-800 meters
Intensity: 5-15% faster than race pace for 1,500-1,600 meters; 100% of HRmax
Frequency: 2-8 repetitions
Recovery: Run-to-recovery ratios of 1:2-1:4
Total volume per session: Approximately .3-2 miles (600-3,200 meters)

SAMPLE SESSIONS FOR THE EARLY PREPARATION PERIOD

Event specialty	Beginner CA[a] = 12-14 TA[b] = 0-2	Intermediate CA = 14-16 TA = 2-4	Advanced CA = 16-18 TA = 4-6
800 m	3 × 200 m, or 1 × 300 m and 1 × 200 m	4 × 200 m, or 2 × 300 m and 1 × 200 m	5 × 200 m, or 3 × 300 m
1,500 m-1 mi	4 × 200 m, or 1 × 300 m and 3 × 200 m	3 × 300 m, or 2 × 300 m and 2 × 200 m	3 × 400 m, or 3 × 300 m and 2 × 200 m
3,000-5,000 m and cross country	3 × 400 m, or 2 × 500 m	4 × 400 m, or 2 × 600 m and 2 × 200 m	4 × 500 m, or 1 × 600 m and 3 × 400 m

[a]CA = chronological age in years.
[b]TA = training age in years.

Developing Race-Specific Fitness

The training methods that we've described in this and the previous chapter are individual building blocks. No single method is sufficient for fully developing the physiological and mental capacities for racing well. By focusing on the individual building blocks—including strength endurance, technique, aerobic fitness, and anaerobic fitness—you can assemble the strongest composite structure of fitness. That's why most daily training sessions should concentrate on only one or two fitness capacities. Trying to develop every capacity at once is like putting the roof on a house before the foundation and walls have been built. Nevertheless, when used at the right times, training that puts it all together, or simultaneously stresses all of the physiological and mental capacities demanded in competition, can spark huge improvements. These methods are race-specific interval training and time trials (practice races).

Race-Specific Interval Training

This interval method involves running at goal race pace over total distances that are similar to the athlete's event specialty. Each repetition should be relatively long, at least one-third of the race distance. For example, a boy who has a goal of 4:45 for 1500 meters might do 3 × 500 meters in 1:35 or 2 × 700 meters in 2:13. In addition to running at goal race pace, these sessions are race-specific because the rest interval is very short, between 20 to 60 seconds, or just enough time to catch your breath and go again.

Preparing for Race-Specific Training Sessions

Race-specific training methods require special preparation because they are so demanding and important for building fitness. Runners should take the necessary steps to restore a high level of energy at least a day or two before a race-specific session. This means using recovery methods such as easy jogging and light stretching to reduce muscle soreness and tightness. It also means eating high-carbohydrate meals to ensure adequate glycogen levels. Immediately before the race-specific session, runners should perform a warm-up complete with jogging, flexibility exercises, and technique strides. It's also good practice to warm up in training shoes and then put on racing flats or spikes for the session, especially for anaerobic intervals, race-specific intervals, and time trials. Light-weight racing shoes can make a big difference in running mechanics and economy, but they obviously don't offer the support and shock absorption of training shoes. By wearing racing shoes in race-specific training sessions, runners condition the muscles and connective tissue in their feet and lower legs to withstand the greater impact.

Sample Sessions: Race-Specific Interval Training

Duration of repetitions: 1/3-1/2 of event specialty
Intensity: Race pace
Frequency: 2-4 repetitions
Recovery: 20-60 seconds
Total volume per session: 60-100% of event specialty

SAMPLE SESSIONS FOR THE EARLY PREPARATION PERIOD

Event specialty	Beginner CA[a] = 12-14 TA[b] = 0-2	Intermediate CA = 14-16 TA = 2-4	Advanced CA = 16-18 TA = 4-6
800 m	2 × 300 m with 60 s recovery	2 × 300 m with 45 s recovery	2 × 300 m with 30 s recovery
1,500 m-1 mi	2 × 500 m with 60 s recovery	2 × 500 m with 45 s recovery	2 × 500 m with 45 s recovery
3,000-5,000 m and cross country	2 × 1,000 m with 60 s recovery[c] 2 × 1,500 m with 60 s recovery[d]	2 × 1,000 m with 60 s recovery[c] 2 × 1,500 m with 60 s recovery[d]	2 × 1,000 m with 60 s recovery[c] 2 × 2,000 m with 60 s recovery[d]

[a]CA = chronological age in years.
[b]TA = training age in years.
[c]Session for 3,000-3,200-meter specialist.
[d]Session for 5,000-meter specialist.

The sample race-specific sessions above are for the beginning of the preparation period for a competitive season. The total session volume is less than the event specialty. For example, a 3,000-meter runner might do an initial session of 2 × 1,000 meters. Over the course of the preparation period the total volume might increase from 60 to 100 percent of the target racing distance. In this progression, you add distance to a base speed, building the race from pieces so that you can cover longer and longer distances.

Time Trials (Practice Races)

As the competitive season approaches, there's no better way to both develop and test fitness than to run a time trial, or practice race. The distance can be 50 to 200 percent of the runner's event specialty. Several weeks before the start of the competitive season, a 3,000-meter runner might do a 1,500-meter to 2,000-meter time trial. Or, once every week or two during the preparation phase, the runner could do a series of time trials at distances both shorter and longer than 3,000 meters.

In addition to stressing the body's physiological systems, time trials are a great way to develop mental fitness, particularly when you use them to practice pacing strategies and tactics. No matter what the outcome, time trials often boost confidence and motivation. If athletes run their goal times, they gain confidence as the racing season approaches. Runners who fall short of their goal times may be disappointed, but the results can boost their motivation to train harder and perform better in the next time trial. In addition, easing up on training before the time trial and simulating a race warm-up is great practice for upcoming races. The simulated race preparation will make runners more comfortable and less nervous in early competitions.

The ultimate time trials are practice races. In the early part of the competitive season, a few races can be designated for practicing pacing and tactical strategies. Practice races fit nicely into the schedules of high school runners in the United States, who typically have two track and field meets a week. You might designate the first, often a dual meet in the middle of the week, as a training session for working on a surging tactic or finishing kick. Then, the second meet, usually a big multiteam competition on the weekend, is for real racing. This gives distance runners the opportunity to experiment with different distances and strategies without excessive pressure.

Using a few early-season meets to practice racing at distances shorter than their event specialties allows runners to progressively develop speed and racing skills. If they can control effort and pace for a short distance, they'll feel confident when moving up to their specialty. In addition, this approach is fun because most young runners enjoy the variety of

Sometimes smaller races can be used as time trials or practices for larger events.

Penn State University

Location: State College, Pennsylvania

Coach: Beth Alford-Sullivan

When planning race-specific training for the women's distance runners at Penn State University, Beth Alford-Sullivan refuses to rely on canned workouts or simple recipes. Instead, Alford-Sullivan is like the master chef who weighs and mixes numerous ingredients, using vast knowledge and experience along with a handful of intuition to create superior results. Says Alford-Sullivan, "Our race-related training depends on many factors, including the athlete's level of fitness and development, her event specialty, the time of the year, and how the athlete is feeling and responding to training."

Sound progression of race-specific training is one cornerstone of the Penn State program. "If we recruit a youngster who ran 50 or 60 low-intensity miles per week in high school, we don't increase the volume in her first two years of college," says Alford-Sullivan. "Instead, we'll maintain the volume and gradually introduce her to higher intensity training. We want that runner to be able to shift pace, run negative splits, and catch up with other abilities that are developed through high-intensity workouts."

To illustrate progression in race-specific training, Alford-Sullivan compares a 1,500-meter runner's interval sessions in her freshman and junior years: "As a freshman, she might begin a workout with a 1,200-meter run at threshold pace, which is a lot slower than race pace. Then she'll do 2 × 400 meters at race pace, followed by another 1,200 at threshold pace. We might finish the workout with a few 150-meter strides. When this athlete reaches her junior year, she'll do more intense, specific training that's right on race pace. For example, she might do a workout of 4 × 600 meters at 1,500-meter pace with 90 seconds to 2 minutes recovery."

The other cornerstone of Alford-Sullivan's training program is balance. "With developing runners, you have to be careful not to ignore any part of the spectrum of training," says Alford-Sullivan. "We want our runners to build both aerobic and anaerobic conditioning, which requires mixing up elements of training to fully develop each system."

When she discusses sample workouts, Alford-Sullivan is quick to point out the finer details that coaches should consider. For example, she has general guidelines for the recovery times between repetitions in interval workouts, but she doesn't always follow the recipe. "I tend to read my runners," she says. "After they finish a repeat on the track, they jog a 200, which takes 70 seconds or so. Then, I gather the athletes and read their body language. If I've got a kid who's bent over or breathing too heavy when it's time to start the next repeat, we'll adjust the recovery. I plan workouts going by science, but I adapt them with intuition and the artistry of coaching."

Alford-Sullivan's approach to race-specific training is clearly a recipe for success. Named the NCAA Cross Country Coach of the Year and selected as an assistant coach for the U.S. Olympic team in 2004, Alford-Sullivan has coached over 30 NCAA All-Americans and guided the Penn State cross country and track teams to the highest levels of collegiate competition.

competing in different events throughout the season. Intermediate and advanced runners might even double in a track meet. For example, after racing 1,600 meters, 3,200-meter specialists could race the 800 later in the meet, a progressive increase in the volume of fast running. When these runners eventually race their specialty they will be prepared to cover the 3,200 meters at goal pace.

Developing Race-Specific Mental Fitness

In chapter 4 we discussed ways to develop mental fitness, focusing on qualities such as self-confidence and motivation, which emerge naturally when runners meet challenging goals for training and racing. We also introduced techniques and strategies such as visualization and establishing a familiar warm-up routine that runners can use to ease nervousness. Mental training methods that promote body awareness, pacing skill, and tactical skill can also be integrated into race-specific training sessions.

Body Awareness Training

Body cues such as breathing rate, sweating, muscle tension, sound of footstrike, and sense of limb movement provide critical information about how hard runners are working. These cues help runners make adjustments to improve technique, save energy, and reduce fatigue. Inexperienced runners typically don't attend to these cues, so we suggest training sessions to practice body awareness. In the middle of a continuous tempo run, for example, the coach can direct runners through a body awareness inventory: How's your breathing? Relaxed or too hard? Are you extending at your ankle joint when you push off the ground? Do you feel any tension in your shoulders? Then, when trouble spots are identified, runners should make adjustments. For example, if you hear and feel yourself taking heavy, plodding steps, try to adjust the stiffness of your leg muscles for a springier stride. Or, if your shoulders are riding up to your ears, relax them.

Pace Work

Skill in judging and adjusting pace separates elite runners from average runners. Pacing isn't easy to master, especially when you're fatigued. Coaches should design training sessions to help runners develop pacing skill, which requires being able to calculate split times. Let's say that George's goal for 5,000 meters is 16:15, which calls for 400-meter splits of 78 seconds each. In an aerobic interval training session of 3 × 1,600 meters at race pace, George's coach will call out the cumulative time at each 400, and George will calculate and call back the split for the lap just run as well as for what the next lap should be to keep on pace. It is

Active Rest As a Training Method

Active rest refers to training methods that include easy jogging, ice whirlpool baths, and massage. It might seem odd to view rest as a training method, but it makes sense when you consider that fitness for distance running isn't developed *during* a training session, it's developed *between* sessions when the body replaces the energy spent and repairs muscle tissue that was broken down. Of course, proper nutrition and adequate rest are the keys to regeneration, but runners can accelerate the process with active recovery methods. On days following high-intensity interval sessions, for example, 20 to 30 minutes of easy exercise (e.g., jogging, cycling, or swimming) along with stretching can increase the rate of oxygen- and nutrient-enriched blood flow, restoring energy to tired muscles. This training session should not drain energy; it's simply meant to accelerate regeneration from the previous day's training.

Other methods that speed recovery include massage, cold treatment, and heat treatment. Research shows that massage decreases muscle tightness and soreness. Athletes can massage their own tired, sore muscles, or the school or club athletic trainer can administer the massage. The application of cold or heat also speeds recovery by increasing the rate of blood flow to damaged muscle tissue. Generally speaking, use cold applications (ice packs and ice whirlpool) immediately following training, especially when muscles and joints are sore or injured. In most cases, apply heat prior to a training session to warm the muscles and prepare them for activity. Coaches should seek guidelines for applying cold and heat treatments from the school or club athletic trainer.

important to calculate splits as quickly as possible so that you can turn your attention to other important cues instead of spending a whole lap trying to solve a math problem.

In another method for developing pacing, which can also be integrated into interval training sessions, the coach gives runners feedback on their pacing by blowing a whistle to indicate the target pace for each 100-meter or 200-meter segment of a repetition. This exercise trains runners to associate their effort with specific paces and to make adjustments when they're off pace.

Tactical Practice

In chapter 4 we described tactical approaches to racing, including even-paced and negative-split running, front running, surging, and kicking. Race-specific training sessions can help young runners master these tactics. As we discussed earlier, fartlek is an excellent method for learning to surge in the middle of races. In addition, aerobic, anaerobic, and race-specific interval sessions can promote specific tactical skills. Consider variations of a race-specific interval session for a 3,200-meter specialist who is shooting for a goal time of 10:00 (see table at the top of page 153).

Tactical skill	Sample session
Even-paced running	3 × 1,000 meters in 3:07, averaging 75 seconds for 400-meter splits
Negative-split running	2 × 1 mile, with the first mile in 5:05-5:07 and the second mile in 4:53-4:55
Front running	2 × 1 mile, with the first mile in 4:50-4:52 and the second mile as fast as possible
Kicking	4 × 800 meters, with the first lap of each 800 in 80 seconds and the last lap in 70 seconds

As you can imagine, there are an infinite number of ways to help runners develop pacing and tactical skill, but each training session devoted to pacing and tactical skill should focus on specific areas for improvement in individual runners and clearly communicate the objectives of the session. For example, a runner who has performed poorly because she lacks a strong kick must learn to hold back on repetitions or parts of repetitions that are intended to set up a finishing sprint.

A team approach to tactical training produces good results and is fun. Coaches can design interval sessions by giving team members instructions to help each other master particular tactics. The runner who needs to develop her kick will benefit when her teammates run in front of her for the steady part of a repetition and then challenge her to pass them on the kicking part. Or, a runner who needs to get accustomed to the mental challenges of front running can start ahead of teammates, who are instructed to closely shadow but not pass the leader.

Striding Ahead

To help you remember the details of race-specific training, we've summarized the methods in table 7.1 (page 154). Race-specific methods spark major improvements in performance when applied correctly. Remember, however, that because they can maximally stress the runner's body, coaches must apply these methods with caution. Successful implementation depends on having a strong foundation of general fitness and progressively increasing training loads over time. Now that you've learned about the general and race-specific training methods, you're ready for the first steps of designing training programs: assessing the runner's readiness and setting racing and training goals.

TABLE 7.1—Methods for Developing Race-Specific Fitness

Method	Intensity	Duration	Frequency (number of repetitions)	Recovery	Total volume
Interval tempo running	75-85% of HRmax	3-10 min per repetition	2-10	30-90 s	2-6 mi (3,200-10,000 m)
Continuous tempo running	75-85% of HRmax	12-40 min	1	None	2-6 mi (3,200-10,000 m)
Aerobic intervals	85-95% of HRmax; 3,000 to 5,000-m race pace	600 m to 1 mi per repetition	2-10	Run-to-recovery ratios of 1:0.5, 1:1, or 1:1.5	.75-5 mi (1,200-8,000 m)
Anaerobic intervals	5-15% faster than 1-mi race pace	200-800 m per repetition	2-8	Run-to-recovery ratios of 1:2 to 1:4	.3-2 miles (600-3,200 m)
Race-specific intervals	Race pace	1/3-1/2 of event specialty per repetition	2-4	20-60 s	60-100% of event specialty
Time trials	Race pace	50-200% of event specialty	1	None	50-200% of event specialty

CHAPTER 8

Program Building

Training young distance runners is a long journey, but instead of traveling by cars, planes, and trains, your vehicles are the training methods described in chapters 6 and 7. Training transports runners from where they are now in terms of fitness and performance to where they desire to go in the future. In this chapter we'll guide you through the first two steps of a five-step process for planning and implementing a young runner's training journey. As illustrated in figure 8.1, the first step involves assessing each runner's starting fitness level and training, racing, and health history, and the second involves setting racing and training goals. Coaches who take these steps can confidently determine the best training methods and loads for individual runners.

Step 1: Assess Starting Fitness and Review History

To establish the best route to your destination, you must first take stock of your starting conditions. In order to set appropriate goals, choose the best training methods, and determine training load progression, coaches must have a clear sense of each runner's initial fitness level as well as training, racing, and health history. This sort of evaluation requires a comprehensive system for keeping records, such as the athlete assessment form on pages 157 to 161.

The best time to make athlete assessments is a few weeks before training begins for an upcoming racing season. The sooner you complete the assessments, the more time you'll have to work on training programs. Some of the information comes from interviews with your runners and records of their past training and racing results, and some comes from fitness tests. In the following sections we walk you through the assessment form.

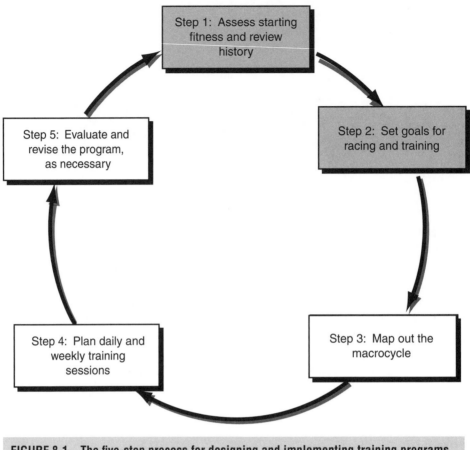

FIGURE 8.1 The five-step process for designing and implementing training programs. In this chapter we focus on the first two steps.

Developmental Status

Section I of the athlete assessment form is for recording information on a runner's developmental status. An awareness of training age helps you make the program progressive, increasing the likelihood that runners will improve from season to season. You can use training age to set restrictions on the racing distances at which runners can compete. Training age also helps you decide which methods to use and avoid for individual athletes. For example, for developing strength endurance, we recommend that runners with less than two years of training use circuit training before progressing to weight training.

Other developmental factors are height, weight, and body composition. Be sure to note changes in these measures since the previous assessment. For instance, if a boy has grown several inches over a summer, it's a red flag that his training should change. He'll need to do extra technique and

Athlete Assessment Form

Name_____

Date_____   Date of last assessment_____

I. Developmental Status

Chronological age: _____ years _____ months

Training age: _____ years _____months

Height: _____   Weight: _____   Body-fat %:_____

Change since last assessment:

Height: _____   Weight: _____   Body-fat %:_____

II. Current Fitness Assessment

FLEXIBILITY

	Poor 1	2	3	4	Excellent 5	Comments
Hip flexors						
Hamstrings						
Calves						

STRENGTH ENDURANCE

Exercise	Score (number of repetitions)
Push-ups	
Curl-ups	
Chin-ups (unassisted)	
Dips (unassisted)	
Leg extensions	

(continued)

TECHNIQUE

	Poor 1	2	3	4	Excellent 5	Comments
Upper-body posture						
Arm action						
Placement and action of the foot on landing						
Action of the leg joints on landing						
Knee lift						
Extension of the leg joints in the takeoff subphase						

CARDIOVASCULAR FITNESS AND AEROBIC FITNESS

$\dot{V}O_2$max (if lab testing is available): _____

Longest continuous aerobic run from previous macrocycle: _____

3,000-meter time trial: _____

ANAEROBIC FITNESS

Time-trial distance	Time
60 meters	
100 meters	
400 meters	

RACE-SPECIFIC FITNESS

Time-trial distance	Time

MENTAL FITNESS

	Poor 1	2	3	4	Excellent 5	Comments
Motivation						
Confidence						
Concentration						
Ability to relax						
Pacing skill						
Tactical skill						

III. Training History: Summary of Previous Macrocycle

Dates of previous macrocycle: _____ to _____

	General preparation	Specific preparation	Pre-competition	Main competition
Training units Average number of units per week				
Strength endurance Average duration of circuit training sessions per week				
Average load lifted in weight training sessions per week				
Hill running: Average volume per week				
Technical skill Average volume of technique drills per week				
Average volume of technique strides per week				
Cardiovascular fitness CAR[a]: Average volume per week				
CAR: Average pace per mile or kilometer				
Aerobic fitness Tempo running: Average volume per week				
Tempo running: Average pace per mile or kilometer				

(continued)

Aerobic intervals: Average volume per week				
Aerobic intervals: Average pace per mile or kilometer				
Fartlek: Average volume per week				
Anaerobic fitness Anaerobic intervals: Average volume per week				
Anaerobic intervals: Average pace per mile or kilometer				
Race-specific fitness Time trials and practice races: Average volume per week				
Time trials and practice races: Average pace per mile or kilometer				
Highest volume of running in a week				
Average volume of running per week				

a CAR = continuous aerobic running

Section IV: Racing History

PERSONAL RECORDS

Event	Time	Date	Meet	Comments
800 meters				
1,500 meters				
1,600 meters				
1 mile				
3,000 meters				
3,200 meters				
2 miles				
5,000 meters				

PERFORMANCES FROM PREVIOUS MACROCYCLE

Date	Meet	Event	Time	Place	Comments

Section V: Health History

Type of injury, illness, or medical concern	Period of injury, illness, or medical concern	Comments

strength endurance training to better control his longer limbs. To help him avoid injuries associated with rapid growth, you should maintain or even reduce his volume of continuous aerobic running and race-specific training until his growth stabilizes.

Weight and body composition help determine whether athletes need to alter their diets for better health and performance. It's especially important to assess whether changes in body weight are due to changes in fat content. The ideal body weight for distance runners depends on their makeup of muscle and fat tissue. If body-fat percentage is within average ranges for teenage distance runners—6 to 12 percent for boys and 12 to 16 percent for girls—they probably don't need to alter their caloric intake. If the values are well outside of this range—less than 6 percent or greater than 20 percent for boys and less than 12 percent or greater than 25 percent for girls—we recommend that they and their parents consult with a physician or nutritionist to decide whether dietary changes are necessary. Assessment of body composition requires specialized training and expertise, so coaches who are not experienced in these techniques should ask a qualified sports physician, athletic trainer, or local fitness specialist to take the measurements.

We have not included biological maturation on the athlete assessment form. Like body-fat composition, an accurate assessment of maturation, or biological, requires expertise beyond the scope of this book. The best measurement of maturation, skeletal age, involves X-raying the bones to determine how much they have ossified, or hardened. Still, you can get a sense of each individual's maturation by observing some of the hallmarks of pubertal change (see table 1.1 on page 6). Obvious changes in secondary sex characteristics, such as lowering of the voice in males and breast development in females, indicate that puberty is underway.

Starting Fitness Levels

In chapters 6 and 7 we described training methods for developing eight fitness capacities: flexibility and mobility, strength endurance, technical skill, cardiovascular fitness, aerobic fitness, anaerobic fitness, race-specific fitness, and mental fitness. The coach must assess the runner's level of fitness in these areas to know which training methods to emphasize in the individual's program (see section II of the athlete assessment form). For some fitness capacities, the most objective tests are administered by exercise physiologists in the laboratory. The best measure of aerobic fitness, for example, is a $\dot{V}O_2$max test on a treadmill. Since most coaches don't have access to this type of testing, we suggest more practical fitness tests in the following sections.

Flexibility

The muscle groups that tend to be tight in distance runners are the hip flexors, the hamstrings, and the calves. The hip flexors, which cross the hip joint in front of the body, are responsible for swinging the leg forward and lifting the knee in the running stride. The hamstrings, which cross the hip and knee joints on the back of the leg, flex the knee during the swing phase and extend the hip at the end of the swing phase and during the stance and takeoff phases. The calf muscles are stretched upon footstrike, creating elastic energy, and they generate propulsive force during takeoff. Tightness in these three muscle groups can impair stride mechanics and cause injuries. For assessing flexibility in these muscles, we recommend the standard tests illustrated in figures 8.2 to 8.4. We've adapted these tests from *Healthy Runner's Handbook*, by Lyle Micheli (1996, pages 9-10).

To obtain objective measures of flexibility, you need a device called a goniometer, which measures joint angles in degrees (you can order a goniometer from fitness specialty stores on the Internet). However, your subjective assessment will suffice for determining whether individuals need to spend more time stretching their hip flexors, hamstrings, and calves. Our assessment form provides an evaluation scale of 1 (poor flexibility) to 5 (excellent flexibility).

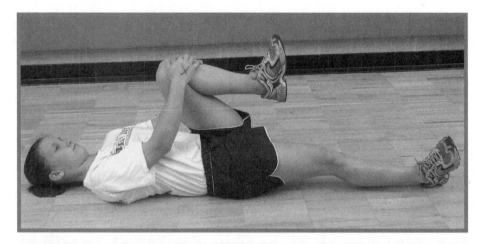

FIGURE 8.2
Hip flexor test

Lying on your back, raise both knees to the chest, grasping them with the hands. Release the right knee only, gently straightening the right leg. Lower the right leg and try to rest it flat on the ground. If you can extend the right leg completely and it's flat on the ground, your right hip flexors are very flexible. The degree to which the right leg bends reflects the level of tightness in your hip flexors. Repeat with the left leg.

FIGURE 8.3
Hamstring flexibility test
Lie facing a wall and prop both feet against it. With the legs straight and buttocks a few feet away from the wall, move the buttocks forward, trying to get as close to the wall as you can. If your buttocks touch the wall, you have very flexible hamstrings. The distance of your buttocks from the wall reflects the tightness of your hamstrings.

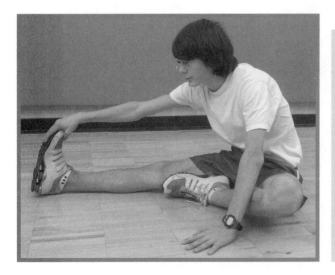

FIGURE 8.4
Calf flexibility test
Sitting with the right leg in front of you and the left leg bent inward, reach forward and grasp the toes of the right foot. Slowly pull the toes toward the body. If the sole forms a right angle with the ground, your calf muscles and Achilles tendon are very flexible. An angle greater than 90 degrees, formed by the top of the foot and the shin, indicates room for improvement. Repeat with the left leg.

Strength Endurance

Coaches should assess runners' strength endurance in order to design effective circuit and weight training sessions. This assessment involves determining the maximum repetitions of certain circuit training exercises that runners are able to do before fatiguing and losing form. You can also use this process to determine how much weight runners should lift for exercises in the weight training sessions (see the instructions for determining repetition maximum values, or RM, on pages 117 and 124).

Coaches can use strength endurance tests to determine whether an athlete has a weak area of the body and whether she is developing strength endurance progressively. For example, if an athlete can do only 15 abdominal curl-ups in the assessment before a cross country season, she will benefit from extra circuit training to develop the abdominal muscles. If she improves to 35 curl-ups in next year's assessment, she and her coach can be confident that the extra training paid off.

Technical Skill

The assessment form includes six features of running biomechanics to evaluate in order to identify strengths and weaknesses. Refer to the technique tips in chapter 5 for details on how to evaluate these features.

Cardiovascular and Aerobic Fitness

The best assessment of these two elements of fitness, a $\dot{V}O_2$max test conducted in an exercise physiology lab, isn't an option for most youth programs. A 3,000-meter time trial is a field test that correlates with lab measures of $\dot{V}O_2$max, because running at race pace for 3,000 meters maximally stresses the aerobic system. The problem with using a time trial to assess changes in aerobic fitness over time is that external factors, such as the weather, can influence performance. If the current assessment is based on a time trial in poor conditions—say, it's hotter and windier than the day of the previous time trial—you could get a false sense of the athlete's aerobic fitness. We've included a space in the assessment form for the results of a 3,000-meter time, but be cautious about how you interpret the results. As for cardiovascular fitness, the assessment should help you decide how much continuous aerobic running the athlete should do in the upcoming macrocycle (a single cross country or track season). We suggest recording the longest continuous aerobic run from the previous macrocycle.

Anaerobic Fitness

Assessment of anaerobic endurance is useful for determining whether runners would benefit from more anaerobic training and for placing runners in their best track events. We recommend a 400-meter time trial because it requires a substantial amount of energy from anaerobic glycolysis. For runners who are slow at the 400, the coach should design progressive training to develop speed and anaerobic fitness. Such training will help slower runners even if they specialize in the longer events, such as 3,000 and 5,000 meters. Training for faster runners may focus on developing the endurance to maintain their speed. Runners with fast 400-meter times have the potential to excel at 800- and 1,500-meter races.

Coaches might also want to test strictly for speed, especially for 800-meter specialists. For this purpose, add time trials for 60 and 100 meters.

Race-Specific Fitness

A great way to assess race-specific fitness is to hold a time trial that approximates race distance. The time trial could be held a few weeks prior to starting the training program. This test is particularly useful for assessing beginners who have limited training and racing experience. The results can be used to plan training sessions and set racing goals for the upcoming season.

A preseason time trial may not be as necessary or useful for intermediate and advanced runners. Coaches will have a good sense of these older, more experienced athletes' race-specific fitness based on their performance in races at the end of the previous season. In addition, these runners may not feel comfortable running a preseason time trial without having trained for it, especially if the weather conditions are poor.

Time trials are an effective way to measure race-specific fitness, especially in beginners.

Mental Fitness

Researchers have not yet developed objective tests for mental fitness in young distance runners. Even so, coaches who have worked with athletes for at least a season should have a good sense of their runners' confidence, motivation, concentration, ability to relax, pacing skill, and tactical skill. You can score these capacities on a scale of 1 to 5.

Training History

Section III of the athlete assessment form summarizes the volume and intensity of training in the previous macrocycle, which is one complete cross country or track season. We've divided the macrocycle into four phases of preparation and competition:

▌ General preparation

▌ Specific preparation

▌ Precompetition

▌ Main competition

Dividing a macrocycle into phases is called periodization (see chapter 9). Coaches can use information from the previous macrocycle to progressively increase training for the upcoming macrocycle. Let's say that Bryce averaged 12 miles a week of continuous aerobic running during the preparation phase of the last cross country season. For the upcoming season, the coach might increase Bryce's average weekly volume to 15 or 16 miles. To progressively build his fitness, the coach would also have to increase Bryce's volume of tempo running, aerobic intervals, and other training methods that involve running.

Here are some guidelines for recording training history in section III.

▌ Average number of training units per week: A training unit refers to the use of a particular method in a daily session. If a runner stretched and performed technique drills in a session, she completed two units—one for flexibility and one for technique. Simply add up the number of units completed in each training phase and divide by the number of weeks in the phase.

▌ Average running volume and intensity per week: For each of the running methods (continuous aerobic running, tempo running, aerobic intervals, anaerobic intervals, and so on), add up the miles, kilometers, or minutes covered in each phase and divide this total by the number of weeks. Then, for runs that you have timed on marked courses or on tracks, calculate the average pace per mile or kilometer.

▌ Average duration of circuit training sessions per week: For each training phase, add up the time taken to complete each circuit training session and divide by the number of weeks.

▌ Average load lifted in weight training sessions per week: First, calculate the load lifted in single weight training sessions by multiplying the number of repetitions of an exercise by the load lifted. For example, if the athlete performed 12 bench-press repetitions with a 50-pound load, the total for that exercise would be 600 pounds ($12 \times 50 = 600$). After figuring the load lifted for each exercise, add them up. To reduce this sum to a more manageable number, divide it by 2,000 pounds, which gives you a measure of tonnage lifted. Then average the loads for all sessions by dividing by the number of weeks in the training phase.

▌ Average volume of technique drills and strides per week: First, add up the total distance (in meters or yards) that the athlete covered in drills and strides during each technique session of each phase. Then, divide this total by the number of weeks in the phase.

As you can see, assessing training background requires detailed daily records. On the following pages we present sample logs that coaches can use to quickly summarize daily and weekly training sessions. The log for recording daily sessions shows the volume and intensity of a continuous tempo run for a runner named Kelsey. The planned dose for the day was 1 × 20 minutes at 80 percent of Kelsey's maximum heart rate (206 bpm), which is around 165 bpm. Kelsey covered 2.7 miles at an average pace of 7:20 per mile. The coach's comments at the bottom of the form show that the session went well. On page 169, Kelsey's tempo run is recorded in a weekly summary. You can calculate weekly totals for each training method at the bottom of this form. Use these weekly totals to determine the average training loads to record on the athlete assessment form.

For coaches who are a bit overwhelmed by the thought of so much recordkeeping, we have a few suggestions for making the process organized and efficient. You can record training results using a standard spreadsheet program on a computer. You can also have your runners log their own training. They can submit their logs to you on a regular

---

Sample Log for Recording Daily Training

Name: *Kelsey*

Date: *Monday, March 21*

Method: *Continuous tempo running*

Planned session: *1 × 20 minutes at 80% HRmax (165 bpm)*

Total volume:

   Distance: *2.7 miles*

   Duration: *20 minutes*

Intensity:

   Average pace per mile: *7:20*

Comments: *Handled the session easily and in good form. Pretty even pace the whole way. Heart rate was 168 at the end of the run.*

Weekly Training Summary

Name: _Kelsey_

Week of: _March 21-27_

Day	Technique training	Circuit training	Weight training	Hill running	Continuous aerobic running	Tempo running	Aerobic intervals	Fartlek	Anaerobic intervals	Race-specific intervals or time trials
Monday						20 min at 7:20 pace (2.7 miles)				
Tuesday										
Wednesday										
Thursday										
Friday										
Saturday										
Sunday										
Week totals										

Record training results using the following measures:

Technique training—distance covered in drills and strides

Circuit training—duration of session in minutes

Weight training—tonnage and duration of session in minutes

Hill running—distance covered

Continuous aerobic running—distance covered or duration and pace per mile or kilometer

Tempo running—distance covered or duration and pace per mile or kilometer

Aerobic intervals—distance covered and pace per mile or kilometer

Fartlek—distance covered or duration

Anaerobic intervals—distance covered and pace per mile or kilometer

Race-specific intervals and time trials—distance covered and pace per mile or kilometer basis for evaluation and calculation of total training volumes and loads. Having runners keep their own training logs not only helps you out, it also benefits them in many ways. For example, daily training logs can be a great source of motivation because they directly reflect hard work and improvement. It's inspiring and fun for runners to look back at challenging workouts that they successfully accomplished. For more inspiration and guidance, runners can fill their training logs with motivational sayings and tips from running magazines and books. Keeping and regularly reviewing a training log is also a great way to figure out which training methods work best, because the log reveals connections between the runner's most successful races and the training that led up to them.

Racing History

Section IV of the athlete assessment form is for recording information about personal records and race results in the previous season. There are two reasons for keeping records of runners' racing histories. First, the coach and athlete can use this information to set performance goals for the upcoming season. Second, the records reveal performance patterns and uncover factors that explain both successful and disappointing outcomes. For example, by examining a runner's times from the previous track season, the coach can determine strengths and weaknesses in the training program. If the runner's 1,500-meter times dropped consistently over the season (4:48, 4:42, 4:37, and 4:34) the coach should feel confident that training produced the desired peaking effect. If the times reveal a plateau or poorer performances as the season progressed (4:48, 4:45, 4:46, and 4:50), the coach should question whether the volume and intensity of race-specific training methods were sufficiently progressive.

Health History

Section V of the athlete assessment form provides space to record injuries, illnesses, and other medical concerns. Coaches can use this information to discover potential causes and solutions to health problems, particularly those involving running injuries. Let's say that David's assessment form showed that he suffered strained calf muscles during the first few cross country races of the season over the last two years. David's coach hypothesized that the injury might have been caused when David switched shoes. All summer long he ran in training flats with a high, supportive heel, which didn't stretch the calf muscles. Then, at the start of the racing season, David began wearing his low-heeled spikes in race-specific training sessions and competitions, which put a lot of strain on his calves. The sudden change in shoes and stress on the calf muscles might very well have caused David's muscle strains. To help David avoid this recurring injury, his coach advised more calf-stretching exercises and had him wear racing shoes in one or two sessions per week during the preparation phase.

Step 2: Set Goals for Racing and Training

In previous chapters we talked about goals as powerful motivators and tools for building confidence. Before we discuss the goal-setting process, let's consider how goals help you make decisions about optimal training. The essential question in designing a young distance runner's program is, "What training session(s) should the runner do (today, tomorrow, next week, and so on)?" To best answer this question, you must think carefully about what the runner is trying to accomplish—you must first consider the runner's goals.

Racing Goals

Setting goals should begin with long-term racing goals. Like the final destination of a journey, long-term goals are powerful motivators. They're the stuff of fantastic dreams. Because long-term goals can't be achieved immediately, they help runners focus on the steps they must undertake to achieve them in the future. For goals to have this powerful influence, coaches and athletes must work together to set them. If runners feel they are a part of the goal-setting process, they will be more focused and motivated.

Carla is a talented and highly motivated 14-year-old whose training age is two years. Carla's best 1,600 meter time as a 13-year-old was 5:47—excellent for her age. Based on her very moderate and progressive training to date, Carla's coach sees the potential for her to break 5:00 for 1,600 meters by age 17, during her senior year of high school. It's a goal that Carla is excited about and willing to work hard for because she knows that a sub-5:00 1,600 will earn her a college scholarship, and she wants to keep running after high school. Before planning training for the upcoming track season, Carla and her coach set the long-term goal of 4:55 in four years, a 52-second improvement.

The stepping stones to this goal will be short-term goals for each year. What strategy should Carla and her coach use to set the yearly goals? They could simply divide the total improvement desired by the number of years: 52 seconds ÷ 4 years = 13 seconds per year. Thus, Carla would shoot for 5:34 at age 14, 5:21 at age 15, and so forth. While this strategy is simple, it may not be very effective because it's unlikely that Carla will improve at a constant rate over the years. Her improvement will be influenced by developmental factors such as growth, maturation, and experience that don't necessarily change in a linear way.

Because Carla has already experienced puberty, her coach figures that growth and maturation won't be major factors as long as Carla can maintain a low body-fat percentage. And because Carla has been training for only two years, her coach predicts large early improvements just due to the effects of training and racing. Finally, a ceiling effect will likely make

Stanford University

Location: Palo Alto, California

Coach: Andrew Gerard

Every cross country enthusiast knows that when a team scores 24 points in a big meet they're impressive, if not dominant. But words like impressive and dominant fall far short of describing the feat when a team scores 24 points in the NCAA championships, one of the most competitive cross country meets in the world. That's just what the Stanford University men accomplished when they won the 2003 NCAA championships in arguably the best team performance ever for collegiate running.

Throughout the 1990s and early 2000s, the Stanford men have dominated collegiate distance running, winning four NCAA championships and finishing in the top five every year since 1996. Stanford's coach, Andrew Gerard, traces their success in the national championships, which are held each year in late November, back to the planning process that typically begins in June. "At the start of a new season," says Gerard, "I look back at my notes from the previous season. The key to successful planning is recordkeeping. I want to know how our training worked in the past in order to plan the future."

For each cross country and track season Gerard keeps three notebooks. In the first he sketches out a general plan for the whole season. "I work backwards, thinking about the end result that we're looking for," says Gerard. "If we're preparing to run under 30:00 for 10K in mid-November, I think about a general plan for how we're going to get there. For example, to break 30:00 a runner will need to handle a certain number of 1,000-meter repetitions at a certain pace. Then I implement the workouts progressively into a schedule, thinking about where they fall in relation to races." Gerard's second notebook is for modifying the training plan. "Especially after races, I take the time to sit down and evaluate the runners' performances," says the coach. "I take notes on what's working in training and why we're doing certain workouts. Then I'll revise the plan if necessary." The third notebook contains his summary of training and racing results and observations from the season. He says, "As training progresses in a new season, it's a great motivational tool for our guys to look back at the records from the previous season. They can see how far they've come in workouts that we repeat from season to season."

Along with his extensive notes, Gerard shapes the Stanford training program by relying heavily on three guiding principles: individualization, progression, and communication. "If you throw everyone into the same workouts," he says, "you get a bell curve. For some runners the workouts will be effective, but for the rest they'll be too easy or too hard." On progression, Gerard says, "Over time, we've got to do everything better—not just run more miles. So to figure out what each athlete needs for improvement, you have to look at the mental, physical, emotional, and tactical aspects of running." Gerard stresses the third principle, open lines of communication, as the foundation of a successful training program. "Communication especially comes into play with daily revision of training," he says. "I don't have a preconceived notion about what a runner can handle on a given day. So we talk about how he's feeling and responding to the previous days' workouts and revise the plan from there.

it harder for Carla to cut big chunks of time when she's 16 or 17 versus when she's 14 or 15. Considering these factors, Carla and her coach set goals to lower her 1,600 meter time by a relatively large amount at age 14 (18 seconds), and by progressively smaller amounts each year thereafter (15, 12, and 7 seconds). The goal times are listed as follows:

Age	Goal	Improvement
14	5:29	18 seconds
15	5:14	15 seconds
16	5:02	12 seconds
17	4:55	7 seconds

In all likelihood, Carla won't improve by exactly 18 seconds and run 5:29 at age 14. She might run a little, or even considerably, faster. If she runs 5:20, she'll be 9 seconds ahead of schedule. When setting goals and planning training for the following year, her coach should respond to this extra improvement by keeping the age-15 goal at 5:14 and increasing the training load of race-specific methods (e.g., aerobic and anaerobic intervals) by a small amount only. The focus of training during the year might be on improving strength endurance and technique. If Carla can run 5:14 at age 15 without putting a lot of extra stress on her body from high-intensity running, she'll leave more room for improvement as she develops. Or, to quote Dr. David Martin and Peter Coe (1997), "Goals are best achieved by doing the least amount of work necessary, not the most, because we want injury freedom as well as continued improvement over the next several years" (page 174). Because Carla has the talent and motivation to become an elite adult runner, she and her coach must design her training so that improvement will continue through her college career and beyond.

It's also possible that Carla might not reach her goal of 5:29 at age 14. Perhaps she is healthy and has a good year, but runs only 5:36. Carla and her coach must decide whether 5:14 is within reach when setting goals and planning training for the next year. If reaching her goal means increasing training loads to levels that might cause injury, then it's best to make the goal a bit slower, perhaps 5:20. If Carla can run 5:20 at age 15, she'll still be in reach of her long-term goal and, importantly, she'll have taken steps to avoid injury.

You can use the same principles to set place goals. A 14-year-old who placed 64th in the district cross country championships might have dreams of placing in the top 5 by age 18. Before each season, the coach and athlete should work out the progression for reaching this goal. As in setting time goals, they should consider how developmental factors will influence the runner's potential for improving his place finish in different meets.

Training Goals

If long-term racing goals mark the final destination of a runner's journey, training goals are intermediate checkpoints along the way. Well-planned training goals guide the selection of daily training methods and loads. When setting these goals for individual runners, coaches should consider three main factors: developmental objectives, training history, and racing goals.

Table 8.1 shows objectives that are based on the developmental principles from chapter 1. These objectives will help you select methods that account for the athlete's maturation, fitness, and experience. Developmentally appropriate training goals for runners up to two years in training age include improving fitness capacities such as strength endurance, cardiovascular fitness, and technique. They don't, however, include developing high levels of anaerobic fitness, which is more appropriate for runners over four years in training age.

To set specific training goals for entire seasons and individual sessions, coaches can apply the individual's training history, as recorded in step 1 of the program-building process. For an upcoming macrocycle, for example, you might set training goals for the following:

▌ Total number of miles or kilometers per week

▌ Average weekly miles or kilometers for each of the different running methods (continuous aerobic running, tempo running, aerobic intervals, and so on)

TABLE 8.1—Developmentally Based Training Objectives

Training age	Objectives
0 to 2 years	Gain experience using all methods of training, each to a small degree Acquire good technique Build a base of strength endurance and cardiovascular fitness Develop the ability to race at an even pace
2 to 4 years	Refine technique Reinforce strength endurance and cardiovascular fitness base Begin to develop race-specific fitness by introducing the advanced training methods: tempo running, aerobic intervals, anaerobic intervals, race-specific intervals, and time trials Improve even-pacing skill and begin to sharpen varied-pacing skill Develop the ability to use various racing strategies
4 to 6 years	Continue using the general methods to develop the fitness base Develop race-specific fitness by increasing the volume of advanced training methods Refine racing strategies that work best for the individual

▌ Paces (minutes per mile or kilometer) for the different running methods

▌ Longest continuous aerobic run and tempo run to be attempted

▌ Average weekly loads of general training methods such as circuit, weight, and technique training

Although concrete scientific guidelines don't exist for how much to increase training loads from one macrocycle to the next, common sense and a long-range view normally shape effective goals. If an athlete's longest continuous aerobic run from the previous macrocycle was 7 miles, 1 or 2 miles is a logical increase that allows room for progressive increases. Or, consider a runner who averaged 2:42 in his best aerobic interval session of 4 × 800 meters. This runner might shoot for a goal of averaging 2:36 to 2:38 for 5 × 800 meters in the upcoming macrocycle.

Of course, the runner's racing goals should influence decisions about optimal training methods and loads. Let's follow up on Carla, the 14-year-old who ran 5:47 for 1,600 meters as a 13-year-old and who is shooting for 5:29 in the upcoming track season. When Carla does race-specific interval training, her goal time for 1,600 meters will set the standard for pacing her repetitions. Race-specific interval training might include the following sessions, all of which are based on the pace required to run 5:29 for 1,600 meters:

▌ 3 × 500 meters in 1:42 to 1:43 with 45 seconds recovery

▌ 2 × 800 meters in 2:44 to 2:45 with 60 seconds recovery

▌ 1 × 1000 in 3:24 to 3:26 and 1 × 500 in 1:42 to 1:43 with 60 seconds recovery

Training goals are motivating if runners understand exactly what they need to accomplish in the training session's volume, intensity, frequency, and recovery. Coaches should clarify the training goals for each session, as well as explain how achieving the goals will take runners a step or two closer to achieving their racing goals down the road.

Striding Ahead

When you work through the first two steps to planning an effective training program, you'll have two products: a formal assessment of the runner's starting point and a set of goals for racing and training. Together these form a roadmap for the runner's training journey. With the starting point, final destination, and intermediate checkpoints clearly defined, you can begin to bridge the gap between these points by refining your travel plans, or deciding how long you'll take to get from point to point, and by choosing the best vehicles, or training methods. That's our focus in the following chapter, where we show you how to assign appropriate methods for different phases of training and competition.

CHAPTER 9

Planning Training

Now that we've taken the first two steps to designing training programs, assessing the runner's starting fitness and setting goals for training and racing, we're ready to begin planning. This chapter focuses on the third and fourth steps, mapping out the macrocycle (season) and planning daily and weekly training sessions (see figure 9.1). Using our travel analogy, these two steps are like making a detailed itinerary for a long journey. Once you set your sights on the starting point and final destination, you're ready to chart your course with the details, including when you'll begin certain stages of the journey, when you plan to reach important landmarks along the way, and what means of transportation, or training methods, you'll use to progress from point to point. You're ready to answer questions such as these:

- When in the course of a season should you implement particular training methods?
- How much should each training method contribute to the total training load as the season progresses?
- How should you combine different training methods from day to day?
- How can you organize training to help runners reach their highest level of performance in the most important competitions?

In this chapter we'll help you answer these questions with a systematic approach to planning training, called periodization.

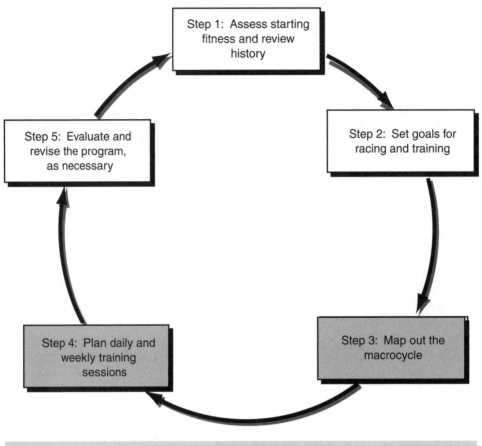

FIGURE 9.1 The five-step process for designing training programs. In this chapter we focus on the third and fourth steps.

Step 3: Map Out the Macrocycle

Periodization involves dividing the duration of a training program into smaller segments and then assigning methods and loads for each segment that will best help the runner meet training and racing goals. The smaller segments are repeated over time in cycles. In figure 9.2 we've divided a four-year high school career into smaller, more manageable chunks of time, beginning with a macrocycle, which lasts from the start of a given season to the start of the following season (a whole cross country or track season). We've divided the macrocycle into three major periods:

▌ *Preparation* emphasizes training
▌ *Competition* focuses on racing
▌ *Transition* allows recovery and regeneration after the season's final race and before a new season begins

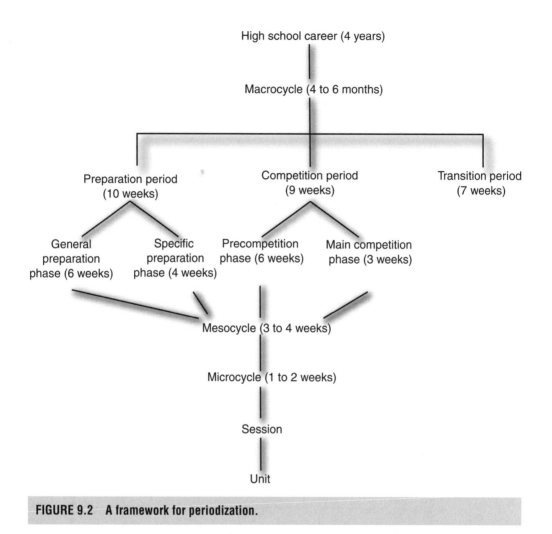

FIGURE 9.2 A framework for periodization.

The preparation and competition periods are divided into subphases, which consist of three- to four-week cycles of training called mesocycles. The next smallest cycle, called a microcycle, lasts one to two weeks. Microcycles are made up of sessions, or single workouts. Finally, a single session consists of units, which are the methods that make up a workout, such as flexibility exercises, continuous aerobic runs, and weight training. If this terminology is confusing, don't worry—we'll discuss the terms in much more detail as the chapter progresses.

Another way to map out a macrocycle is to create a periodization chart, which we've done in figure 9.3. This chart is a sample macrocycle for a cross country season, spanning six months from the first day of training on July 1 through the competitive period ending on November 4. The chart includes the transition period from the end of the cross country season the week of November 11 to the beginning of

Athlete: _____

Cross country   Track

	July	August	September	October	November	December	January
Season	Cross country						Track
Periods	Preparation		Competition		Transition		Preparation
Phases	General preparation	Specific preparation	Precompetition	Main competition	Transition		General preparation
Mesocycles	1 · 2	3	4	5 · 6			1

Microcycles: 7/1, 7/8, 7/15, 7/22, 7/29, 8/5, 8/12, 8/19, 8/26, 9/2, 9/9, 9/16, 9/23, 9/30, 10/7, 10/14, 10/21, 10/28, 11/4, 11/11, 11/18, 11/25, 12/2, 12/9, 12/16, 12/23, 12/30

Meets:
- Lower Richland: Dual (9/9)
- Sumter: Dual (9/16)
- Francis Marion Invtl. (9/23)
- Coaches' Classic Invtl. (9/30)
- Rock Hill Invtl. (10/7)
- District (10/21)
- Regional (10/28)
- State (11/4)

FIGURE 9.3 Periodization chart for cross country.

180

training for outdoor track the week of December 30. The main competition phase would be longer for elite cross country runners to compete in postseason regional and national championships in the weeks following the state championship.

For many young runners, the calendar year includes two macrocycles, one for cross country and one for outdoor track. This is called a double-periodized year. When you include a macrocycle for indoor track, you have a triple-periodized year.

The sample periodization chart on page 180 gives you a framework for designing the training program. Let's begin to fill in this framework by

1. focusing on the main training objectives for each phase,
2. identifying the methods for accomplishing training objectives in each phase, and
3. determining how much each method should contribute to the entire training load in each phase.

While our example for carrying out these steps is a cross country season, the principles and practices apply to planning for track season as well.

General Preparation Phase

In the sample periodization chart on page 180, we've divided the preparation period into two phases: general preparation and specific preparation. The general preparation phase is primarily for building a base of technical skill, strength endurance, and cardiovascular fitness. In the specific preparation phase general methods gradually decrease while race-specific methods become more prominent. The general preparation phase covers 6 weeks, or about one-third of the preparation and competition periods, which total 19 weeks. Devoting one-third of the macrocycle to general preparation enables runners to build a strong base before increasing the volume of race-specific training. Remember, the stronger the base, the greater the potential for developing race-specific fitness. For beginners, coaches might even choose to lengthen the duration of the general preparation phase to up to one-half of the macrocycle.

Table 9.1 lists the objectives and methods for the two preparation phases, along with recommendations for how much each training method should contribute to the total training load during a microcycle (one to two weeks). We've based the percentages on the amount of time that runners devote to training per week. Let's say that during the general preparation phase for cross country, a runner trains for 6 hours (360 minutes) a week. We recommend devoting approximately 30 percent of the training load to developing cardiovascular fitness, so the runner would spend approximately 108 minutes of the microcycle training for

TABLE 9.1—Training Objectives, Methods, and Loads for the General and Specific Phases of the Preparation Period

Main objectives	Key methods	Relative training load (%)	Units per microcycle
GENERAL PREPARATION PHASE			
Flexibility	Stretching exercises	10	3-6
Mobility	Games (ultimate Frisbee, keep-away, flag football)	10	2-4
Strength endurance	Circuit training, weight training	20	2-4
Technical skill	Technique drills, strides	10	2-4
Cardiovascular fitness	Continuous aerobic running, cycling, swimming	30	2-4
Aerobic fitness	Interval tempo running, fartlek	7.5	1-2
Anaerobic fitness	Anaerobic intervals	2.5	1-2
Race-specific fitness	Race-specific intervals, time trials	0	0
Recovery between training sessions	Easy jogging, cycling, swimming	10	2-4
SPECIFIC PREPARATION PHASE			
Flexibility	Stretching exercises	15	3-6
Mobility	Games	5	1-2
Strength endurance	Circuit training, weight training, hills	15	2-4
Technical skill	Technique drills, strides	10	2-4
Cardiovascular fitness	Continuous aerobic running	20	1-3
Aerobic fitness	Continuous tempo running, interval tempo running, aerobic intervals	15	2-4
Anaerobic fitness	Anaerobic intervals	5	1-2
Race-specific fitness	Race-specific intervals, time trials	5	1-2
Recovery between training sessions	Easy jogging, cycling, swimming	10	3-6

cardiovascular fitness (360 × .30 = 108). According to the last column of table 9.1, you should spread this training across two to four units in the microcycle, which means in a one-week microcycle the runner might do a 40-minute run on Monday and a 68-minute bike ride on Thursday to total 108 minutes of cardiovascular training.

We want to provide coaches with a solid framework for deciding how much training to assign, but individual differences and needs ultimately determine the right load for each runner. For example, physically mature track runners who specialize in the middle distances, 800 and 1,500 to 1,600 meters, might need slightly less training for cardiovascular fitness, perhaps 20 to 25 percent of the total load in the general preparation phase, and more training for anaerobic fitness than we recommend in table 9.1. Nevertheless, our guidelines are based on scientific and developmental principles of training, and they will give you a sound starting point that you can adapt as necessary.

Note that half of the training load during the general preparation phase is devoted to developing cardiovascular fitness (30 percent) and strength endurance (20 percent). The key methods for developing strength endurance include circuit training, weight training, and hill running. For at least the first mesocycle of this phase (three to four weeks), it's best to use circuit training to build a base for weight training and hill running. We recommend devoting another 30 percent of training to developing flexibility (10 percent), mobility (10 percent), and technical skill (10 percent). In the case of a runner who trains 6 hours (360 minutes) in a one-week microcycle, about 36 minutes of that time would be spent stretching, 36 minutes playing mobility games, and 36 minutes doing technique work.

Even though general training methods dominate the general preparation phase, race-specific methods are still part of the program. We recommend devoting 10 percent of training to developing aerobic fitness (7.5 percent) and anaerobic fitness (2.5 percent). During this phase the main methods for developing aerobic fitness are tempo running and fartlek. Anaerobic fitness will come from the short bursts of fast running in mobility games such as ultimate Frisbee and flag football. Finally, the general preparation phase also features recovery methods, such as easy jogging and swimming, to speed regeneration after demanding workouts. Because the training intensity is fairly low during this phase, recovery methods account for only about 10 percent of the training load.

Specific Preparation Phase

In the sample periodization chart on page 180, the specific preparation phase lasts four weeks, or one mesocycle. This may not seem like a long time for developing a high level of fitness in preparation for racing, but it doesn't take as long to build race-specific fitness as it does to build general fitness. In addition, the type of training you do during the specific preparation phase will carry over into the precompetition phase.

As you can see in table 9.1, the major difference between the two preparation phases is that the specific phase involves less general training and more race-specific training than the general phase. The percentage of training time devoted to developing aerobic fitness doubles from 7.5 percent to 15 percent of the program. In a one-week microcycle, this increase could come from adding an extra tempo run, fartlek session, or aerobic interval session. We've also increased anaerobic and race-specific fitness training. Cardiovascular fitness and strength endurance, which accounted for 50 percent of the training load in the general preparation phase, now make up only 35 percent of training in the specific preparation phase. The shift from general to specific training methods builds a bridge from the preparation to competition periods, preparing runners for racing.

Precompetition Phase

Our sample macrocycle for cross country divides the competition period into two phases: precompetition (six weeks) and main competition (three weeks). The precompetition phase emphasizes training methods that build race-specific fitness by simulating the physical and mental demands of competition. It also includes low-key races that runners can use to experiment with pacing strategies and tactics before the more important races of the main competition phase.

Table 9.2 shows our recommendations for the percentage contribution of training methods in the precompetition and main competition phases. The major difference between the specific preparation phase and the precompetition phase is the increase in the amount of race-specific training, including race-specific intervals and time trials or practice races. We've increased training for race-specific fitness from 5 percent to 15 percent. Other advanced, high-intensity methods, such as aerobic intervals and anaerobic intervals, continue to make up a relatively large portion of the training load at 15 percent. Runners will need to spend more time recovering, using methods such as easy jogging and swimming, because of the increase in high-intensity training, so we've increased the contribution of recovery methods from 10 percent to 20 percent.

You should view races in the precompetition phase as stepping stones to the major races in the main competition phase. The objective of racing during precompetition is to gain experience, skill, and comfort in competition, and experimenting with different tactics is one key to meeting

TABLE 9.2—Training Objectives, Methods, and Loads for the Precompetition and Main Competition Phases of the Competition Period

Main objectives	Key methods	Relative training load (%)	Units per microcycle
PRECOMPETITION PHASE			
Flexibility	Stretching exercises	15	3-6
Mobility	Games (ultimate Frisbee, keep-away, flag football)	0	0
Strength endurance	Circuit training, weight training, hills	15	1-3
Technical skill	Technique drills, strides	5	1-2
Cardiovascular fitness	Continuous aerobic running	15	1-2
Aerobic fitness	Continuous tempo running, interval tempo running, aerobic intervals	10	2-4
Anaerobic fitness	Anaerobic intervals	5	1-3
Race-specific fitness	Race-specific intervals, time trials	15	2-4
Recovery between training sessions	Easy jogging, cycling, swimming	20	3-6
MAIN COMPETITION PHASE			
Flexibility	Stretching exercises	20	3-6
Mobility	Games	0	0
Strength endurance	Circuit training, weight training, hills	10	1-3
Technical skill	Technique drills, strides	10	1-3
Cardiovascular fitness	Continuous aerobic running	0	0
Aerobic fitness	Interval tempo running, continuous tempo running, aerobic intervals	15	2-4
Anaerobic fitness	Anaerobic intervals	5	1-3
Race-specific fitness	Race-specific intervals, time trials	15	1-3
Recovery between training sessions	Easy jogging, cycling, swimming	25	3-6

Racing during precompetition helps young runners to gain experience, skill, and comfort in competition, as well as to experiment with different training tactics.

this objective. Runners can practice a different racing plan in each early-season meet, such as even pacing, negative-split pacing, or front running. Such practice prepares runners for the many tactical scenarios that could arise in more important competitions, and it helps runners find racing strategies that work best for them.

Some runners, especially beginners, might set new personal records every time they race during the precompetition phase, but that shouldn't be the objective of early-season competitions. Runners should focus on tactics, technique, and time goals that gradually lead to new PRs. The risk of setting PRs in early races is that runners might not continue to improve as the competition period progresses, which could dampen motivation to excel in major races at the end of the season.

One of the major questions about racing in the precompetition phase is whether runners should train through, which means competing without taking recovery days before and after the race. Some coaches believe that if runners reduce their training before early-season races, they'll lose fitness and valuable training time. If runners toe the starting line tired from hard training sessions in the previous days, however, they risk poor performance, injury, and a loss in confidence. Even when runners aren't out to set PRs in early-season races, they should still be physically rested and mentally sharp, which will help them improve their fitness, experience, and confidence through racing. Later in the chapter we discuss how to taper, or reduce the training load, in the days leading up to races.

Main Competition Phase

The most demanding training should draw to a close by the end of the precompetition phase so that runners can focus on challenging themselves in competition and setting new PRs. If training has gone well up to this point, don't worry about improving fitness through increasing the training load. Instead, use races to sharpen your fitness.

The main competition phase consists of a handful of important races at the end of the season. For beginners who haven't yet reached the performance level to qualify for championship meets, important races might be the last few dual meets and invitationals of the season. For intermediate and advanced runners, the important races are city, regional, state, and national championships. Coaches should emphasize peaking for the last races of a season regardless of the runner's development, because beginners who get accustomed to peaking in the last few dual meets of a season will be preparing for championship meets later in their careers.

The main objective of training during the main competition phase is maintaining race-specific fitness and form by running at speeds approximating race pace. We've assigned 35 percent of training time to advanced methods for sharpening aerobic fitness (15 percent), anaerobic fitness (5 percent), and race-specific fitness (15 percent). Training sessions in this phase should be designed so that the fast running is not so intense that it leads to extreme lactic acid accumulation and fatigue. In interval training, for example, the repetitions should be relatively short and the recovery intervals relatively long so that the athlete is running fast but not draining energy. Runners should finish interval training sessions feeling light and energized, as if they could do several more repetitions with little trouble. Fast running that doesn't drain energy sharpens mental fitness because it makes you feel fast. When race-week training consists only of easy, slow running, runners often feel sluggish and tired, which might lead to doubts and worries about upcoming races.

Another important method for maintaining race-specific fitness and form during the main competition phase is technique strides (repetitions of 100 to 150 meters at race pace), which runners might do in several sessions during the week of a race.

In the main competition phase many training sessions involve fast running, so a significant amount of time—approximately 20 percent of the load—should be devoted to warming up and stretching. And recovery is vital during this phase, particularly in the last few days before the race and a day or two afterward, so we recommend that recovery methods make up 25 percent of training.

Transition: Recovering, Regenerating, and Reflecting

Our discussion of periodization has focused on the preparation and competition periods. We can't forget the transition period, though, because it is a critical part of the young runner's program and development. Transition is the rest period between seasons or macrocycles. The objectives during the transition period are to recover from the stress of training and racing and to regenerate physical and mental energy for the upcoming macrocycle.

Bingham High School

Location: South Jordan, Utah

Coach: Jeff Arbogast

Jeff Arbogast, better known as Coach Arb to his athletes, doesn't believe in gearing training programs toward a single, all-important peak in each competitive season. "Once you reach a peak," he explains, "you have nowhere to go." Using a construction analogy to describe the program at Bingham High School, Coach Arb says, "We're not building pyramids with broad bases that narrow to single peaks. Instead, we're building skyscrapers. We're digging a deep foundation and laying down stories—big, flat, wide stories—and securing each one before adding another. Each floor of the building sends our kids to the next level."

Over 22 years at Bingham, the master architect has crafted a blueprint for success, winning a total of six state championships and two national championships for girls' and boys' cross country. At last count, over 75 Bingham distance runners have gone on to compete in college cross country and track. To top off these achievements, Coach Arb was named National Cross Country Coach of the Year for boys in 2001 and for girls in 2002.

Using periodization, Coach Arb plans the four-year Bingham training program down to the last detail. Each year is composed of four macrocycles: summer training, cross country, indoor track, and outdoor track. Each macrocycle consists of three main training components: speed, endurance, and resistance.

To illustrate his skyscraper philosophy, Coach Arb takes a single training session, for developing speed and endurance, and he explains how the workout evolves over the four macrocycles. In early June, at the start of the summer training macrocycle, the Bingham runners do mile repeats one day a week at an altitude of 4,500 feet, shooting for 5,000-meter race pace. Boys and girls who have been training for at least one year do 5 × 1 mile, while less experienced runners do up to three repeats. The runners do this session every Wednesday for two months through the end of July, when it moves to a venue at 9,800 feet and transforms into 5 × 1,200 meters. At the start of the cross country macrocycle in September, the core speed-endurance session evolves into 5 × 800 meters at faster than race pace. Around the middle of cross country season, Coach Arb adds a twist: 2 × 200 meter kickers at the end of the session. "What matters," he says, "is being able to run fast when tired." For the last two macrocycles, indoor track and outdoor track, the core speed-endurance session evolves into 5 × 700 meters and then 5 × 600 meters at paces faster than 1,600- to 3,200-meter race pace.

The key to Coach Arb's philosophy is to capitalize on the speed developed in track season, rather than to reach a peak and have to start all over again with traditional base training, which involves a lot of long, slow, distance running. "We look at track training and racing as a means to an end, which is building speed for the next four macrocycles," says Coach Arb. At the start of the new summer training macrocycle, the Bingham runners are ready to run faster mile repeats than they did the year before. "Everything we do has a reason—we don't want to waste a step. We owe that to the kids," says Coach Arb.

In our sample macrocycle, the transition period lasts seven weeks, from early November to the end of December (see figure 9.3). This period will be several weeks shorter, however, for advanced runners who compete in postseason regional and national championships.

For runners, transition is a time to take a break from distance training; use this time to relax and to participate in other sports and activities just for fun. For coaches, the transition period is a time to reflect on each runner's training and racing over the previous months and to plan the upcoming macrocycle. During the transition, coaches can begin planning by completing the assessment process that we discussed in chapter 8.

Step 4: Design Daily and Weekly Training Sessions

Thus far we've mapped out a macrocycle by dividing it into phases, identifying the training objectives for each phase, and assigning how much each training method contributes to the total training load. Using this framework, we're ready to take the next step, planning daily training sessions and organizing them over microcycles (one- to two-week periods) and mesocycles (three- to four-week periods). At this point, the following questions are most important:

▌ In a training session that has more than one unit, in what order should runners do the different units?

▌ On which days of the week should runners do the most demanding (and least demanding) sessions?

▌ How many days should separate workouts that stress similar parts of the body and physiological systems?

▌ How should a particular training method progress over the microcycles and mesocycles of a season?

We'll answer these questions by presenting guidelines for planning daily and weekly training sessions. To illustrate how to apply the guidelines, we've designed four sample microcycles, one for each phase of the preparation and competition periods (see pages 190 to 194). The sample microcycles are intended for an intermediate cross country runner (training age: two to four years) who races 3,000 to 5,000 meters. The training loads in the sample microcycles correspond to the recommendations in tables 9.1 and 9.2, on pages 182 and 185.

Sample Sessions: General Preparation Phase
(Intermediate Level, 7-Day Microcycle for Cross Country)

Monday	**Unit 1: Cardiovascular fitness (continuous aerobic running)** 35-40 min at 70-75% of HRmax
	Unit 2: Mobility and anaerobic fitness 20-min game of ultimate Frisbee
Tuesday	**Unit 1: Warm-up and flexibility** Stretching exercises[a]
	Unit 2: Technical skill (drills[b]) High-knee marching—3 $\times$ 30 m Basic skipping—3 $\times$ 60 m Butt kicks—3 $\times$ 30 m High-knee running—3 $\times$ 40 m
	Unit 3: Strength endurance (circuit training[c]) 1 $\times$ 4-station circuit
Wednesday	**Unit 1: Warm-up and flexibility** Stretching exercises[a]
	Unit 2: Aerobic fitness (interval tempo running) 4 $\times$ 4 min at 80-85% of HRmax with 60 s recovery, or 30 min fartlek
Thursday	**Unit 1: Recovery** 20-30 min of easy jogging or swimming
Friday	**Unit 1: Cardiovascular fitness** 70 min of cycling, or 35-40 min of running at 70-75% of HRmax
	Unit 2: Mobility and anaerobic fitness 20-min game of flag football
Saturday	**Unit 1: Warm-up and flexibility** Stretching exercises[a]
	Unit 2: Technical skill (strides) 12 $\times$ 150 m
	Unit 3: Strength endurance (circuit training[c]) 1 $\times$ 4-station circuit
Sunday	Rest

[a]See guidelines for stretching and illustrations of exercises on pages 105 and 100 to 104.
[b]See illustrations and instructions for technique drills on pages 128 to 129.
[c]See illustrations and instructions for circuit training on pages 109 to 114.

Sample Sessions: Specific Preparation Phase
(Intermediate Level, 10-Day Microcycle for Cross Country)

Monday	**Unit 1: Cardiovascular fitness (continuous aerobic running)** 45-50 min at 70-75% of HRmax
	Unit 2: Mobility and anaerobic fitness 20-min game of ultimate Frisbee
Tuesday	**Unit 1: Warm-up and flexibility** Stretching exercises[a]
	Unit 2: Aerobic fitness (interval tempo running) 4 × 6 min with 60 s recovery at 80-85% of HRmax
Wednesday	**Unit 1: Warm-up and flexibility** Stretching exercises[a]
	Unit 2: Technical skill (drills[b]) High-knee marching—3 × 40 m Basic skipping—3 × 70 m Butt kicks—3 × 40 m High-knee running—3 × 50 m
	Unit 3: Strength endurance (weight training[c]) 2 sets of lower- and upper-body exercises
Thursday	**Unit 1: Warm-up and flexibility** Stretching exercises[a]
	Unit 2: Anaerobic fitness (anaerobic intervals) 4 × 400 m at 5-15% faster than race pace for 1,500-1,600 m with 3-4 min recovery
Friday	**Unit 1: Recovery** 20-30 min of easy jogging or swimming, or rest by taking the day off completely
Saturday	**Unit 1: Warm-up and flexibility** Stretching exercises[a]
	Unit 2: Aerobic fitness (aerobic intervals) 4 or 5 × 800 m at 5,000-meter race pace with a 1:1 recovery[d]
Sunday	**Unit 1: Recovery** 20-30 min of easy jogging or swimming, or rest by taking the day off completely
Monday	**Unit 1: Warm-up and flexibility** Stretching exercises[a]
	Unit 2: Strength endurance (hill training) 6 × 300 m uphill with easy jog recovery (downhill)

(continued)

Sample Sessions *(continued)*

Tuesday	**Unit 1: Warm-up and flexibility** Stretching exercises[a]
	Unit 2: Technical skill (drills) See the previous Wednesday's session
Wednesday	**Unit 1: Warm-up and flexibility** Stretching exercises[a]
	Unit 2: Race-specific fitness (race-specific intervals) 2 × 1000 m at race pace with 90 s recovery

[a]See guidelines for stretching and illustrations of exercises on pages 105 and 100 to 104.
[b]See illustrations and instructions for technique drills on pages 128 to 129.
[c]See illustrations and instructions for weight training on pages 119 to 123.
[d]1:1 recovery means that the interval between repetitions lasts as long as the repetition itself.

Organizing Different Units in a Single Training Session

Most daily training sessions consist of more than one unit. For example, on a day when runners stretch and do technique drills, they complete two units of training. In such a session, the coach could even add a unit of circuit training without overdoing it. The effectiveness of the session greatly depends on the way that the individual units are ordered, so pay attention to the following guidelines. These are not hard and fast rules, but they are usually the best way to organize a session.

Low-intensity units should precede high-intensity units. Monday's session in the sample microcycle for the general preparation phase (see page 190) consists of two units of training. The first unit, a continuous aerobic run at 70 to 75 percent of maximal heart rate, is performed at a relatively low intensity compared to the second unit, which is a game of ultimate Frisbee. The first unit shouldn't cause severe muscular fatigue. Instead it should warm up the muscles and prime the cardiovascular system for the bursts of anaerobic sprinting and jumping that the runner will do in the second unit.

A unit of high-intensity, race-specific training should not precede a unit of low-intensity, general training on the same day (except for doing stretching exercises after a tempo run or an interval session). If you did an intense anaerobic interval session before a continuous aerobic run, you'd risk overtraining and injury.

A warm-up unit of jogging and stretching should precede units of race-specific training. Stretching exercises prepare the muscles for intense work and prevent injuries during fast running. Therefore, any session that involves high-intensity, race-specific training methods should be preceded by a thorough warm-up that includes 10 to 15 minutes of jogging and a complete stretching routine. It's a good practice to also do some light stretching after running sessions.

Runners should not do technique units when overly fatigued. In all of the sample microcycles, units of technique training are early in the session, following a warm-up with stretching exercises. Technique training should not follow a unit that causes deep muscle fatigue, such as circuit training or anaerobic intervals, because the fatigue will prevent runners from executing and learning good form.

Sample Sessions: Precompetition Phase
(Intermediate Level, 7-Day Microcycle for Cross Country)

Monday	**Unit 1: Cardiovascular fitness (continuous aerobic running)** 40 min at 75% of HRmax
	Unit 2: Strength endurance (circuit training[a]) 2 × 4-station circuit
Tuesday	**Unit 1: Warm-up and flexibility** Stretching exercises[b]
	Unit 2: Race-specific fitness (race-specific intervals) 3 × 1,000 m at race pace with 90 s recovery
	Unit 3: Anaerobic fitness (anaerobic intervals) 3 × 300 m at 5-15% faster than race pace for 1,500-1,600 m with 3-4 min recovery Or, replace units 2 and 3 with a 5,000-meter race (dual meet)
Wednesday	**Unit 1: Recovery** 20-30 min of easy jogging or swimming
Thursday	**Unit 1: Warm-up and flexibility** Stretching exercises[b]
	Unit 2: Aerobic fitness (continuous tempo running) 15-20 min at 80-85% of HRmax
Friday	**Unit 1: Recovery** 20-30 min of easy jogging or swimming
Saturday	**Unit 1: Warm-up and flexibility** Stretching exercises[b]
	Unit 2: Race-specific fitness 5,000-meter time trial or invitational cross country race
Sunday	**Unit 1: Recovery** 20-30 min of easy jogging or swimming

[a]See illustrations and instructions for circuit training on pages 109 to 114.
[b]See guidelines for stretching and illustrations of exercises on pages 105 and 100 to 104.

Units of continuous aerobic running should precede units of strength endurance training. In a session that includes running and strength endurance training, run first. For example, a continuous aerobic run should precede circuit or weight training, as illustrated in the session on the first Monday of the sample microcycle for the precompetition phase (page 193). The muscle fatigue caused by the strength endurance unit could lead to injury if it is followed by a run.

Sample Sessions: Main Competition Phase
(Intermediate Level, 7-Day Microcycle for Cross Country)

Monday	**Unit 1: Warm-up and flexibility** Stretching exercises[a]
	Unit 2: Aerobic and anaerobic fitness (aerobic and anaerobic intervals) 3 × (1 × 600 m and 1 × 200 m), running the 600 at 5,000-meter race pace and the 200 at a controlled sprint, with complete recovery between sets
Tuesday	**Unit 1: Warm-up and flexibility** Stretching exercises[a]
	Unit 2: Technical skill (strides) 8 × 150 m at race pace
	Unit 3: Strength endurance (circuit training[b]) 1 × 4-station circuit
Wednesday	**Unit 1: Warm-up and flexibility** Stretching exercises[a]
	Unit 2: Aerobic fitness (interval tempo running) 4 × 3 min at 75-80% HRmax with 90 s recovery
Thursday	**Unit 1: Recovery** 20-30 min of easy jogging
Friday	**Unit 1: Recovery** 20-30 min of easy jogging
	Unit 2: Technical skill (strides) 8 × 150 m at race pace
Saturday	5,000-meter cross country race
Sunday	**Unit 1: Recovery** 20-30 min of easy jogging or swimming, or complete rest

[a]See guidelines for stretching and illustrations of exercises on pages 105 and 100 to 104.
[b]See illustrations and instructions for circuit training on pages 109 to 114.

Organizing Training Sessions in a Microcycle

Let's say that you're planning an upcoming microcycle, and you've decided to combine a continuous aerobic run with mobility games on one day and stretching with an interval tempo session on another day. On what days of the microcycle will you place these two sessions? What will you plan for the other days of the microcycle? This section will help you figure out how to arrange sessions within microcycles. The sample microcycles on pages 190 to 194 are either 7 or 10 days long. To illustrate the pattern of training during the general preparation phase, for example, we chose a seven-day microcycle for simplicity: It's convenient to think about training on a weekly basis. Still, coaches may need to adapt the sample seven-day microcycle if the training sessions do not allow runners to recover sufficiently. Beginners may need an extra day or two of recovery during the middle of the week, particularly before the interval tempo session on Wednesday. If so, add these recovery days, lengthening the microcycle, perhaps to 9 or 10 days.

On the other hand, some intermediate and advanced runners may be able to handle more units of training than we've prescribed. One way to increase their training load is to schedule additional units on two or three mornings of each microcycle. Coaches can use morning sessions for recovery methods, continuous aerobic running, or even strength endurance training. These extra units will help young runners who have the desire and potential to continue beyond high school prepare for the two-a-day sessions that are part of the training program for many college and world-class runners.

Repeat key training methods for a given phase regularly in the microcycle. You can't reach a high level of fitness by applying a certain training method only once or even a few times—peak fitness comes from progressively stressing the body and mind numerous times. Within a phase of training, you should repeat the training methods that stress the most important fitness capacities for that phase. For example, a primary objective of the specific preparation phase is to develop a high level of aerobic fitness using methods such as tempo running and aerobic interval training. During this phase runners should repeat these methods several times in a microcycle. A general rule is to repeat key methods at least once or twice in a 7- to 10-day period. In the 10-day microcycle for the specific preparation phase (page 191), we've included two units for developing aerobic fitness: an interval tempo run on the first Tuesday and aerobic intervals on Saturday. If these two training sessions were spread out over a longer period, such as once every three weeks, they wouldn't stress the aerobic system enough to lead to positive adaptations. Including the tempo run that we've scheduled on Wednesday of our sample microcycle for the general preparation phase (page 190), our hypothetical cross country runner would do a total of 10 tempo runs, one per week, over the 10 weeks of the entire preparation period.

To prevent boredom from repeating methods, coaches should vary elements such as the training venue for continuous aerobic running, the exercises in weight training, and the lengths of repetitions in interval training. When two continuous aerobic runs are scheduled in a microcycle, for example, it's a good idea to plan them for different courses. On the first day, runners might train on a flat dirt road in the country. On the second, they might run on a hilly golf course. Or, if two or three circuit training sessions are planned in the microcycle, you can vary the exercises in the circuit and change the venue of the workout each time.

Avoid using the same training method two days in a row. While you should repeat key training methods in a microcycle, developing fitness isn't simply a matter of training, training, and more training. Instead, repeated cycles of training with sufficient recovery do the trick. At least one day should separate the use of a particular method. If a runner does circuit training on a Monday, he should wait at least until Wednesday before repeating the method, allowing the stressed muscles to restore energy and to undergo the physiological adaptations that improve strength endurance. This doesn't necessarily mean that Tuesday should be devoted to recovery methods or complete rest. If, for example, the circuit session on Monday primarily stressed muscles of the upper body, the runner's legs might be fresh enough to allow for a continuous aerobic run on Tuesday.

Stretches should be done before any high-intensity race-specific training session, but after a jogging warm-up.

Two exceptions to this rule exist. First, recovery methods can be used two days in a row, particularly in the days leading up to a race. Second, elite runners who compete in track meets that feature semifinals the day before the finals should do back-to-back days of race-specific training to simulate these racing demands.

Low-intensity or recovery days should both precede and follow high-intensity days. When coaches plan high-intensity sessions such as race-specific intervals or anaerobic intervals, they should also plan enough recovery so that runners are physically regenerated and mentally fresh for the next challenging workout. One day of recovery exercise (e.g., easy jogging, cycling, or swimming) is usually sufficient. Be aware, however, of individual differences in recovery rates. Some runners, particularly beginners, may need more recovery or complete rest before they are ready to train hard again. On the day before a demanding session, runners should use either recovery methods or low-intensity methods such as continuous aerobic running or technique strides.

Assign race-specific training methods on the days of the week that competitions are usually held. In the sample microcycle for the specific preparation phase (page 191), we've scheduled a session of aerobic intervals for Saturday. In the sample microcycle for the precompetition phase, Saturday might be set aside for a 5,000-meter time trial. Both of these sessions closely simulate the physical and mental demands of competition. We've scheduled the sessions for Saturday because that's the day of the most important races during the main competition phase for cross country. This instills a pattern in which runners condition their bodies and minds for the challenge of competition at the end of the week.

It's also a good idea to schedule race-specific training sessions at the time of day that the most important races will be held. If cross country races are scheduled for 8:00 A.M., the coach should plan several race-specific training sessions for that time. These sessions could be held on successive Saturdays during the specific preparation and precompetition phases.

The race microcycle should include sessions with low volumes of fast running and sessions of recovery. The sample microcycle for the main competition phase (page 194) illustrates this guideline. During the race week, Monday, Tuesday, Wednesday, and Friday include units of fast running. One objective of these sessions is to activate the neuromuscular pathways that will be used in the race. Another objective is to boost the runner's comfort and confidence in her ability to maintain race pace. The most important thing to remember about these sessions is that they should not be so intense that they drain energy. For example, the interval session scheduled for Monday and the 150-meter technique strides on Tuesday and Friday are for practicing pacing and good form rather than for stressing the physiological systems in order to reach a higher level of fitness. The key to avoiding fatigue during these sessions is to shorten the repetition distance and lengthen the rest interval.

Organizing Microcycles in a Mesocycle

After arranging units within sessions and sessions within microcycles, the next step is to organize the microcycles within a mesocycle, tying together individual weeks of training into a block of three to four weeks. Follow these guidelines to organize the microcycles within a mesocycle.

Repeat key methods throughout the mesocycle, gradually increasing the training load. Let's say that, for the specific preparation period, you've set up a three-week mesocycle that's made up of three one-week microcycles. You've planned a continuous tempo run for the first Monday of the first microcycle. You should repeat tempo running several times throughout the mesocycle, perhaps assigning it for the next two Mondays. This cyclical pattern ensures that runners stress particular elements of fitness, adapting for improvement on a regular basis. Of course, for improvement to occur, the training load for each method has to increase systematically. Over three successive Mondays in a mesocycle, you might increase the duration of the continuous tempo run from 14, to 16, to 18 minutes.

Increase training loads over the successive microcycles in a mesocycle, adding one unloading microcycle at the end of each mesocycle. A common practice in periodization is to set up mesocycles in a pattern that increases the training load over the first two to three weeks and decreases it in the last week, as illustrated in figure 9.4. Figure 9.4 shows an increase in running volume over the first two weeks of two successive mesocycles, each lasting three weeks. In the first mesocycle, we've scheduled 25 and 32 miles of running in successive seven-day microcycles. Then, after a week of reduced volume, the runner starts the second mesocycle at 32 miles and increases to 37 miles across the two weeks. This progression will result from increasing the volume for all the running methods (continuous aerobic running, tempo running, and aerobic and anaerobic intervals). The intensity will also increase as the pace gets faster each time the runner performs the unit.

The volume drops during the third week of both mesocycles. The third week is called an unloading microcycle because the training load decreases. In the unloading microcycle, cut training volume by 25 to 50 percent of the highest volume in the mesocycle. We've lowered the mileage by 40 percent from the second (32 miles) to the third (19 miles) week of the first mesocycle. The unloading microcycle gives runners a little extra recovery from training and refreshes their mental outlook for the

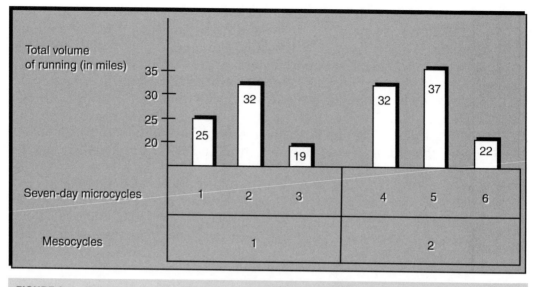

FIGURE 9.4 **Building and unloading microcycles in two successive mesocycles.**

next mesocycle. Considerable improvement in performance can result as the body and mind regenerate and fitness levels rise.

During the precompetition and main competition phases of the season, plan mesocycles so that the unloading microcycles lead up to races. The reduction in training load will result in a timely regeneration for the physical and mental demands of competition.

Striding Ahead

This chapter's guidelines for using periodization to plan daily and weekly training will give you a solid framework for designing your program. For the best outcomes, however, you must consider which patterns of training work best for individual athletes. Let's say that, for a given runner, you've planned one recovery day following high-intensity anaerobic interval sessions throughout the precompetition phase. If the runner is not fully recovering after one recovery day, adjust the schedule by adding an extra recovery day following anaerobic interval sessions. This sort of flexibility and revision in planning training is the theme of the next chapter.

Before moving on, we want to make one more point about planning daily and weekly training: It's vital for the coach to discuss upcoming training plans with runners. An open line of communication is crucial to finding out which training methods work best for each individual. A great way to start the conversation is to hand out a weekly workout schedule a few days before it begins. The runners and coach can discuss the plan and make suitable changes. In addition, runners can use their plans to prepare physically and mentally for the challenges of particular sessions. For example, athletes who know that they will be running a time trial on Saturday can prepare by eating a high-carbohydrate meal and getting a good night's sleep on Friday. During the week, runners can plan their strategies for the time trial and perform mental imagery to fine-tune mental fitness.

CHAPTER 10

Program Evaluation

Coaches who plan training following the steps in chapter 9 gain a world of confidence in their programs. They know where their athletes are going as well as how to help them get there successfully and safely. The detailed planning that characterizes periodization lessens the chances of major obstacles blocking a runner's journey to performance goals. Nevertheless, no matter how much forethought goes into planning training programs, minor setbacks and detours are inevitable, such as injuries, illness, loss of motivation, personal problems, and even stretches of bad weather. In this chapter we discuss how to evaluate training programs and get back on course in the event of unexpected detours. This revision is the final step in the five-step process for designing training programs (see figure 10.1).

Evaluating Training and Racing Outcomes

The two sure signs of a successful program are healthy and motivated runners who are racing at higher and higher levels. In chapter 8 we talked about assessing factors such as improvement, health, and motivation after each season—the first step to planning training for the following season. To make necessary adjustments in your program *during* the season, you must evaluate your runners' training and racing on a day-to-day basis.

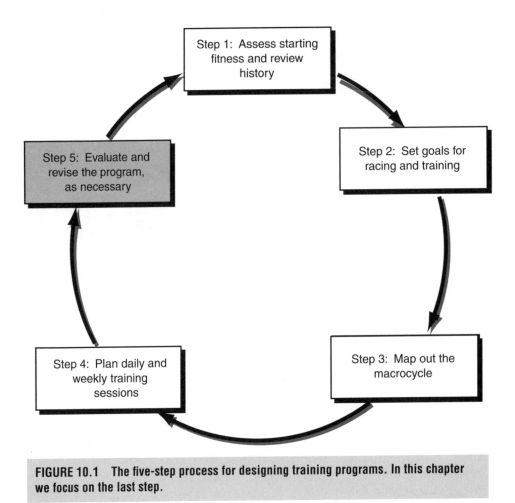

FIGURE 10.1 The five-step process for designing training programs. In this chapter we focus on the last step.

Evaluating Training Performance

Sometimes it's easy to take a wrong turn in training without realizing it. Coaches need to watch closely and make sure that runners stay on track. One way to do this is to check the actual contributions of different training methods to the total training load against the amount planned. Let's say that for a given runner you've planned to devote approximately 25 percent of training during the general preparation phase to developing strength endurance. During a given week, the runner's training time for these methods totaled less than 10 percent—maybe he had to miss practice on the day of a planned circuit training session. Usually it's no problem to miss one workout. If, however, the runner repeatedly misses out on a particular training method, he won't develop the fitness to reach his racing goals. Later we'll discuss strategies for getting back on course when the actual training load deviates from the planned program.

Another way to evaluate training on a daily basis is to use indicators such as heart rate and running time to make sure that runners are meeting training objectives. Say, for example, that the objective of a session is to develop cardiovascular fitness with continuous aerobic running. If the runner's pace is too fast, as indicated by a heart rate above the intended range of 65 to 75 percent, she may not be able to maintain it long enough to experience important improvements in the aerobic system. Sometimes it's tempting to let the runner keep going because she's feeling good and working hard. The workout may even lead to a breakthrough in confidence. Remember, though, that if the runner strays too far off course and doesn't accomplish the planned objectives, she could face consequences such as injury and illness.

Healthy and motivated runners who are improving are a good indication that a program is successful.

Finally, coaches can evaluate the training program by asking runners for feedback. The question "How do you feel?" is a powerful assessment tool. Here are a few variations:

▮ How are your legs feeling after yesterday's interval workout? Are they sore?

▮ How is your breathing? Are you working harder than we planned?

▮ How did your technique feel on that last stride? Can you tell whether your arms are crossing the front of your body or not?

▮ Do you think you had enough recovery time yesterday to work hard today?

▮ Are you psyched to run these 200s in under 35?

▮ Did you like that workout? How would you change it to make it better?

Evaluating Racing Performance

The ultimate test of an effective training program is whether runners are performing up to their capabilities and improving in races. If runners are meeting their racing goals there's no need to change the program other than to progressively increase training loads. As the saying goes, "If it ain't broke, don't fix it!" If, however, runners' performances aren't up to par, the coach must search for reasons and revise the program accordingly.

Runners might not reach their racing potential for several reasons. Some runners shine in training sessions but flicker out in races. For these runners, psychological factors such as nervousness, lack of confidence, poor concentration, or ineffective tactics are likely limiting competitive performance. To figure out the source of the problem, you must become a detective:

▍ Is the runner tight and anxious before the race starts? Maybe he's too nervous.

▍ Does the runner truly believe that she can achieve her goal? Maybe she lacks confidence.

▍ Does the runner fall behind on uphill sections of cross country courses? Maybe he's not concentrating on the right cues for good uphill running technique.

▍ Does the runner finish the race with too much energy left? Maybe she isn't pacing herself properly.

The answers to these questions will help you adapt the training program to focus on the aspects of mental fitness that need improvement.

In another scenario, a runner has a high level of mental fitness but simply lacks the physical fitness to achieve his goals. This is evident in competitions where the runner starts out on goal pace and in good position but fades as the race progresses. If your evaluation doesn't indicate low levels of mental fitness, the explanation is likely that the runner is not physically prepared. Carefully examine records of recent sessions to see whether the athlete has conditioned his body for the physical demands of racing. For example, Vijay's goal is to break 2:10 for 800 meters, but he has struggled to run just 2:16. A careful review of Vijay's recent training shows that he has been far from hitting goal times in race-specific sessions. The fastest 400-meter repetition he ran in training was only 67 seconds, a 2:14 pace for an 800-meter race. He has also only done a few 200-meter repetitions that were faster than race pace. A clear reason for Vijay's disappointing racing performance exists: He simply has not prepared his body for running under 2:10. Remember, it's vital to keep records of daily training in order to make this type of assessment.

Revising the Training Program

Part of the challenge of coaching distance runners is adjusting the program to account for individual differences and to meet individual needs. This is the art of coaching. It requires creativity and flexibility to steer runners

University of Notre Dame

Location: Notre Dame, Indiana

Coach: Tim Connelly

At the University of Notre Dame, where Tim Connelly has coached since 1988, a thoughtful approach to planning and revising training has resulted in a great deal of success. From the mid-1990s and into the 2000s, the Notre Dame women have consistently been among the top cross country teams in the Big East and NCAA championships.

Connelly maps out the Notre Dame training program months before a racing season begins. "I lay out the whole season by planning the general types of training we'll do, figuring out which races each athlete will run, and identifying when we want to be most ready to compete," says Connelly. "For cross country, I start planning early in the summer. I know that in August and September we're going to do a lot of tempo running and fartlek. And by October we want to build up to a key interval workout of 4 × 1 mile at race pace. But I fine-tune the specific details of our workouts as we get closer to them. For example, we use early cross country races to determine how fast we'll run our structured intervals."

To ensure that the best laid plans don't go awry, Connelly sometimes has to put the reins on highly motivated runners who tend to push too hard in training. "If we're running 4 × 1 mile in early October, and the goal pace for a given runner is 5:20, I don't get too concerned if she starts out 4 or 5 seconds under pace," Connelly says. "But I do get concerned if she runs the first mile in 5:05. That's when I remind the athlete that we don't need to be ready right now—instead, we need to be ready for the championship meets in November. To help the runner hit the goal pace, I'll tell her to stay in the pack with teammates who are running 5:20s. It's like water torture for highly motivated runners, but they understand that if they're hitting goal paces in workouts in October, they'll be ready for the most important races at the end of the season."

Connelly's progressive approach to planning is an insurance policy against having to make major revisions in training—the sort of revisions that come as a result of injuries. "We train hard to compete, and we have a lot of highly motivated athletes. So sometimes the most difficult thing for our runners to do is to back away from training," he says. "But the best way to deal with injuries is to avoid them in the first place. If I see that a runner is struggling in a workout, we'll back off. Sometimes you have to be willing to call it a day. But I help our runners understand that backing off from training is not the beginning of the end of the world."

Among other outstanding features, the Notre Dame program is characterized by consistency. "If you can run for 18 months straight," says Connelly, "you're going to improve. Success comes from the long uninterrupted stretches of challenging training at a level that allows continual progression. That's a definite key for high school runners who want to compete in college."

toward their goals. These coaching skills are essential because, as we've said, the road to the runner's goals can have potholes and detours. In this section we'll talk about strategies for avoiding setbacks and for getting back on course should setbacks occur.

Getting Back on Course After Detours in Training

Table 10.1 summarizes strategies for getting back on course after detours in training. For example, a common setback occurs when runners simply fail to improve their fitness, reflected in a lack of progress in training sessions. In this situation, coaches should look for signs of overtraining and undertraining. Overtraining refers to excessive amounts of stressful work that break the body down so that it can't recover within a few days. Some signs of overtraining include long-lasting fatigue and muscle soreness, injury, illness, difficulty falling asleep at night and waking in the morning, changes in mood, and loss of motivation. Some signs of undertraining are a lack of progress in workouts that are easy for the runner to complete and failure to improve in races. A runner who is undertraining is simply not challenged physically and mentally by workouts.

TABLE 10.1—Detours and Setbacks in Training: Strategies for Revising the Program

Potential detours and setbacks	Ways to get back on course
Lack of improvement in fitness over time	Look for signs of overtraining and undertraining Identify and remove developmentally inappropriate training methods Cut back on excessive training loads if overtrained Add to training loads if undertrained
Failure to meet training objectives for a given session	Stop the session if the runner is extremely fatigued and losing form Adjust target heart rates and paces to set the right intensity
Common cold, upset stomach, or other short-term illnesses	Take time off from training until health completely returns See family physician for treatment
Injuries	Take time off from training until injury completely heals See the school's athletic trainer or family physician for treatment Use supplemental training methods if possible (swimming, cycling, water running, circuit and weight training)
Unexplained off days	Be positive and upbeat: "It's only a bad day, we'll make up for it" Seek the source of the problem and eliminate it in the future

If you find that overtraining or undertraining is the root of the problem, you must identify the inappropriate methods and make adjustments accordingly. Consider a runner who has been training for less than a year and who complains of muscle soreness for several days after doing anaerobic interval sessions. To avoid serious injury, the coach must cut back on the volume of running covered in anaerobic interval sessions. If you've planned for the method to account for five percent of the total load in a given phase, you might cut back one or two percent. Over the next few seasons and years this form of high-intensity work can be increased as the runner matures and develops the conditioning to handle it.

Undertraining and overtraining often result when the actual training load deviates from planned loads. Let's go back to the runner who missed a circuit training session. At the end of the week, the coach evaluates this runner's program and finds that the contribution of strength endurance falls short of the planned load. For just one workout the coach might not make any adjustments. If, however, the runner misses several sessions, especially if the cause is injury or illness, the coach is faced with a dilemma. Should the runner skip over the lost training and advance to where his teammates are? Should he pick up where he left off and try to catch up? Or should he go back to the start of the training journey and rebuild a fitness base?

The answers to these questions depend on how much training the runner has missed and how much fitness he has lost. No firm guidelines exist for getting back on course after missing training. Generally speaking, however, the more fitness lost, the farther back you must go in the training journey, using general methods such as continuous aerobic running and circuit and weight training to rebuild fitness. The danger of advancing a runner to where he would have been had he not missed training is that he likely won't be able to handle the advanced loads and might suffer an injury or illness.

Another bump in the road is failing to meet training objectives in daily sessions. Usually this is the result of running too fast or too slow, thus missing out on the intended training effect. Don't hesitate to change the workout on the spot if you sense this is the case. Take the runner whose 3,200-meter goal is to break 10:00. In a race-specific interval session of $3 \times 1,000$ meters, he's shooting for 3:05 to 3:10, a range that includes his race pace of 3:07. However, the runner struggles to hit 3:10 on the first repetition, and then starts to fade on the last two repetitions. If you sense that the struggling runner can't complete the last two repetitions in 3:05 to 3:10, you might shorten the distance from 1,000 to 800 or 600 meters. Then in future sessions for developing race-specific fitness, you might shorten the distance of each repetition or make the runner's goal times slower. This might mean revising his overall goal of breaking 10:00. In contrast, if this runner is hitting 3:05 easily, his future sessions should have faster goal times, and his goal to break 10:00 might be lowered to sub-9:45.

Even though changes to the training program are inevitable to keep runners on course, it's important for coaches to understand that they should not make changes hastily and without careful thought. Sometimes runners veer off course from training plans simply because they have bad days. Typically, the younger the training age, the more bad days the runner will experience. Many circumstances may cause disappointing results in a training session: a sleepless night, an upset stomach, a side stitch, bad weather, a demanding test in school, or even an argument with a friend. When runners are having extremely bad days, the coach should stop the session and, on a very upbeat note, suggest that they try it again the next day. It's important to try again so that runners can regain confidence. It doesn't make sense to let young runners fail to achieve training objectives and risk losing confidence if there's a good reason for a temporary setback. When things aren't going very well, the coach should seek the source of the problem, let runners know that it's only a bad day, and try to eliminate that problem in the future.

Dealing With Side Stitches

One of the most common setbacks in training and racing is the side stitch, or a sharp pain just under the ribs, typically on the right side of the body. Exercise scientists are stumped about the exact cause of side stitches, but they have found some clues. First, stitches tend to occur in runners who are just starting to train and are relatively unfit. It's possible that these runners get stitches because their respiratory muscles—the diaphragm and muscles attached to the ribs—fatigue and cramp due to insufficient blood flow and oxygen delivery. Like the leg muscles, the respiratory muscles work very hard during high-intensity running, and stitches seem to occur when runners breathe vigorously. Because highly fit runners tend to experience fewer stitches, it's possible that they have conditioned their breathing muscles to receive and use more oxygenated blood. Thus, one key to getting rid of stitches is to improve your fitness through progressive increases in training.

Second, stitches tend to occur in runners who train soon after drinking a lot of water or eating. Food and water in the stomach can cause pressure that triggers pain by pulling on muscle and connective tissue. A solution is to allow several hours for food to digest before running. However, don't avoid drinking water just to prevent a stitch—you could risk dehydration. Instead, drink several small cups of water rather than one or two large cups in the hours before training and racing.

If you get a side stitch while you're running try this bit of advice from the experts: stop, bend over at the waist, and massage the area in which you have pain. Another method is to tighten the abdominal muscles and breathe deeply. At first this might worsen the pain, but within a minute or so the stitch should go away. If the pain from a side stitch persists over several days, you should seek medical attention because of the possibility of a strained or torn muscle.

Getting Back on Course After Detours in Racing

Shortcomings in mental fitness are among the primary reasons for setbacks in races (see table 10.2). As we've discussed, some runners who are in great shape physically and have impressive training sessions may fall short of their racing goals because they lack mental fitness. In this situation, the coach must evaluate each runner for specific weaknesses in mental fitness and then design training and racing experiences to improve those weaknesses. Consider Julia, a runner who has been getting nervous before races and who has not been performing up to par. Julia's coach notices that she is relaxed, talkative, and playful before her everyday training sessions, which have been very successful. On race days, however, she isolates herself from teammates and takes on a serious attitude. Sensing that Julia might be putting too much pressure on herself before races, her coach suggests that she hang out, warm up, and joke around with her teammates to help her relax. Julia and her coach agree to try this plan for one race, and they find that being around teammates before the race helps Julia relax and forget about being nervous, enabling her to race faster than ever.

TABLE 10.2—Detours and Setbacks in Racing: Strategies for Revising the Program

Potential detours and setbacks	Ways to get back on course
Shortcomings in mental fitness	Evaluate elements of mental fitness: confidence, concentration, pacing and tactical skill, relaxation, anxiety, fear, and motivation Design training and racing experiences to improve mental fitness in weak areas
Shortcomings in physical fitness	Evaluate elements of physical fitness: technique, strength endurance, cardiovascular fitness, aerobic fitness, and so on Evaluate recent training sessions to determine whether they simulate racing demands Design training to improve weak areas and stress the body to meet racing demands
Injuries or illnesses	Hold off on racing until completely recovered and healthy Stay on treatment and therapy schedules; use supplemental training methods if possible
Unexplained off days	Seek the source of problem and eliminate it in the future Use poor performance as a source of motivation to do better next time Put running in its proper perspective Race again as soon as possible Try not to drop out of the race

If a lack of confidence is the problem, the coach might tailor training sessions to ensure successful outcomes because success in training breeds confidence for racing. This might mean making goal times for repetitions in interval sessions easier to reach, or prescribing sessions that the runner enjoys and always seems to master. In addition, you should bolster the athlete's confidence by reminding him about recent workouts and races that went well. Other training changes might include extra attention to relaxation techniques, more work on pacing control, and time set aside for visualization of successful racing outcomes.

Pinpointing weaknesses and making changes in training to eliminate them are also the keys to getting a runner back on course when she lacks the physical fitness to attain her racing goals. In this case, the coach must analyze the racing performances to detect physical weaknesses. Perhaps the runner's form falls apart in the last half of the race. This indicates that she needs to work on strength endurance and technique. Maybe the runner can't respond to midrace surges and finishing sprints. She probably needs more varied-pace training that stresses the FT muscle fibers and anaerobic energy pathways.

Probably the most common reason for disappointing performances in distance running is simply having an off day. As with off days in training, the key to preventing them in races is to seek the source of the problem. If you have an upset stomach and a side stitch, perhaps you ate too soon before competing. A painful blister that makes you slow down could be the result of wearing a new pair of spikes without first breaking them in. Perhaps you feel tired before the race starts because you didn't sleep well the night before due to nervousness. Once you have an idea of what caused an off day, you can devise a plan for eliminating the problem in the future. To avoid the side stitch, try eating an hour earlier. To prevent blisters, wear new shoes a few times in training before you race in them. To be fresh and well rested on race day, take your mind off racing the night before by watching television, reading a favorite book, or listening to relaxing music before you go to sleep.

Often there's no obvious reason for what went wrong in a race. You're healthy, fit, and have been training well. You feel great before the race starts. But during the race, it all falls apart, and you can find no clear explanation for the disappointing result. This is a scenario that even the world's best distance runners experience many times in their careers. Successful runners and coaches take advantage of these disappointments to get back on course for future races. If you use poor performance as a source of commitment to do your best in the next race, you can raise your level of motivation and determination to succeed. Coaches must repair the emotional wounds of bad races as quickly as possible and direct the runner's focus to the next race. It's important to race again as soon as possible after unexplained off days, because you don't want to allow doubts about fitness and ability to build when there's likely no reason for the uncertainty.

Sometimes runners have a few unexplained bad races in a row. From our own experiences, we know well the disappointment that comes from this sort of setback, but we also see an opportunity for coaches and parents to help young runners put athletics into perspective. When young runners realize that the sun will come up tomorrow and that the coach, family, and friends will be there with encouragement, they learn a wonderful lesson about sport and about life. Young runners who love to train and race have many sessions and competitions to look forward to down the road. Bad races are just temporary detours along the way.

One last bit of advice about setbacks in racing: It's important to try to finish every race you start unless you suffer an injury or experience pain during the event. Some runners get in the habit of dropping out of races because they're fatigued or they've fallen off pace for a PR. These runners may never fully challenge themselves because the thought

Motivation and confidence-building sometimes include reminding runners of races or practices where they succeeded in meeting their goals.

of quitting is always present. Even if you have to slow down to a jog on off days, you should try to finish the race. However, under no circumstances should coaches or parents encourage runners to finish races when they are experiencing pain and extreme discomfort from an injury, cramp, or health-threatening response to very hot or cold weather.

Dealing With Injuries

Given the physical demands of distance running, a fine line separates peak performance and injury risk. Over a long career, despite following a sound training program, few runners will completely avoid getting hurt, so it's important for coaches, parents, and runners to know the causes, symptoms, and approaches to treating and rehabilitating running injuries. Common causes of injuries include the following:

▌ Training errors—Sudden, sharp increases in training volume and intensity; overuse (running more miles than the body can handle); failure to take sufficient recovery time between demanding workouts; running too much on very hard or very soft surfaces

- Anatomical abnormalities—Flat feet, high arches, excessive pronation or supination, knock knees, bowed legs, inwardly rotated thigh bones, unequal leg lengths
- Muscle imbalances—Differences in the strength of opposing muscle groups (hamstrings and quadriceps, calf and tibialis anterior, hip flexors and hip extensors); differences in the flexibility of opposing muscle groups; excessively tight or loose muscles
- Poor technique—Excessive turning and twisting motions, overstriding, striking too hard on the heel or forefoot
- Inappropriate footwear—Insufficient cushioning, inadequate control for excessive pronation or supination, insufficient arch support, overly worn shoes
- Suboptimal nutrition—Insufficient intake of calories, fluids, calcium, electrolytes, or other nutrients

If you consider the causes of running injuries, you might find that some aspect of your training program increases injury risk. By eliminating the risk factor or adding training methods that counteract it, you can prevent injuries. For example, impact-related injuries, such as shin splints and stress fractures, are often caused by running long distances on hard surfaces such as asphalt road. Runners can reduce their risk for these injuries by training on dirt roads and trails.

Common Running Injuries

To prevent and treat running injuries, you'll benefit from knowing their causes, symptoms, and rehabilitation methods. An extensive discussion of running injuries is beyond the scope of this book, but you should at least know some characteristics of common running injuries.

Stress fractures are tiny breaks that occur in the bones of the feet, shins, thighs, and hips. The symptoms include localized pain and tenderness on the surface of the affected bone. This injury is commonly caused by overuse, or the excessive loading of the bones from the repetitive stress of running on hard surfaces. Stress fractures tend to occur in girls who, as a result of inadequate caloric intake and excessive training, experience athletic amenorrhea, or cessation of normal menstruation. Cyclical increases in estrogen levels, which occur with regular menstruation, are necessary for maintaining bone density. Diagnosing a stress fracture is typically complicated because the fracture may not show up on X-rays for several weeks after the onset of symptoms. To avoid serious bone damage and to promote healing, athletes who experience the symptoms of stress fractures should stop running and see a sports doctor. If a stress fracture is diagnosed, rehabilitation involves alterations in training and diet, a change in footwear or the use of orthotics, and cardiovascular training methods such as swimming, pool running, and cycling that don't stress the affected bone.

Plantar fasciitis is inflammation of the band of connective tissue that runs along the insole of the foot from the heel to the arch. This injury is characterized by gripping pain and tenderness in the arch, close to the fleshy part of the heel. The pain is especially intense in the morning and during running. Plantar fasciitis is common in runners who have flat feet and who overpronate. Recovery time from this injury can often require several weeks or months of reduced or no running. Doctors may prescribe exercises for strengthening muscles in the feet, orthotics, anti-inflammatory medication, and steroid injections.

Achilles tendinitis is the degeneration and inflammation of the Achilles tendon, which connects the calf muscles to the heel bone. The main symptoms of this overuse injury are pain, tenderness, and swelling along the tendon. The pain is especially severe when athletes run on their toes, up hills, and in low-heeled racing flats or spikes. Runners with tight calf muscles are at particular risk, so should regularly stretch these muscles. In some cases, rehabilitation time can be lengthy because the Achilles tendon receives limited blood flow and is stressed in daily activities such as walking. The main treatments—icing, anti-inflammatory medication, and ultrasound—increase blood flow to the tendon in order to reduce inflammation and promote healing. Swimming and deep-water running are good training methods for maintaining fitness while the tendon heals.

Patellofemoral pain syndrome results from cartilage degeneration behind the kneecap. Runners with this syndrome experience stiffness and grinding pain in the knee, especially after sitting for long periods and bending the knee in activities such as squatting and stair climbing. Patellofemoral pain syndrome occurs most often in runners with knock knees, bowed legs, and flat feet. Another cause is strength imbalances between the hamstrings and quadriceps. Doctors recommend anti-inflammatory medicine and exercises that strengthen the quadriceps and stretch the hamstrings.

Osgood-Schlatter syndrome refers to inflammation, tenderness, and pain where the patellar tendon (in front of the knee) attaches to the tibia, or shin bone. This syndrome, which is unique to young athletes, develops due to a combination of rapid bone growth and repetitive stress. During the adolescent growth spurt the bones grow faster than the muscles and connective tissue. When growth of the tibia outstrips that of the patellar tendon, the tendon pulls hard on its attachment site at the top of the shin. The excessive tugging causes irritation and pain. In addition, the force can lead to small bony formations and fractures. In most cases, the swelling and pain go away with reduced running and skeletal maturation.

Iliotibial band syndrome refers to inflammation and pain caused by rubbing of the iliotibial band tendon against the lateral (outside) of the knee. The iliotibial band runs along the lateral side of the thigh from the hip to the knee. In adult runners the syndrome is typically caused by a combination of repetitive stress from running and tightness of the iliotibial band and the muscles around it. In young runners an additional cause is rapid growth of the femur. Runners should cease running, ice the injured area, and stretch the iliotibial band (see figure 6.2h on page 102) and hamstring muscles (see figure 6.2k on page 103).

Shin splints is a term referring to pain and tenderness along the shin bone. When the pain runs along the inner side of the shin from a few inches below the knee to the ankle, doctors refer to the injury as **medial tibial pain syndrome**. The pain associated with this syndrome is caused by inflammation of the tissue that lines the bone. When the pain is on the outer side of the shin, the cause is often **compartment syndrome**—swelling of the muscles in the lower leg, which overstretches the elastic sheath that covers the muscles and creates pressure on nerve endings in the muscles. Runners with shin pain should consult a sports doctor because appropriate treatment depends on the cause, which is difficult to self-diagnose, and because continuing to run without appropriate treatment can result in stress fractures.

To effectively deal with injuries, you must heed their symptoms and understand the best approaches to treatment and rehabilitation (see the sidebar on pages 212 to 213). While some injuries require immediate medical treatment, others, especially those caused by chronic overuse, may not pose an immediate danger. In some cases runners can self-treat these injuries, ideally under the supervision of a sports doctor or certified athletic trainer. Self-treatment of many running injuries involves RICE, which stands for rest, ice, compression, and elevation. Rest can mean a complete cessation of all training for at least a few days, but for many injuries it's possible to keep training with supplemental methods in order to maintain fitness. For example, runners with knee pain will make their injuries worse if they continue to run, but they can maintain a high level of cardiovascular and muscle fitness by swimming and doing upper-body circuit training.

Some leg and foot injuries that keep you from running are not affected by activities such as cycling and deep-water running. In deep-water running, the athlete mimics the running action while suspended in a pool by a flotation vest. Cycling and deep-water running can elevate the heart rate for prolonged periods, so they're great for maintaining cardiovascular fitness. The duration of supplemental training depends on the injured runner's familiarity with the exercise. For example, injured runners who have never done deep-water running might start out with only 10 or 15 minutes a day and gradually build up to a duration that approaches their longest continuous aerobic run. Runners who are accustomed to riding bicycles can start cycling at 45 minutes or more.

The second component of RICE, applying ice to the injured area, is often very effective for reducing swelling and pain as well as for promoting healing. Injuries that involve chronic inflammation, such as plantar fasciitis and Achilles tendinitis, respond especially well to ice treatment. Simply apply a plastic bag filled with crushed ice to the injured area. To avoid freezing the skin, place a thin cloth between the bag and the injured area. You can also freeze water in a paper cup and use it to perform an ice massage. A general guideline is to apply ice two or three times a day for 10 to 20 minutes each time. We strongly recommend that runners consult a sports doctor or athletic trainer for an injury-specific icing protocol.

Compression of the affected area is also often an effective treatment for injuries that cause swelling. The most common method of compression is applying an elastic bandage. The placement of the bandage depends on the injury and the individual. Athletic trainers know the proper techniques for wrapping injuries.

The fourth component of RICE, elevation, involves raising the injured area to reduce blood flow to it, thereby reducing swelling. A runner who has a knee injury, for example, should lie on a bed or couch, elevating the affected leg with a pillow or two. The leg should be raised to a level slightly above the heart.

Going Off-Course for Variety and Fun

Sometimes when you're traveling on a long journey, the most effective and fun way to reach your destination is to venture off on side roads and unpaved paths. It's the same with training for distance running—it can be worthwhile to experiment with training methods and doses that deviate from the planned program. Occasional training detours that add variety and fun are essential because they keep young runners motivated, interested, and engaged. If young runners are limited to completing the assigned workouts day after day, week after week, and month after month, they will very likely become bored with running.

The key to cultivating interest in training is to make the program as varied as possible. You can use different training methods, exercises, and drills from day to day, and you can change the training venue and environment as often as possible. Every so often, surprise your athletes with a change that spices up the day's training. For example, instead of announcing ahead of time that the team will do its continuous aerobic run on the beach, a 10-mile drive from school, you might just show up at practice that day with a van and pile everyone in. Or, on a day scheduled for an interval tempo session, you might change the workout to a controlled fartlek just for variety. You might even surprise the team once or twice every few weeks by canceling practice altogether and taking the team to the movies.

Training methods that are inherently fun should be a regular part of the program. Especially in the general preparation phase, coaches should include games such as basketball, soccer, ultimate Frisbee, and keep-away several times each week. You can also spice up training methods that aren't inherently fun, such as recovery sessions, by adding variety and making them playful. For example, on a recovery day during the spring, runners can go swimming in a local pond or river, or they can go mountain biking. In winter, a recovery session might be 20 minutes of cross-country skiing. If the recovery session is an easy 20-minute run, the whole team can run together, talking and joking along the way. If the course goes through a park, you can play a game that awards points to the first runner who spots a chipmunk, sparrow, deer, or other animal that might appear. If the course goes through an urban neighborhood, you might substitute different makes and colors of cars for animals.

Sometimes experienced coaches and runners unexpectedly change training and racing plans on a hunch that a detour might lead to a breakthrough. A coach might postpone an important race-specific interval session until the next day if the wind is blowing hard on the day that the session is scheduled. A 1,500-meter runner might abandon a racing plan to sit and kick over the last 300 meters if she feels strong and has the energy to surge and break up the field with 800 meters to go. You should act on these hunches every so often because they might be shortcuts on the road to your goals. Then again, they might take you miles off course, but you can learn important lessons from such detours if you keep track of how you veered off course and avoid those roads in the future.

Above all, the most important feature of a training program is an atmosphere of fun because without it, young runners aren't motivated to improve themselves through hard work and dedication. Coaches and parents foster this atmosphere when they adopt the philosophy that youth sport is about doing your best and enjoying the journey on the road to self-improvement. When they're not pressured to win, young athletes are truly motivated by the challenge of this journey. Still, they want to have fun along the way. Successful coaches and parents realize this and use their creativity to make sure that training and competitive experiences are challenging and fun.

Coaches who follow sound, scientific guidelines for designing and adapting training will surely challenge their young runners with sessions that develop physical and mental fitness. But as complex as designing training can be, it can sometimes be easy compared to creating an atmosphere of fun and enjoyment, which requires thought and ingenuity on a daily basis. Our advice to coaches who want to add more fun to daily training is to listen carefully to your athletes to find out what they enjoy most about running and about their lives as teenagers. Maybe they'd like it if you played music over the speaker system at the track every once in a while. They might enjoy dressing up in running costumes on special holidays such as Halloween and St. Patrick's Day; they'd like to see you in costume, too! They enjoy team parties and awards banquets where everyone is recognized. Your runners rely on you to build team morale and camaraderie with special experiences and events that add excitement to their training.

Striding Ahead

We congratulate you on your efforts to learn about training for young distance runners and applying the science of distance running to the artistry of coaching, parenting, and running itself. We leave you with one last bit of advice for ensuring successful and safe training journeys in the future: Keep asking for directions! You can always learn more about training. As sport science and training theory evolve, so too will new ideas and training methods for you to consider applying to your own program to make it even better.

You will be rewarded in many ways by learning more about running. Reading books and running magazines, attending clinics, and discussing ideas and strategies with others who share your interest are all ways to keep learning. If you're a coach, you'll experience the incredible satisfaction of improving your ability to help young athletes achieve their goals. In addition, your own experience will be enriched because you'll be engaged in an exciting discourse among other coaches and sport scientists about the best methods for developing young runners. Perhaps you'd like to learn more about exercise physiology, or maybe you want to set up a computer system for keeping training records and tracking your athletes' progress. To advance your coaching skills, you'll need to keep seeking knowledge about training for young runners.

If you're a parent, you'll do a great service to your child by learning more about nutrition, the effects of training on maturation and growth, and other areas that influence the young runner's health. If your child's experiences in distance running are positive, they have tremendous potential for establishing behaviors and values that will contribute to a lifetime of good health. It's your responsibility, along with the coach and family physician, to ensure that your child has good experiences in training and competition. To meet this responsibility, you'll need to continue learning about youth distance running.

If you're a young runner, you should realize that learning more about distance running is vital to progressing and developing in future years. The coach takes the wheel at the beginning of the training journey, but as you gain experience over the years, you gain more control over your own training program. After all, who knows better than you what training is working and what's not? As an advanced runner, you can learn about your body and how it responds to training and racing, and you can share some of the responsibility of directing the journey with your coach. When you and your coach work together in this way, you increase your potential for success. Most important, if you commit to learn more about running, you'll gain knowledge and experience that will be the source of a lifetime of good health.

We wish you success in your journey in youth distance running. Perhaps our paths will cross along the way!

REFERENCES

American College of Sports Medicine: Position Statement. 2000. Nutrition and athletic performance. *Medicine and Science in Sports and Exercise.* Available: www.ms-se.com/pt/pt-core/template-journal/msse/media/1200.pdf.

Bar-Or, O., and V.B. Unnithan. 1994. Nutritional requirements of young soccer players. *Journal of Sports Sciences* 12:S39-S42.

Brukner, P., and K. Bennell. 1997. Stress fractures in female athletes: Diagnosis, management, and rehabilitation. *Sports Medicine* 24:419-429.

Butts, N.K. 1982. Physiological profiles of high school female cross country runners. *Research Quarterly for Exercise and Sport* 53:8-14.

Christensen, D.L., G. van Hall, and L. Hambraeus. 2002. Food and macronutrient intake of male adolescent Kalenjin runners in Kenya. *British Journal of Nutrition* 88:711-717.

Cunningham, L.N. 1990. Physiologic comparison of adolescent female and male cross-country runners. *Pediatric Exercise Science* 2:313-321.

Daniels, J. 1998. *Daniels' running formula.* Champaign, IL: Human Kinetics.

Kraemer, W., and S. Fleck. 1993. *Strength training for young athletes.* Champaign, IL: Human Kinetics.

Loosli, A.R., and J. Benson. 1990. Nutritional intake in adolescent athletes. *Pediatric Clinics of North America* 37:1143-1152.

Martin, D.E., and P.N. Coe. 1997. *Better training for distance runners.* 2nd ed. Champaign, IL: Human Kinetics.

Micheli, L.J. 1996. *Healthy runner's handbook.* Champaign, IL: Human Kinetics.

Newsholme, E., T. Leech, and G. Duester. 1995. *Keep on running.* Chichester, England: John Wiley & Sons.

Noakes, T. 2003. *Lore of running.* 4th ed. Champaign, IL: Human Kinetics.

Sundberg, S., and R. Elovanio. 1982. Cardiorespiratory function in competitive endurance runners aged 12-16 years compared with ordinary boys. *Acta Paediatrica Scandinavica* 71:987-992.

Wahl, R. 1999. Nutrition in the adolescent. *Pediatric Annals* 28:107-111.

INDEX

Note: The italicized *f* and *t* following page numbers refer to figures and tables, respectively.

ABOUT THE AUTHORS

Larry Greene knows all about the challenges facing young runners. He was the Florida state high school champion in cross country in 1977 and in the 2-mile run in 1978. He also finished 10th in the national Junior Olympic Cross Country Meet as a senior. Greene's high school accomplishments earned him a scholarship to Florida State University, where he set the school record for the indoor 3,000-meter run and qualified for the NCAA championship meet three times.

After college, Greene competed and excelled as a distance runner. In 1984 he ran the fastest half-marathon in the world (1:01:27) and finished fourth in the 10,000-meter run at the U.S. Track and Field Championships. In 1987 he finished third in the half-marathon at the U.S. Olympic Festival.

Greene is a senior instructor in the department of integrative physiology at the University of Colorado at Boulder. He received an MS in movement science from Florida State University in 1988 and a PhD in exercise science from the University of South Carolina in 1993. A former cross country and track coach at the youth and university levels, Greene served as the director of the Carolina Marathon Youth Cross Country Run from 1990 to 1993. His leisure-time interests include running, cycling, and cross-country skiing.

Russ Pate has been an exercise physiology instructor and researcher since 1972. He is also a lifelong distance runner. Pate has a personal best time of 2:15:20 in the marathon, plus he has competed in the marathon at three U.S. Olympic Trials. A professor of exercise science and associate dean for research in the Arnold School of Public Health at the University of South Carolina, Pate has focused his research on the relationship between physical activity and health in children and adolescents.

Pate has served as president of the American College of Sports Medicine (ACSM) and as chairman of the Physical Fitness Council of the American Alliance for Health, Physical Education, Recreation and Dance. He also has been recognized with Scholar Awards from both organizations. In addition, he is a member of the North American Society of Pediatric Exercise Medicine.

Pate received a PhD in exercise physiology from the University of Oregon in 1974. He received the T.K. Cureton Award, presented by the National Fitness Leaders Association in 1995, and in 1996 he received the ACSM's Citation Award. In his free time, Pate enjoys running, traveling, and spending time with his kids.